Motivating Learners, Motivating Teachers

CAMBRIDGE LANGUAGE TEACHING LIBRARY

A series covering central issues in language teaching and learning, by authors who have expert knowledge in their field.

For a complete list of titles please visit: www.cambridge.org/elt/cltl

A selection of recent titles in this series:

Meaningful Action
Earl Stevick's Influence on Language Teaching
Edited by Jane Arnold and Tim Murphey

The Roles of Language in CLIL
Ana Llinares, Tom Morton and Rachel Whittaker

Materials Development in Language Teaching (Second Edition)
Edited by Brian Tomlinson

Values, Philosophies, and Beliefs in TESOL
Making a Statement
Graham Crookes

Listening in the Language Classroom
John Field

Lessons from Good Language Learners
Edited by Carol Griffiths

Teacher Language Awareness
Stephen Andrews

Language Teacher Supervision
A Case-Based Approach
Kathleen M. Bailey

Conversation
From Description to Pedagogy
Scott Thornbury and Diana Slade

The Experience of Language Teaching
Rose M. Senior

Learners' Stories
Difference and Diversity in Language Learning
Edited by Phil Benson and David Nunan

Task-Based Language Teaching
David Nunan

Rules, Patterns and Words
Grammar and Lexis in English Language Teaching
Dave Willis

Language Learning in Distance Education
Cynthia White

Group Dynamics in the Language Classroom
Zoltán Dörnyei and Tim Murphey

Testing for Language Teachers (Second Edition)
Arthur Hughes

Motivational Strategies in the Language Classroom
Zoltán Dörnyei

The Dynamics of the Language Classroom
Ian Tudor

Using Surveys in Language Programs
James Dean Brown

Approaches and Methods in Language Teaching (Second Edition)
Jack C. Richards and Theodore S. Rodgers

Teaching Languages to Young Learners
Lynne Cameron

Classroom Decision Making
Negotiation and Process Syllabuses in Practice
Edited by Michael P. Breen and Andrew Littlejohn

Establishing Self-Access
From Theory to Practice
David Gardner and Lindsay Miller

Collaborative Action Research for English Language Teachers
Anne Burns

Affect in Language Learning
Edited by Jane Arnold

Developments in English for Specific Purposes
A Multi-Disciplinary Approach
Tony Dudley-Evans and Maggie Jo St John

Language Learning in Intercultural Perspective
Approaches through Drama and Ethnography
Edited by Michael Byram and Michael Fleming

Motivating Learners, Motivating Teachers
Building vision in the language classroom

Zoltán Dörnyei
Magdalena Kubanyiova

CAMBRIDGE
UNIVERSITY PRESS

CAMBRIDGE
UNIVERSITY PRESS

University Printing House, Cambridge CB2 8BS, United Kingdom

Cambridge University Press is part of the University of Cambridge.

It furthers the University's mission by disseminating knowledge in the pursuit of education, learning and research at the highest international levels of excellence.

www.cambridge.org
Information on this title: www.cambridge.org/9781107606647

© Cambridge University Press 2014

This publication is in copyright. Subject to statutory exception and to the provisions of relevant collective licensing agreements, no reproduction of any part may take place without the written permission of Cambridge University Press.

First published 2014

A catalogue record for this publication is available from the British Library

ISBN 978-1-107-60664-7 Paperback

Cambridge University Press has no responsibility for the persistence or accuracy of URLs for external or third-party internet websites referred to in this publication, and does not guarantee that any content on such websites is, or will remain, accurate or appropriate.

Contents

Acknowledgements viii
Introduction 1
    Why write a book about vision in language education? 1
    Why focus on both learners and teachers in the same book? 3
    What is the point of mixing the terms 'vision' and 'motivation'? 3
    What is this book intended to offer? 4
    Who are we and how have we come to write this book? 5

Part I Theoretical overview 7

1 The role of vision in motivating human behaviour 8
    1.1 What is 'vision' and why does it matter? 9
    1.2 Vision, motivation and the self 11
    1.3 Mental imagery 14
    1.4 Language learning motivation and future L2 self-guides 20
    1.5 Motivation and vision in language teachers' development 22
    1.6 Summary 28

Part II Motivating language learners through vision 31

2 Creating the language learner's vision 34
    What do we mean by 'constructing' a vision? 34
    Why is 'agency' important? 35
    Towards designing a 'visionary' programme 36

Contents

2.1	Understanding students' current identity concerns and lived experiences	38
2.2	Providing regular tasters of desired future states	45
2.3	Applying guided imagery	48
2.4	Applying guided narratives	57
2.5	Ensuring ample exposure to role models	62

3 Strengthening the vision through imagery enhancement — 65

3.1	Training imagery skills	66
3.2	Building creative visual and narrative tasks into the teaching routine	72
3.3	Encouraging students to keep learning journals	77
3.4	Harnessing the power of virtual worlds	78
3.5	Strengthening the whole group's vision	82

4 Substantiating the vision by making it plausible — 90

4.1	Cultivating realistic beliefs about language learning	90
4.2	Creating channels for constructive reality self-checks	92
4.3	Eliminating obstacles and barriers	97

5 Transforming the vision into action — 99

5.1	Providing students with models of self-relevant roadmaps	101
5.2	Mapping out pathways to success through visualisation	103
5.3	Providing students with individual guidance	105

6 Keeping the vision alive — 107

6.1	Including regular reminders and 'priming stimuli' in the teaching content	107
6.2	Engaging learners' transportable identities	109
6.3	Helping to re-envisage 'broken' visions	112

Contents

7 *Counterbalancing the vision by considering failure*	114
7.1 Offering regular reminders of the negative consequences of not succeeding	115
7.2 Foregrounding the ought-to self	116
7.3 Integrating images of feared selves into visualisations?	118
Part III Motivation and vision for language teachers	**123**
8 *(Re-)igniting the flame of teacher vision*	125
8.1 Understanding who we are for insights into who we want to become	125
8.2 Engaging with the 'whys': values, moral purposes and teaching philosophies	130
8.3 Generating images of ideal language teacher selves	136
8.4 Sparking creative tension	138
9 *Guarding the flame of teacher vision*	145
9.1 Staying connected to the original vision in the face of detrimental ought-to self-images	145
9.2 Building resilience through vision boosters and safety zones	147
9.3 Processing our fears and turning adversity into allies	150
9.4 Sustaining hope	154
Conclusion	157
References	163
Index	176

Acknowledgements

We are grateful to the following colleagues and friends for their kind help in collecting illustration material for this book: Alan Maley, Alastair Henry, David Lasagabaster, Jim King, Julia Chenjing You, Letty Chan, Martin Lamb, Michael Magid, Mike Gow, Mostafa Papi, Neil McClelland, Peng Ding, Peter Edwards, Sarah Mercer, Stephen Ryan, Tae-Young Kim, Tatsuya Taguchi and Tetsuya Fukuda. We would also like to express our thanks to our editors at Cambridge University Press, Jane Walsh, Anna Linthe and Jo Garbutt, who generously supported our project right from the beginning. Finally, our sincere thanks are also due to three anonymous reviewers and the content editor of this book, Verity Cole, who have made some genuinely useful suggestions on how to improve both the content and the presentation of the material. Thank you all!

The authors and publishers acknowledge the following sources of copyright material and are grateful for the permissions granted. While every effort has been made, it has not always been possible to identify the sources of all the material used, or to trace all copyright holders. If any omissions are brought to our notice, we will be happy to include the appropriate acknowledgements on reprinting.

Extract on p. 8 from *To Reach the Clouds* by Philippe Petit, published by Faber and Faber, 2008. Originally published by Pan Macmillan, 2002. Copyright © 2008, 2002;

Extract on pp. 40–41 adapted from *Teach with Your Heart: Lessons I Learned from The Freedom Writers* by Erin Gruwell, published by Broadway Books, 2007. Copyright © 2007;

Extract on pp. 39 and 43 adapted from *Identity and Language Learning* by Bonny Norton, published by Pearson Education Ltd, 2000. Copyright © 2000;

Extract on pp. 44–45 adapted from *A validation and application of the L2 Motivational Self System among Chinese learners of English* by Michael Magid, The University of Nottingham, 2011. Copyright © 2011;

Acknowledgements

Extract on p. 50 from *Innovation in Language Learning and Teaching – Motivating English learners by helping them visualise their ideal L2 self: Lessons from two motivational programmes* by Michael Magid and Letty Chan, published by Taylor and Francis, 2012. Copyright © 2012;

Extract on p. 53 from *Spinning Inward: Using Guided Imagery with Children for Learning, Creativity and Relaxation* by Maureen Murdock, published by Shambhala Publications, 1987. Copyright © 1987;

Extract on p. 75 from 'Our Story' from Freedom Writers Foundation, http://www.freedomwritersfoundation.org/our-story. Copyright © 2013;

Extract on pp. 76–77 adapted from 'The role of transportation in the persuasiveness of public narratives' from *Journal of Personality and Social Psychology* by Melanie C. Green and Timothy C. Brock, The Ohio State University, 2000. Copyright © 2000;

Extract on p. 78 from *The Freedom Writers Diary Teacher's Guide* by Erin Gruwell and The Freedom Writers Foundation, published by Broadway Books, 2007. Copyright © 2007;

Extract on p. 82 from *Massively Multiplayer Online Games as support tool for learning a second language* by Dawid Krystowiak, The University of Birmingham, 2012. Copyright © 2012;

Extract on p. 84 from 'About' from Freedom Writers Foundation, http://www.freedomwritersfoundation.org/about.html. Copyright © 2013;

Extract on p. 93–94 from *Creative Visualization: Use the Power of Your Imagination to Create What You Want in Your Life* by Shakti Gawain, published by Nataraj Publishers, 2002. Copyright © 2002;

Extract on p. 95 from 'The ideal self as the driver of intentional change' from *Journal of Management Development* by Richard E. Boyatzis and Kleio Akrivou, published by Emerald Group Publishing, 2006. Copyright © 2006;

Extract on p. 112 from *Re-imagining ideal L2 selves in the study abroad context: A study of Vietnamese postgraduate students in the UK* by Tra Mi Thi Do, The University of Birmingham, 2012. Copyright © 2012;

Extract on pp. 114–115 adapted from *A validation and application of the L2 Motivational Self System among Chinese learners of English* by Michael Magid, The University of Nottingham, 2011. Copyright © 2011;

Acknowledgements

Extract on p. 117 from *A validation and application of the L2 Motivational Self System among Chinese learners of English* by Michael Magid, The University of Nottingham, 2011. Copyright © 2011;

Extract on pp. 135–136 adapted from *NLP for Teachers: How to Be a Highly Effective Teacher* by Richard Churches and Roger Terry, published by Crown House Publishing, 2007. Copyright © 2007;

Extract on p. 138 from *Seeing through teachers' eyes: Professional ideals and classroom practices* by Karen Hammerness, published by Teachers College Press, 2006. Copyright © 2006;

Extract on p. 139 from 'Putting theory into practice: Letting my students learn to read' by Lynne Doherty Herndon, from *Teachers' Narrative Inquiry as Professional Development* edited by Karen E. Johnson and Paula R. Golombek, published by Cambridge University Press, 2002. Copyright © 2002.

Introduction

In order to offer a brief introduction to this book, we would like to start out by answering five key questions: (1) Why write a book about vision in language education? (2) Why focus on both learners and teachers in the same book? (3) What is the point of mixing the terms 'vision' and 'motivation'? (4) What is this book intended to offer? (5) Who are we, the authors, and how have we come to write this book?

Why write a book about vision in language education?

There is a straightforward answer to this question: because vision matters a lot. This has been recognised by many for a long time (see e.g. Levin 2000; van der Helm 2009); for example, in one of the best-known biblical proverbs that talks about prophetic vision, we are told, 'Where there is no vision, the people perish' (Proverbs 29:18), and John Dewey, the eminent American philosopher and educational reformer (1859–1952), stated as early as 1897 in his famous *My Pedagogic Creed* that the central issue in education is vision-building, or as he termed it, *image-formation*:

> I believe that the image is the great instrument of instruction. What a child gets out of any subject presented to him is simply the images which he himself forms with regard to it.
>
> I believe that if nine-tenths of the energy at present directed towards making the child learn certain things, were spent in seeing to it that the child was forming proper images, the work of instruction would be indefinitely facilitated.
>
> I believe that much of the time and attention now given to the preparation and presentation of lessons might be more wisely and profitably expended in training the child's power of imagery and in seeing to it that he was continually forming definite, vivid, and growing images of the various subjects with which he comes in contact in his experience.
>
> (Dewey 1897: 79–80)

In keeping with his view, we have come to believe that vision is one of the single most important factors within the domain of language learning: where there is a vision, there is a way. The main objective of this book is therefore to explain what exactly is involved in the vision to learn a foreign/second language (L2), where the significance of this vision lies and in what ways it can be generated and nurtured consciously by the teacher. When we talk about motivating learners in the following chapters, we do not necessarily mean providing them with entertainment and laughter (although those can often, but not always, be very welcome ingredients of the classroom learning process). Instead, what we mean by *motivating* in this book is to help students to 'see' themselves as potentially competent L2 users, to become excited about the value of knowing a foreign language in their own lives and, subsequently, to take action. This action will sometimes be genuinely enjoyable and seemingly effortless, as witnessed by students who are absorbed in watching a gripping foreign language movie, browsing foreign language websites or competing with other teams in a classroom language quiz. At other times, however, the going may get tougher, and even though such low points are inevitable in any sustained activity, too many learners abandon the study of an L2 as a result of their diminishing motivation. Along with the researchers, practitioners and materials writers whose work we will cite and discuss in this book, we believe that such demotivation is not inevitable, as many people are ready to invest effort in difficult tasks when they have a clear vision of where the process can take them. This vision is what our book is about.

✎ Illustration: The power of vision: 'I have a dream!'

On 28 August 1963, Martin Luther King, Jr gave a speech in Washington DC about racial equality and an end to discrimination. This speech has been seen as a defining moment of the American Civil Rights Movement. At the end of the speech, he departed from his prepared text and finished with describing an extended vision of a brighter future, punctuated with eight occurrences of the now legendary phrase, 'I have a dream ...':

> I have a dream that one day this nation will rise up and live out the true meaning of its creed: 'We hold these truths to be self-evident, that all men are created equal.' ...
>
> I have a dream that my four little children will one day live in a nation where they will not be judged by the color of their skin but by the content of their character ...

The power of this vision has been evidenced by history.

Introduction

Why focus on both learners and teachers in the same book?

The answer to this question has to do with how classrooms work. We are interested in transforming classrooms into learning environments that truly facilitate the study of foreign languages. Such a transformation of classroom practice has to begin with the teachers, because they are the people in the best position to shape classroom life. As evidenced by so many inspiring examples around the world, teachers *can* become transformational leaders, and the engine of this transformational drive is the teacher's vision for change and improvement. The good news about this vision is that it is highly contagious: it has the potential to infect the students and generate an attractive vision for language learning in them. Therefore, the rationale for combining the topics of teacher and student motivation in one book is actually quite simple: the two are inextricably linked because the former is needed for the latter to blossom.

What is the point of mixing the terms 'vision' and 'motivation'?

This is an important question, and in fact we could even go one step further and ask: should a vision-based approach replace previous motivational frameworks?[1] The answer is no. The plurality of motivational constructs has to do with the multi-faceted nature of human behaviour and with the various levels of abstraction that we can approach it from. The undeniable fact is that the range of potential motives that can affect human behaviour is vast: people might decide to do something for as diverse reasons as physical needs, financial benefits, moral or faith convictions, cognitive curiosity or because they fancy someone who already does it – the list is virtually endless. Various motivation theories highlight different clusters of these motives in order to explain certain specific behavioural domains under focus, such as, for example, voting, mating, learning or working behaviours. Zoltán's earlier book in the Cambridge Language Teaching Library series – *Motivational Strategies in the Language Classroom* (Dörnyei 2001) – surveyed a wide selection of diverse motives that are relevant to sustained learning behaviours in foreign language classes, and the approach offered in the current book does not replace or invalidate the motivational strategies presented there.

---

[1] For an overview of different approaches to understanding motivation in language education, see Dörnyei (2001, 2014) and Dörnyei and Ushioda (2011).

So, what is the point in shifting the attention to vision? The reason for doing so is that we understand 'vision' to be one of the highest-order motivational forces, one that is particularly fitting to explain the long-term, and often lifelong, process of mastering a second language. While the day-to-day realities of one's L2 learning experience are the function of multiple factors related to diverse aspects of the learning environment or the learner's personal life, the concept of vision offers a useful, broad lens to focus on the bigger picture, the overall persistence that is necessary to lead one to ultimate language attainment. In other words, while individuals pursue languages for a variety of purposes, and an equally wide array of reasons keep their motivation alive, the vision of who they would like to become as second language users seems to be one of the most reliable predictors of their long-term intended effort.

In sum, we are firm believers in the ultimate motivational potential of vision, and therefore in the following chapters we shall explore how this vision can be generated and under what conditions it can work best. If it is true that vision can have a substantial impact on motivation and action – and a massive body of research from across a wide range of scientific disciplines suggests that it can – then why not explore this potential in our language classrooms?

What is this book intended to offer?

We hope to provide an accessible discussion that avoids too much jargon and that is not theorising for its own sake but rather serves practical purposes. We have found in our own experience that when teachers genuinely care for student learning, they need some solid framework to understand the key parameters of their professional work in order to make the most of it. The analysis of vision lends itself to this purpose: the nine chapters of this book are intended to present a firm foundation which those teachers wishing to establish a motivational practice in their language classes can build upon. The theoretical principles will be accompanied by a wide range of illustrations from research practice, interviews, anecdotes and celebrity quotes in order to bring the topic alive; we hope to be persuasive and engaging enough to generate real zeal and conviction in our readers so that their excitement, in turn, can be transmitted to their students. This book, then, is a platform to present our own vision about the subject and a call to readers to join us in our visionary journey towards making language learning more engaging and rewarding for our learners.

In our discussion of the pedagogic implications of vision, we will present a number of ideas for classroom activities, with the caveat that this

Introduction

is not a 'recipe book' whose main aim is to provide teaching resources. Instead, as stated above, our chief objective is to offer insights, clarity and explanation about a fascinating subject in the hope that this will enrich our classroom colleagues' creative work with their students. Thus, we genuinely agree with the well-known social psychologist Kurt Lewin (1952: 169), who concluded: 'There is nothing more practical than a good theory.' (Practical resources concerning vision in language education can be found in two recipe books: Arnold, Puchta and Rinvolucri 2007 and Hadfield and Dörnyei 2013.)

Who are we and how have we come to write this book?

Interestingly, we both come from Central Europe and were born only a few hours' drive away from each other – Zoltán in Hungary, Maggie in Slovakia – but it wasn't until we were both in England that we met, when Maggie started her PhD studies at the School of English, Nottingham University, where Zoltán was teaching. Zoltán began his career as a language teacher and teacher trainer in Budapest, and moved to Nottingham, where his wife comes from, at the end of the 1990s. By that time he had more or less turned into a full-time researcher of L2 applied linguistics, with his main specialisation area being the motivational background of second language acquisition. He was interested in undertaking Maggie's supervision because she shared his belief in the capacity of good scholarship to make tangible differences in the actual practice of real classrooms, and as part of the first phase of Maggie's PhD research, we launched an innovative in-service teacher-training course in Slovakia. As will be explained in more detail in Part III, this course was a mixed success. On the one hand, the participants – teachers working in various sectors of the Slovakian educational system – loved it and engaged with it meaningfully, covering a lot of ground and producing excellent course evaluation feedback. On the other hand, however, Maggie's subsequent research revealed very little evidence that the participants would try to incorporate the newly learnt knowledge and skills in their actual teaching practice. This puzzling experience led to a major turn in Maggie's PhD research in order to understand the anatomy of teacher-training failure, and the outcome of this work has been summarised in her recent book, *Teacher Development in Action: Understanding Language Teachers' Conceptual Change* (Kubanyiova 2012).

Interestingly, the original idea for this book was not related to this book at all: it concerned our preparing together the second edition of Zoltán's *Motivational Strategies* book (Dörnyei 2001). Yet, it soon became clear that we were both interested in more than merely updating an existing collection of motivational techniques: we wanted to explore our more general ideas about transforming language teaching practice by generating a constructive vision of change. At this point we also realised that our research interests – Zoltán focusing primarily on students, Maggie on teachers – were conveniently complementary, which suggested the structure of this book. Accordingly, we rewrote our original book proposal for Cambridge University Press, and to our delight, the editors of the Cambridge Language Teaching Library series – Jane Walsh, Anna Linthe and Jo Garbutt – embraced the project right from the beginning.

Part I
Theoretical overview

1 The role of vision in motivating human behaviour

> You can't depend on your eyes when your imagination is out of focus.
> Mark Twain (1835–1910)

Let us start our exploration of the nature of vision and its role in human behaviour with an extraordinary story about how far and (literally) how high vision can take us; the following is a true story adapted from Philippe Petit's (2002) autobiography:[2]

> It is winter, 1968, and a young, eighteen-year-old Frenchman, Philippe Petit, is sitting with a toothache in the waiting room of a dentist in Paris. Philippe has been practising wire walking for a few months and as he is waiting for his turn to be seen by the dentist, he is looking at some newspapers when suddenly he freezes: *'I am staring at an illustration and reading over and over a short article about a fantastic building whose twin towers, 110 stories tall, will rise over New York City in a few years and "tickle the clouds"'* (p. 4). At this point the Twin Towers of the World Trade Center only exist in an architect's imagination, but a powerful seed has been sown in Philippe's mind: *'So it is as a reflex that I take the pencil from behind my ear to trace a line between the two rooftops – a wire, but no wirewalker'* (pp. 4–6).
>
> Four years later, in 1972, Philippe comes across another article, this time in the French Magazine *Paris Match*; as he recounts, *'It tells of two pillars already towering above lower Manhattan. A full-page aerial shot portrays the towers as if they were already out of reach. I can hear the cranes bustling to complete the structure on schedule. I can smell the smoke, feel the incessant activity, the urgency ... The article is so disturbing that I throw it into the large red box labelled* PROJECTS *and try to forget about it. I cannot. The towers keep erupting in my conversations, my thoughts, my dreams'* (p. 8).

The rest is history: two years later, in 1974, Philippe illegally rigged a tightrope between the Twin Towers of the World Trade Center, and on Wednesday, 7 August, shortly after 7:15 am, he stepped off the South Tower and walked the steel cable a quarter of a mile above the street

---

[2] In the summary of Philippe's story, italics indicate literal quotes from his autobiography. Philippe's remarkable adventure has also been made into an Oscar-winning documentary film, *Man on Wire* (2008).

The role of vision in motivating human behaviour

level for over 40 minutes, making eight crossings between the towers as well as spending some time sitting and lying on the wire and giving knee salutes. The vision that was originally planted in a Paris dentist's waiting room six years earlier had borne fruit and had become fully realised.

Philippe's extraordinary story raises the question of what the secret of a 'vision' is: how can it suddenly appear out of nothing and then assume such astonishing power that it can drive someone like Philippe Petit to do such an incredibly risky thing as to walk on a steel wire a quarter of a mile above the streets of Manhattan?

1.1 What is 'vision' and why does it matter?

According to the *Oxford English Dictionary*, a vision is 'the ability to think about or plan the future with imagination' or 'a vivid mental image, especially a fanciful one of the future'. The term has been used widely both in the media and in a variety of diverse contexts in everyday life, so much so that van der Helm (2009) actually talks about 'the vision phenomenon' to cover 'the ensemble of claims and products which are called "visions" or could be called as such' (p. 96). In his insightful analysis, he distinguishes between seven different types of vision: religious, political, humanistic, business/organisational, community, public policy and personal visions. Within these contexts, he argues, the actual meaning of vision is fairly homogeneous, capturing three defining aspects: (1) the *future*, (2) the *ideal* and (3) the *desire for deliberate change*.

Our interest in this book concerns *personal vision*, which has to do with 'giving meaning to one's life, with helping to make shifts in professional careers and with coaching yourself in realising a personal dream' (van der Helm 2009: 98). This is the understanding of the term *vision* that is implied, for example, in self-help manuals (i.e. all the *How to ...* books sold at airport bookshops), and we have selected it to be the central theme of this book because it captures a core feature of modern theories of L2 motivation: the emphasis on the learner's desire to approximate a preferred future state, the sort of ideal self a language learner might envision for him-/herself. It is this directional nature of the vision, the *pull towards* an imagined future state, that makes the concept useful within the context of human motivation, because the attractive visionary target mobilises present potential in order to move in the preferred future direction, that is, to change in order to appropriate the future.

A key question we need to address in order to understand the exact nature of vision is in what way it is dissimilar to a 'goal' – after all, a goal also represents directional intentions to reach future states. There is one fundamental difference between the two concepts: unlike an abstract, cognitive goal, a vision includes a strong *sensory element*: it involves tangible images related to achieving the goal. Thus, for example, the vision of becoming a doctor exceeds the abstract goal of earning a medical degree in that the vision involves the individual's actually seeing him-/herself receiving the degree certificate or practising as a qualified doctor. That is, the vision to become a doctor also involves the sensory experience of *being* a doctor. More generally, the main feature of a vision is that it subsumes both a desired goal and a representation of how the individual approaches or realises that goal. In this sense, a vision can be understood as a *personalised goal* (Markus and Ruvolo 1989) that the learner has made his/her own by adding to it the imagined reality of the actual goal experience. Talking about the vision of an organisation, Ira Levin (2000: 95) articulates this sensory element when she says that effective visions 'should outline a rich and textual picture of what success looks like and feels like'. She goes on to say that a vision 'should be so vivid as to enable the listener or reader to transport himself or herself to the future, so to speak, to witness it and experience it'. Vision, thus, has significant motivational capacity; as Taylor and his colleagues (1998) argued in their seminal paper 'Harnessing the Imagination', adding sensory information to a desired future goal enhances people's motivation to achieve it (see ILLUSTRATION 1.1 for an L2 learning-related example). As we shall see later, this aspect of vision has been systematically utilised in several disciplines, most notably in sport psychology, where generating a powerful vision in an athlete can make the difference between a good and a gold-medal-winning performance.

> Illustration 1.1 'When I think about my vision ...' (from Magid 2011: 214)
>
> Extract from an interview with a learner of English:
>
> When I think about my vision, I feel excited and I have a strong desire to make it come true. The feeling of excitement motivates me to learn English. I realised that I need to put more time and effort into learning English to achieve my vision. That's the way that my vision encourages me!

In the following sections we explore in more detail the motivational capacity of vision, first by looking at one specific motivation theory in psychology – possible selves theory – that is particularly relevant in this context, and then by examining the implications of this theory for language learning contexts both for learners and for teachers.

The role of vision in motivating human behaviour

1.2 Vision, motivation and the self

How can we best understand the motivational dimension of vision? Or to put it another way, which theoretical approach to motivation can best accommodate the visionary aspect? In order to capture the whole breadth of vision, we would need a motivation construct that concerns human behaviour in a holistic manner. This is particularly true for language vision, because a foreign language is more than a mere communication code that can be learnt similarly to other academic subjects; instead, the knowledge of a language is part of the individual's personal 'core', involved in most mental activities and forming an important part of one's identity. Therefore, an adequate motivation theory of language vision would require a paradigm that approaches motivation from a whole-person perspective, which makes psychological theories of human identity and the self likely candidates for this purpose.

1.2.1 'Possible selves'

Over the past three decades, personality psychology has increasingly turned to investigating the active, dynamic nature of the self-system – that is, the 'doing' side of personality – by examining how the self regulates behaviour and how various self-characteristics are related to action (see Cantor 1990). Indeed, in a comprehensive review of the topic, Leary (2007: 318) concludes that the popularity of the self as a psychological construct is largely due to its ability to link people's thoughts or behaviours to 'self-motives', such as motives for self-enhancement, self-verification, self-expansion or self-assessment, all within the broad effort to promote and maintain one's self-image through action. Because motivation research, by definition, also focuses on human action, there emerged in the 1980s a promising interface between the two psychological fields.

Within the dynamic approach of linking the human self with human action, the notion of *possible selves* offers the most powerful, and at the same time the most versatile, motivational self-mechanism: first introduced by Markus and Nurius in 1986, the concept of the possible self represents individuals' ideas of what they *might* become, what they *would like* to become and what they are *afraid of* becoming in the future. That is, possible selves include the manifestations of one's future goals and aspirations, allowing people to experience what it would be like to be in that future state.

What is particularly significant from the point of view of our current discussion is that possible selves also involve *images* and *senses* (a point that we will elaborate on below in a separate section); as Markus and Nurius (1986) emphasised, possible selves are represented in the same imaginary and semantic way as the here-and-now self, that is, they are a *reality* for the individual: people can 'see' and 'hear' their possible future self (see also Ruvolo and Markus 1992). This means that, in many ways, possible selves are similar to dreams and visions about oneself. Indeed, Markus and Nurius (1987: 159) confirm, 'Possible selves encompass within their scope *visions* of desired and undesired end states' (our emphasis) – thus, possible selves can be seen as the 'vision of what might be'.

1.2.2 The ideal and the ought-to selves

From the point of view of education, one type of possible self, the *ideal self*, is of particular interest, because it refers to the representation of the characteristics that someone would ideally like to possess – that is, the representation of hopes, aspirations and wishes (see Higgins 1987, 1998). The assertion that someone who has a powerful ideal self – for example a student who envisions him-/herself as a successful businessperson or scholar – can use this self-image as a potent *self-guide* with considerable motivational power requires little justification. This is expressed in everyday speech when we talk about someone following or living up to their dreams.

A complementary future self-guide that has educational relevance is the *ought-to self*, referring to the attributes that one believes one ought to possess – that is, the representation of someone's sense of personal or social duties, obligations or responsibilities (see Higgins 1987, 1998). Thus, in contrast to the ideal self, which concerns the individual's own visions for him-/herself, the ought-to self represents other people's visions for the individual. This 'imported' self-image is particularly salient in some Asian countries where students are often motivated to perform well to fulfil some family obligation or to bring honour to the family's name (see e.g. Magid 2012).

The motivational aspect of the two self-guides (ideal and ought-to) was clearly explained by Higgins's (1987, 1998) *self-discrepancy theory*, which states that people have a feeling of unease when there is a discrepancy between their actual real-life self and their aspired future self. This psychological tension, then, spurs the desire for action towards reducing the gap, and it thus becomes a potent source of motivation. This makes perfect sense and the resulting motivational power can indeed be significant (although, as we shall see below, some conditions need to be in place for the natural process of discrepancy-reduction to exert its full effect).

The role of vision in motivating human behaviour

1.2.3 Conditions for the motivating capacity of future self-guides

The question that most teachers would probably want to ask at this point is this: OK, if future self-images are indeed so instrumental in impacting motivation, does this mean that if my students can develop a vivid and realistic vision of themselves as successful learners, they will be guaranteed to become keen and active members of my class? Regrettably, not necessarily. It has been widely observed in various educational contexts that although visionary future self-guides have the capacity to motivate action, this does not always happen automatically but depends on a number of conditions. The following list contains some of the most important prerequisites (see Dörnyei and Ushioda 2011); this list will be highly relevant – and will be discussed further in Chapter 2 – when we consider ways of generating an L2 vision in learners, because the essence of all the vision-enhancing practices is to ensure that these conditions are met.

- The learner *does have* a desired future self-image. People differ in how easily they can generate a successful possible self and therefore not everyone is expected to possess a developed ideal or ought-to self-guide.
- The future self is sufficiently *different* from the current self. If there is no observable gap between current and future selves, no increased effort is felt necessary and no motivation emerges.
- The future self-image is *elaborate* and *vivid*. People vary in the vividness of their mental imagery, and a possible self with insufficient specificity and detail may not be able to evoke the necessary motivational response.
- The future self-image is perceived as *plausible*. Possible selves are effective only insofar as the individual does indeed perceive them as *possible*, that is, realistic within the person's individual circumstances. Thus, a sense of controllability (i.e. the belief that one's action is conceivable and can make a difference) is an essential prerequisite.
- The future self-image is *not* perceived as *comfortably certain* to reach, that is, within one's grasp. The learner must not believe that the possible self will happen automatically, without a marked increase in expended effort.
- The future self-image is in harmony – or at least does not clash – with other parts of the individual's self-concept (e.g. a conflict between the ideal and the ought-to selves), particularly with expectations of the learner's family, peers or other elements of the social environment.
- The future self-image is accompanied by relevant and effective *procedural strategies* that act as a *roadmap* towards the goal. Once our

vision generates energy, we need productive tasks into which to channel this energy or it will ebb away.
- The future self-image is *regularly activated* in the learner's working self-concept. Possible selves can be squeezed out of someone's working self-concept by other contenders for attention and will therefore become relevant for behaviour only if they are primed by frequent and varied reminders.
- The desired future self-image is offset by a counteracting *feared possible self* in the same domain. Maximal motivational effectiveness is achieved if the learner also has a vivid image about the *negative consequences* of failing to achieve the desired end state.

1.3 Mental imagery

We saw above that the distinguishing feature of desired future possible selves is the sensory images they carry, and this makes possible selves appropriate to describe the motivational dimension of vision. *Mental imagery* (as such internal images are usually referred to in psychology) is something we are all familiar with, because a significant amount of human thinking, problem-solving, creating, hoping, learning, planning, musing and daydreaming happens in pictures that stimulate all our senses. The process involves generating an imagined reality that we can see, hear, feel and taste. This quasi-perceptual experience is often described in everyday parlance as 'visualising', and Shakespeare coined an expressive term in *Hamlet* to describe the process: 'seeing in the mind's eye'.

Neurobiological research has confirmed that people activate similar neural mechanisms when they see or hear something and when they imagine seeing or hearing the same event (Moulton and Kosslyn 2009). Likewise, studies of brain damage have shown that such injuries often produce parallel deficits in one's ability of perception and the use of imagery (Reisberg and Heuer 2005). That is, to put it bluntly, the brain cannot tell the difference between an actual physical event and the vivid imagery of a simulated scenario (Cox 2012). For this reason, mental imagery lends itself to versatile applications in a range of diverse areas and can be used for the purpose of preparation, repetition, elaboration, intensification or modification of behaviours. For example, as we shall see in Section 3.1 in detail, virtually all world-class athletes use *guided imagery* as an integral part of their training programme, because it is a well-documented fact in sport psychology that imagery can be used for mentally practising specific performance skills, improving confidence, controlling anxiety, preparing for competitive situations and enhancing actual performance (cf. Morris, Spittle and Watt 2005).

1.3.1 Potency and frequency

Throughout this book we offer many quotes and illustrations to describe the power of mental imagery, but perhaps nothing is so spectacular as Albert Einstein's case. As Norton (2013) relates, while Einstein was still a teenager, he repeatedly imagined himself chasing after a beam of light and visualised how the world would look from this perspective. He recalled later that this thought experiment had played a memorable role in his development of the concept of special relativity (see also Finke 1990, which discusses various discoveries and inventions in visualisation). The potency of mental simulation is also demonstrated by Beethoven, who began to lose his hearing at the age of 26 and composed some of his best-known music – such as his Ninth Symphony – while being totally deaf. And to prove that visualisation is not restricted to cognitive or artistic creation but can even have tangible financial outcomes, ILLUSTRATION 1.2 describes a fascinating research project in the business world that was even reported in mainstream television news bulletins in many countries because some clever technology succeeded in triggering off people's mental imagery in a targeted way to increase their pension saving intentions.

Illustration 1.2 The impact of future images on people's saving habits

In a study focusing on people's savings for the time after their retirement, Hershfield *et al.* (2011) utilised people's vision of their future selves in an ingeniously powerful way: the researchers devised an instrument that, by means of virtual reality hardware and software, allowed the participants to interact with realistic visual computer simulations of their future selves. That is, people could actually see their future images on the screen as a result of the computer's 'ageing' of their current appearance. This short-circuiting of present and future self-images had a dramatic effect on the participants' financial disposition: in all cases, those who interacted with their virtual future selves exhibited an increased tendency to allocate more resources towards their future retirement funds!

With regard to the frequency of mental imagery, Klinger's (2009) research on daydreaming (see ILLUSTRATION 1.3) shows that various forms of daydreaming are a surprisingly common part of our mental activities, with as much as half of human thought qualifying for it, and as Markus (2006: xii) points out, within this category the time people spend envisioning their futures is enormous. As she adds, in the USA it is actually 'both a birthright and a moral imperative to tailor one's personal version of the American Dream', which is also reflected in the phrase, 'if you dream it, you can become it'.

Illustration 1.3 On daydreaming

Eric Klinger (2009) describes a series of experiments in which he and his colleagues investigated the thought flow of research participants as they went about their everyday activities. At a given signal by the researcher, the participants were asked at quasi-regular intervals to note down their latest thoughts and rate them on a series of scales. Three of the findings are particularly noteworthy from the point of view of this book:

- It appears that about half (!) of human thought qualifies as *daydreaming* (i.e. thoughts that are undirected and primarily based on imagination). Although this proportion is reduced by the intensity of the task, the results indicate that even in high-pressure, demanding tasks our minds seem to wander into imaginary worlds for about 10% of the time on average. This suggests that imagination-driven daydreams are an integral part of our thought processes.
- Our daydreams are often visual and are heavily influenced by daydreamers' future goals. It appears therefore that although daydreams are predominantly spontaneous and undirected, much of human daydreaming in fact involves explorations of future visions.
- We appear to be in charge of the daydreaming flow to some extent as we can influence not only when to stop but also what to daydream about.

In sum, this research programme has shown that daydreaming about our future in images constitutes a significant portion of our thoughts as we plod through our daily tasks. These daydreams, then, seem to function as reminders of our future aspirations, and sometimes even give us clues about how to attain them.

1.3.2 Imagery in psychology: Paivio's theory of imagery functions in performance

Within psychology, the role of imagery was foregrounded by an influential cognitive theory, the *dual coding theory*, proposed by Canadian psychologist Allan Paivio (1986; for an educational discussion, see Clark and Paivio 1991). He was initially interested in the powerful mnemonic effects of imagery – that is, the use of imagery as a memory aid – but his research expanded into a more comprehensive theory of cognition. Paivio suggested that cognition is made up of two interacting mental subsystems, verbal and non-verbal, and that visual and verbal information is processed differently and stored separately in long-term memory. This means, in effect, that we code environmental information in two different modes, which is well illustrated by the fact that, for example, we can think of an 'orange carrot' both as a verbal phrase and a mental image. Thus, Paivio's theory proposed that a basic dimension of human mental operations is a non-verbal imagery system whose critical functions include 'the analysis of scenes and the generation of mental images (both functions encompassing other sensory modalities in addition to visual)' (1986: 53–4).

Paivio's dual coding model is particularly relevant to our book because it highlights motivational and emotional functions as a central component, and Paivio further elaborated on the links of this functional aspect to mental imagery within the area of sport psychology: his description of the cognitive and motivational functions of imagery in sport performance (Paivio 1985; cf. also Hall *et al.* 1998) initiated a great deal of research on specifying the various behaviour-modificational roles that imagery can play in our mind. The key aspect of Paivio's framework of imagery functions is the separation of cognitive and motivational functions. The former involve imagery used by athletes for mental rehearsal to plan, refine and practise various strategies, routines and perceptual-motor skills (e.g. specific movements), while motivational functions concern keeping up one's motivation, psyching oneself up for specific events, inducing relaxation and imaging oneself working towards and achieving specific goals (e.g. winning an event). Thus, as Cox (2012: 277) summarises, an athlete can use imagery 'to plan a winning strategy (cognitive function) or to get energised for competition (motivational function)'. (We will come back to imagery in sport in Section 3.1, where we discuss imagery training.)

1.3.3 Imagery in language education

Educational research has also shown that what worked for Albert Einstein or successful Olympic athletes also works in the classroom for both teachers and learners, and the field of language education has seen an increase of interest in the role of imagery in learning and teaching. Since the publication of a pioneering volume by Earl Stevick in 1986 called *Images and Options in the Language Classroom* that drew attention to imagery, as well as a dedicated book chapter by Jane Arnold in 1999 entitled 'Visualization: Language Learning with the Mind's Eye', two practical recipe books have appeared focusing on this topic (Arnold *et al.* 2007; Hadfield and Dörnyei 2013) alongside a number of more general publications incorporating some aspects of imagery within creative approaches to L2 lesson planning (Thornbury 1999) and teaching various language skills, such as L2 writing (Wright and Hill 2008) or grammar (Gerngross, Puchta and Thornbury 2006).

Furthermore, our current book demonstrates that imagery is also a key concept in modern theories of language learning motivation as it is at the heart of desired possible language selves, distinguishing them from abstract future goals. Therefore, familiarising ourselves with the various procedures of (guided) imagery in Sections 2.3 and 3.1 will be an ideal starting point for learning how to make the most of the motivational power of vision in the language classroom.

1.3.4 Remembering the past to imagine the future

Szpunar and McDermott (2009) highlight the intriguing fact that the reason why we can imagine our future vividly is due to our ability to recollect *past* occurrences. Indeed, the detail with which we can visualise future occasions – complete with faces of specific people, what they are wearing, the lighting in the room and other concrete details – is all related to our ability to recall similar details about past events that we have either experienced personally or heard someone else describe. In both cases, what we do, in effect, is insert mental images in our present consciousness. This ability to be aware of our past or future in the present is sometimes referred to as *mental time travel* (Dowrick 2012), and the past–future link has been found to be so strong that individuals who are unable to 'travel' in their past – that is, unable to fully re-experience it – seem also unable to set on an imaginary journey into their future.

Neuropsychological evidence confirms the past–future link because the brain regions known to be engaged when we recall our past become similarly activated when we envision a personal future event. This finding is important as it implies that if students find it difficult to 'see' themselves in the future, it may be possible to stimulate their imagination by encouraging them to remember and visualise themselves in specific past events (especially ones that involve successful L2 experiences, including the 'tasters' of L2 selves referred to in Section 2.2). Thus, the inclusion of guided imagery (see Section 2.3) which features the students during a past event may be a useful starting point for those who seem unable to generate future images of themselves.

1.3.5 Imagery perspective

When we imagine ourselves in the future, we have two options: we can see the event from either a *first-* or a *third-person perspective*. The difference is that while in the first-person perspective we are looking at the imagined scene through our own eyes (i.e. as if it was actually happening to us right now), a third-person perspective allows us to visualise the event

The role of vision in motivating human behaviour

from an observer's perspective, watching ourselves and our surroundings as if we were watching a movie in which we played a part. The question that inevitably springs to mind for anyone interested in implementing guided imagery as a tool for creating ideal L2 selves is: does it matter which perspective we choose? The latest research on imagery perspective shows that it may well do, as illustrated by Libby *et al.*'s (2007) study of US voters in ILLUSTRATION 1.4.

Illustration 1.4 On third-person imagery

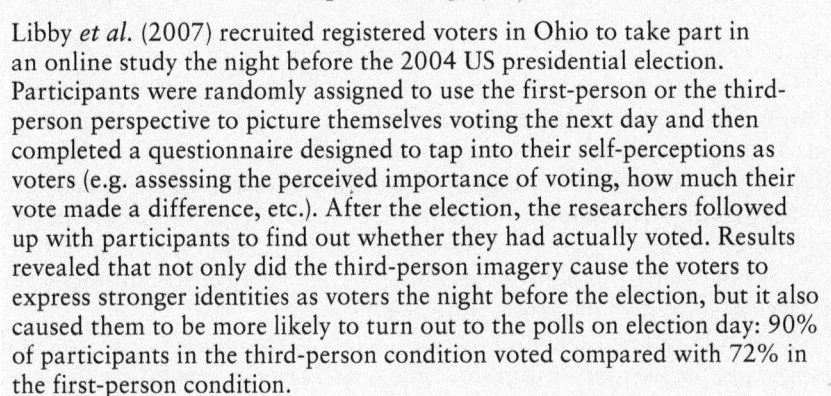

Libby *et al.* (2007) recruited registered voters in Ohio to take part in an online study the night before the 2004 US presidential election. Participants were randomly assigned to use the first-person or the third-person perspective to picture themselves voting the next day and then completed a questionnaire designed to tap into their self-perceptions as voters (e.g. assessing the perceived importance of voting, how much their vote made a difference, etc.). After the election, the researchers followed up with participants to find out whether they had actually voted. Results revealed that not only did the third-person imagery cause the voters to express stronger identities as voters the night before the election, but it also caused them to be more likely to turn out to the polls on election day: 90% of participants in the third-person condition voted compared with 72% in the first-person condition.

The significance of imagery perspective has also been shown to have educational implications. In a study by Vasquez and Buehler (2007), students were asked to imagine carrying out an important academic task that they had to perform within the next few weeks. Those who imagined this from a third-person perspective reported significantly higher achievement motivation than those who were instructed to imagine performing the same task from the first-person perspective. How can we explain this intriguing phenomenon? The emerging consensus among scholars is that when we imagine something in the first-person perspective, our focus is on the experience itself, but we tend to switch to the third-person imagery when we want to integrate that experience into our self-concept and this, in turn, appears to have implications for what we do (Libby and Eibach 2009, 2011). Linking this finding back to possible selves research, it suggests that imagining our future selves from the first-person perspective is associated with the self-enhancing function, while the third-person perspective may be linked to 'action-readiness' (Oyserman 2009; Oyserman, Bybee and Terry 2006). Translated into

19

practical terms, guided imagery from the first-person perspective may be effective if our primary purpose is to enhance the students' positive feelings about themselves or to improve their attitudes towards the L2, while the third-person perspective may be more powerful if we want the students' L2 visions to motivate specific actions such as learning behaviours. Thus, both perspectives have a useful place in a comprehensive 'visionary programme'.

1.4 Language learning motivation and future L2 self-guides

As we saw in Section 1.2, vision is a powerful motivational construct whose essence can be captured by the psychological concept of possible selves. This concept has been successfully adapted to language learning situations under the rubric of 'possible L2 selves' or 'future L2 self-guides'; let us have a brief look at how this understanding has emerged in the history of L2 motivation research, leading to the development of Zoltán's theory of the L2 Motivational Self System, which is fully compatible with possible selves theory and which also embraces the experiential nature of 'vision' discussed earlier.

With a long-term learning process such as the mastery of a second language, the learner's ultimate success will largely depend on the level of motivation; without sufficient motivation, even individuals with the most remarkable abilities cannot accomplish long-term goals, and neither are appropriate curricula and good teaching enough on their own to ensure student achievement. This truth is clearly expressed in arguably the oldest English proverb that is still in regular use today (first recorded in the twelfth century): 'You can lead a horse to water, but you can't make it drink.' Indeed, most teachers would agree that you can give someone the opportunity to do something, but you cannot force them to do it if they do not want to, which means in educational terms that motivation is essential for students to take ownership of their learning in order to succeed. Accordingly, the concept of language learning motivation has been the target of intensive research in second language acquisition (SLA) research for over five decades, with several books and literally hundreds of articles published on the topic (see Dörnyei and Ushioda 2011 for an overview). It is useful to divide the evolution of motivation research during this period into three broad phases:

- *The social psychological period* (1959–1990), which was initiated and characterised by the work of social psychologist Robert Gardner and his associates in Canada (e.g. Gardner 1985; Gardner and

The role of vision in motivating human behaviour

MacIntyre 1993). The best-known concepts stemming from this period are *integrative* and *instrumental orientation/motivation*, the former referring to the desire to learn an L2 of a valued community so that one can communicate with members of the community and sometimes even become like them, the latter to the concrete benefits that language proficiency might bring about (e.g. career opportunities, increased salary).

- *The cognitive-situated period* (during the 1990s), which widened the perspective of the study of L2 motivation by importing a range of contemporary cognitive theories from educational psychology. Besides wishing to bring L2 motivation theory in line with mainstream motivational psychology, a second general objective in this period was to adopt a more *situated* analysis of motivation in specific learning settings, particularly in L2 classrooms. The best-known concepts associated with this phase are *intrinsic* and *extrinsic motivation* (i.e. performing a behaviour for its own sake or as a means to an end), *attributions* (i.e. how one explains past successes and failures), *self-confidence / efficacy* as well as *situation-specific motives* related to the learning environment, such as motives related to the L2 course, the L2 teachers or the learner's peer group (see Dörnyei 1994).
- *New socio-dynamic approaches* (first decade of the twenty-first century), which have been characterised by an interest in *motivational change / evolution* and the relationship between motivation and *identity* in specific social contexts. The best-known concepts originating in this period are the *process-oriented conceptualisation of motivation* (Dörnyei 2000), motivation as *investment* (Norton 2000), a *dynamic systems perspective* in motivation (i.e. research that integrates the various factors related to the learner, the learning task and the learning environment into one complex system; see Dörnyei and Ushioda 2011) and the concepts of the *ideal* and *ought-to L2 selves*, which will be described in detail below.

1.4.1 The L2 Motivational Self System

In 2005, Zoltán proposed a new approach to the understanding of L2 motivation (Dörnyei 2005), conceived within an 'L2 Motivational Self System', which integrated a number of influential L2 theories (e.g. Gardner 2001; Noels 2003; Norton 2001; Ushioda 2001) with the findings of 'self research' in psychology (described in the previous sections). The model consists of the following three main constituents (for a more detailed discussion, see Dörnyei 2009):

Motivating Learners, Motivating Teachers

- *Ideal L2 self*, which concerns the L2-specific facet of one's *ideal self*: if the person we would like to become speaks an L2 (e.g. the person we would like to become is associated with travelling or doing business internationally), the ideal L2 self is a powerful motivator to learn the L2 because we would like to reduce the gap between our actual and ideal selves.
- *Ought-to L2 self*, which concerns the attributes that one believes one *ought to* possess to avoid possible negative outcomes, and which therefore may bear little resemblance to the person's own desires or wishes.
- *L2 learning experience*, which concerns situation-specific motives related to the immediate learning environment and experience (e.g. the positive impact of success or the enjoyable quality of a language course).

Thus, the L2 Motivational Self System suggests that there are three primary sources of the motivation to learn a foreign/second language: (1) the learner's internal desire to become an effective L2 user, (2) social pressures coming from the learner's environment to master the L2 and (3) the actual experience of being engaged in the L2 learning process. This model is therefore fully compatible with possible selves theory and also embraces the experiential nature of 'vision' discussed earlier: the first two components involve future self-states that the learner envisages and experiences as if they were reality, while the third component focuses on the direct experience associated with the actual self.

1.5 Motivation and vision in language teachers' development

The new conceptualisation of L2 motivation in terms of language identity and vision offers a fresh perspective on a motivational teaching practice (we will discuss the practical implications in detail in Part II of this book). Yet, research on language teachers' development also suggests that novel ideas, however powerful and attractive they may be, do not necessarily translate into transformed teaching practices. Consider a far from unique scenario from Maggie's experience as a teaching practice supervisor, in which two student teachers processed their newly learnt knowledge in a strikingly different way (see ILLUSTRATION 1.5). It is clear that while one of the two trainees seemed to have got things right and this manifested itself in the actual class she conducted, the other perceived and then transmitted the new methodological input in a rather ineffective way.

Illustration 1.5 Same idea, different impact (adapted from Kubanyiova 2012: xiii)

As part of their supervised teaching practice on an MA in TESOL course, student teachers were preparing to teach an English class of undergraduates for one semester. To inspire them and help them enlarge their repertoire of suitable tasks and activities, a series of practical workshops was organised; one of these demonstrations included a choral reading task and two of my supervisees decided to try it out in their own lessons. The two teachers used exactly the same materials and performed the same activity with students of similar language proficiency, age, motivation, socioeconomic background and previous language learning history, in a similar-size classroom at the same time of the day. Yet, the outcome was strikingly different. In one teacher's class, the classroom atmosphere was soaked with enthusiasm and engagement: the learners eagerly debating over the right kind of intonation, practising pronunciation of difficult words, often eliciting the teacher's help, the whole class roaring with laughter as they were performing the task together, begging the teacher to let them 'do it again'. In the other teacher's class, however, there was such a strong sense of tension, reluctance, embarrassment and boredom, which was intensified by the teacher's command to 'do it again'.

How can we explain the very different responses of the two language teachers to the new material and, consequently, the profound differences these responses had on the learners' classroom engagement? One of the growing domains in applied linguistics that can shed some light on this question is language teacher cognition research.

1.5.1 Language teachers' cognitions

'Teacher cognition' refers to 'the unobservable cognitive dimension of teaching', typically summed up as what teachers 'know, believe and think' (Borg 2003: 81). This research area is primarily concerned with understanding the teachers' mental lives and how these shape their classroom practices. This is a relatively new line of inquiry in applied linguistics (it was launched only in the 1990s) and yet over its short life span an extensive range of theoretical concepts have been explored, including – to give a flavour of this richness – teachers' beliefs, conceptions, emotions, identities, selves, ideologies, knowledge, maxims, philosophies, principles, theories and values. As a result, applied linguists have started to acknowledge and appreciate the complex dynamics which underlie the teachers' understanding, interpretation and implementation of new ideas in their classrooms.

Differences in classroom behaviours such as the ones illustrated above are now seen to occur as a function of the 'unobservable dimension' of the teachers' cognitions related to the L2, to language pedagogy in general, to the particular teaching context, to the students and, last but not least, to the teachers themselves. When teachers enter the classroom, they carry with them the baggage of their prior beliefs about how languages are learnt and how they should or should not be taught, as well as memories of the diverse images and models of good and bad teaching that they have encountered and subsequently internalised or rejected throughout their teaching careers. As a consequence, the extent to which teachers would transform their language classrooms into motivating environments as a response to some new input received – for example, a teacher development course, talking to colleagues or reading this book – depends on an intricate tapestry of multiple influences. Yet, amidst this complexity, there is an important finding that has emerged from research on language teachers' conceptual change and that allows us to orientate ourselves: the teachers' vision of themselves in the future plays a central role in how they engage with new ideas and, consequently, how they grow as professionals.

Coming back to the different practices of the two teachers in the above illustration, the contrasting uptake and implementation of the newly learnt knowledge in their course was likely to be related to their prior beliefs about what language teaching should be like. These beliefs shaped their vision of themselves as classroom practitioners – determining how they related to the learners and how they acted out the teacher's role – to the extent that, as we saw, in the case of one of these teachers the whole process became counterproductive. Teacher cognition research would suggest that this was likely to be more than a methodological issue (after all, both teachers carried out the same procedures), highlighting the possible roots of the differences in the teachers' mindsets.

1.5.2 The centrality of vision and motivation in language teachers' mental lives

The focus on images of teaching and the self is not new in the teacher cognition literature: Johnson (1994) and, more recently, Golombek (2009) have included the construct of *images of teaching* in their discussion of language teacher knowledge and beliefs. Goodman (1988) has referred to *guiding images* as visual representations of pre-service teachers' philosophies of teaching derived from their images of past experiences as children, pupils, student teachers and their future expectations. Stuart and Thurlow (2000: 117) have concluded that pre-service teachers need to have a 'personalised vision of what their classroom could be', and Thornbury (1999: 4) also talks about 'lesson images', referring to the mental scripts of lesson plans that guide experienced teachers' classroom conduct; as one accomplished teacher in his study claimed, 'I have a vision. I sort of know exactly how it's going to go. I've imagined what will happen' (p. 4). These and similar studies in both the general educational and the applied linguistics literature suggest that how language teachers come to view themselves exerts a powerful influence on the kinds of learning opportunities they create in their language classrooms.

Teacher motivation has surprisingly not held a prominent place in language teacher cognition research, because motivation research in general has tended to focus on the students, with the teachers seen only as the administrators of certain motivational strategies. The few existing investigations on the teachers' own disposition have been largely restricted to studying issues such as the teachers' job satisfaction, stress and burnout (prompted by the large-scale phenomenon of teachers leaving the profession). Things have started to change, however, because as Dörnyei and Ushioda (2011) summarise, it has been increasingly recognised that the teacher's level of enthusiasm and commitment is one of the most important factors that can affect learners' motivation to learn. As they conclude, 'if a teacher is motivated to teach, there is a good chance that his or her students will be motivated to learn' (p. 158). Similarly, it requires little justification that in order for teachers to deepen their knowledge and transform their practices, they must be motivated to invest mental energy in reflection, a process that has been found instrumental for any meaningful development of language teachers to occur (see Johnson 1999; Kubanyiova 2012).

In her research with EFL teachers in Slovakia, Maggie found two broad motives that led her research participants into careers in teaching: the love of English and the desire to be valued (Kubanyiova 2006). What she later also discovered was that while these motives did shape the teachers' classroom behaviours and their reflections on their own practices, they were almost always accompanied by references to images related to broader self-identification and future self-concept themes. Her conclusion was that if we want to understand what motivates teachers to do what they do, we need to gain insights into their images of who they yearn to become – that is, their *ideal language teacher selves* (cf. Kubanyiova 2012).

1.5.3 Possible selves and language teacher development

We have seen earlier that the concept of *possible selves* offers a powerful bridge between the students' visions of themselves in the future and their actual learning behaviours. Teachers, like learners, hold multiple personalised and socially constructed images of themselves in future states, which can be either positive, such as aspirations, hopes and desires, or negative, representing identity-related fears and worries. Although most empirical research to date has focused on the impact of possible selves on students' – rather than teachers' – engagement and achievement, some recent work has begun to apply the concept to explain the role these future visions play in teaching and teacher development (see Hiver 2013 and Kubanyiova 2009 for L2-specific research).

To explain the role of possible selves in language teachers' development, Maggie proposed a theoretical model of Language Teacher Conceptual Change (LTCC; see Kubanyiova 2012), which highlights the role of the teachers' ideal, ought-to and feared selves in shaping the ways in which language practitioners approach the question of their lifelong professional development. Within this model, the *ideal L2 teacher self* subsumes the language teachers' future self-images of identity goals, hopes and aspirations, and the motivation to engage with new ideas is energised by the teachers' realisation of the discrepancy between their actual (i.e. present) and ideal (i.e. desired) selves. The *ought-to L2 teacher self* refers to the teachers' images of who they believe they should become, related to the self-relevant representation of responsibilities, obligations and normative pressures with regard to their work. These ought-to images may come from a variety of sources, including students' expectations, school policies, the wider sociocultural context or the requirements of a specific teacher-training course. Finally, the teachers' vision of the negative consequences and fears for the future has been conceptualised as the *feared L2 teacher self*, which represents a deterrent vision of who the teacher might become if he/she does not live up to his/her ideal or ought-to images.

In the light of these considerations, let us return to the initial question of why new ideas, however powerful and attractive, do not necessarily translate into transformed teaching practices. We can list at least three reasons (see Kubanyiova 2012 for a fuller explanation):

- The novel approaches, ideas, techniques or materials simply do not tap into those professional self-images that are salient in the teacher's current self-concept. In other words, teachers may appreciate the ideas and perhaps even try them out in the classroom if they absolutely have to, but because they do not represent the kind of teacher they would ideally like to become, there is no compelling reason to engage with them at a deeper level. This developmental path has been dubbed the 'Nice-but-not-for-me' route.

- The new content does not create emotional dissonance, that is, a salient recognition of a discrepancy between the teacher's actual and future selves. In this case, although the new ideas may closely correspond with the teachers' desired image of themselves, they believe, rightly or wrongly, that they are already part of what they do. Because there is no gap to be bridged, there is no real need for the teachers to engage with the ideas any further and thus no change occurs. This reaction has been termed the 'Couldn't-agree-more' route.
- The new ideas threaten the teacher's sense of self. The teachers in this third scenario may be inspired and willing (or perhaps feel pressured) to pursue a modified future image of themselves that the new material has evoked, but they soon discover that this new image clashes with – and thus threatens – other images of their future selves that are more important in their self-concept. If this threat outweighs any benefits that the new teaching ideas might bring about, the teachers are unlikely to pursue this 'Nice-but-too-scary' route any further.

1.5.4 Creating conditions for language teacher conceptual change

What makes the latest theorising in language teacher cognition research particularly appealing for the purpose of our book is that it sheds light on some important principles for promoting teacher learning and for creating conditions for transformational change within teachers. We explore these conditions in Part III in detail, but let us conclude this section with a metaphorical image that summarises the main principles of language teacher conceptual change in relation to vision.

Inspired by the title of John Ortberg's (2001) book *If You Want to Walk on Water, You've Got to Get Out of the Boat*, let us imagine a scene of participants in a training course focusing on 'Walking on Water': they are sitting in their small boats in the middle of the sea, intently listening to what the instructor has to say. There is a lot of excitement and fervent engagement with the topic as they are made familiar with the latest developments in the art of walking on water. But when the invitation finally comes from the trainer to come and join her on the sea and try walking on water for themselves, many (if not most) choose to remain in their boats. The question is, why? Some just like to be out in the sea and although they are really enjoying the course, they never really thought of themselves as water-walkers and, to be honest, never really intended to learn, let alone use, this skill in their lives. Some others believe that they have already mastered the technique and, therefore, while in total agreement with what the trainer has to say, are convinced that the invitation is not really for them but for their novice peers. Finally, a small group of trainees may begin to feel the pressure to step out of the boat and may even find the courage to do so, as soon as their feet touch the water, they realise how cold, deep and dangerous the sea really is, and thus they quickly return to the safety and cosiness of their boats.

Based on the insights from our research into language learning motivation and language teachers' conceptual change, we can offer the following advice to the 'Walking on Water' course leader on how to inspire the trainees to get out of their boats (adapted from Kubanyiova 2012):

- *Inspire a vision (resonance)*. The course participants are unlikely to feel the need to get out of the boat if the course content does not *resonate* with their vision of who they want to become. Working with them on developing such a vision seems to be the single most important element of any course whose aim is to inspire meaningful learning experience and a lasting transformation.
- *Rock the boat (dissonance)*. It is much more comfortable to remain in the boat than to risk drowning in the rough seas, yet we can hardly live up to our visions by staying put. The course leader must make this *dissonance* salient by (gently) rocking the boat and slowly shaking the course participants out their comfort zones.
- *Spread a safety net (hope)*. Rocking the boat when all that the course participants can see is rough and dangerous waters can be a genuinely frightening experience (even in language teaching practice), and it is likely to put off many teachers from sticking their necks out ever again. Spreading safety nets and providing plenty of models and practice runs can turn the threat into a challenge and give the participants *hope* that walking on water is not something people are born with, but rather a skill that anyone can develop if they learn to trust their vision and persevere in their practice.

1.6 Summary

This theoretical introduction may have felt like a smorgasbord of colourful ideas, with references to diverse people such as Martin Luther King, Jr and Albert Einstein, and drawing on wide-ranging academic disciplines from sport psychology and teacher cognition research to neurobiology. One might rightly wonder whether all this is really interrelated and connected to language education, that is, whether there is indeed a meaningful link between, say, the foundation of the theory of relativity and the teaching of the present perfect tense in the language classroom. We will revisit this question in the concluding chapter of this book, but it is important to note here that our intention was not at all to present an impressive cacophony of elements that might be interesting in themselves but which do not come together as a cohesive whole. Instead, we hoped to illustrate that vision is indeed one of the highest-order motivational constructs that transfers freely from one domain to another and thus has broad relevance. Yet, admittedly, assuming this general relevance and the transferability of lessons learnt in specific disciplines is somewhat speculative, because the exact manner in which vision operates in shaping human behaviour has not been tested empirically in its entirety, particularly not in the field of language education. In this sense, this book itself is rather 'visionary' in nature, which highlights the need for further research in order to work out the exact details of the 'big picture'.

The good news is that as far as applied linguistics is concerned, this further research is on its way. There seems to be a rapidly growing body of research on the relationship between L2 motivation and future self-images (for recent reviews, see Dörnyei and Ushioda 2011; Henry 2011; Kormos, Kiddle and Csizér 2011; Magid 2012; Papi and Abdollahzadeh 2012), and promising results have been reported in longitudinal studies with regard to employing various self-enhancement activities, including guided imagery, to facilitate student commitment to and engagement with language learning (e.g. Fukada *et al.* 2011; Jones 2012; Magid and Chan 2012; Sampson 2012). Furthermore, Zoltán has recently completed a study with Letty Chan (Dörnyei and Chan 2013), which provides strong empirical evidence for the multi-sensory nature of future self-guides, highlighting the positive link between a broad imagery capacity (including both visual and auditory components) and the learners' ideal and ought-to L2 selves.

Thus, although empirical research has not yet fully caught up with the current theoretical developments concerning vision and the various practical proposals for enhancing it within the context of language education, researchers have been offering more and more pieces of jigsaw to validate a vision-based approach. Future research will still be needed, though, to test out how these various pieces fit together and to evaluate the effectiveness of the overall framework offered in this book. Accordingly, we would like to encourage teachers to adapt the ideas presented in the following chapters critically and creatively to their specific contexts, and we would also like to invite them to contribute to validating and refining the various proposals through their own classroom-based research. In sum, we believe that vision has great potential for language education, but for the time being, please use it with care!

Part II
Motivating language learners through vision

> When the soul wishes to experience something, she throws an image of the experience out before her and enters into her own image.
> *Meister Eckhart (1260–1327)*

The material in the previous chapter has helped us to build a case for the place of vision in language education. In this chapter we explore how the theoretical insights can be translated into action and, more specifically, how language teachers can integrate vision into their classroom teaching practice in order to motivate their learners. Let us start with a brief reminder of what we have learnt from the 'possible selves' research so far. We know that a positive vision of ourselves is a motivational resource that can impel us to action, although we have also seen that this is not always an inevitable outcome. Because we are interested in vision that energises actual learning and teaching behaviours, let us recap the criteria that possible selves need to fulfil in order to possess such motivational power.

First, future self-images need to be directly linked to a positive social identity that we personally value, because without this link there would be little incentive to become the person that we have envisaged. We also need to be aware of a clear discrepancy between our present self and the possible future self, because if there is no observable gap between current and future selves, no increased effort is felt necessary. However, as we saw earlier, and especially in the latest research on language teachers' conceptual change, there would still be little motivation to act on the awareness of this difference if we did not feel uneasy about that gap between the actual and the possible self: to put it broadly, we must be bothered. At the same time, the imagined future self needs to be felt plausible rather than an unrealistic fantasy, which is highlighted by the term *possible* self, and we also know that the more vivid the future self, the more power it has. It further reinforces our commitment to work towards the desired future self if it is regularly cued, or activated, in our everyday life, and to say that our future vision is unlikely to take us very far if we cannot see a clear pathway to it requires little justification. Finally, it is often the case that however valued our desired future self may be or however elaborate

Motivating Learners, Motivating Teachers

our plan for reaching it, we may still choose to do little to pursue it if the fear of what might happen in case our desired future does not materialise is not sufficiently vivid in our mind's eye.

[margin note: risk]

If we take all of these conditions into account, we end up with a useful framework for developing an effective motivational intervention programme aimed at enhancing learner vision in the language classroom. An outline of this programme is presented in TOOLBOX 2.1 below, where the conditions for the motivational capacity of desired future selves are matched with specific aspects of motivational classroom practice. It is these key aspects that form the structure of Part II, with each aspect discussed in a separate chapter.

> **Toolbox 2.1 A framework for developing a vision-centred teaching practice**
>
> | Motivational conditions for desired future language selves | Key facets of a vision-centred motivational practice |
> |---|---|
> | The learner has a desired future self-image (vision) which is related to but is also different from his/her current self-concept. | *Creating the language learner's vision* |
> | The vision is elaborate and vivid. | *Strengthening the vision through imagery enhancement* |
> | The vision is perceived as plausible but not comfortably certain, and it does not clash with other parts of the individual's self-concept, particularly with the expectations of the learner's family and peers. | *Substantiating the vision by making it plausible* |
> | The vision is accompanied by relevant and effective procedural strategies that act as a roadmap towards the goal. | *Transforming the vision into action* |
> | The vision is regularly activated in the learner's working self-concept. | *Keeping the vision alive* |
> | The learner is also aware of elaborate information about the negative consequences of not achieving the desired end state. | *Counterbalancing the vision by considering failure* |

It is important to emphasise at this point that the set of motivational principles and facets we will discuss here should not be seen as a linear, step-by-step programme that requires each principle to be fully

Motivating language learners through vision

implemented before moving on to the next. For example, it is generally true that learners will benefit from first experimenting with various visions in order to construct one for themselves that they can then strengthen and nurture. Yet, it is also the case that learners come with a variety of past experiences and future hopes, and while sometimes one tiny impulse is enough to awaken some powerful L2 image that is both meaningful and clear in the learners' minds, in other situations more extensive groundwork is needed. Furthermore, although our suggestions below appear to be categorised into neat clusters, in reality the line separating one motivational facet from another is often blurred: for example, guided imagery exercises that we refer to in the chapter on creating the vision (Chapter 2) can also function as image enhancers (Chapter 3).

The best way to look at the principles for motivating through vision, then, is to use them as a framework for students to reflect on their own motivation and learning (cf. Allwright and Hanks 2009) and as a user-friendly guide for teachers to make informed decisions about the tools that may be needed in specific situations. For example, if it appears to be the case that students do not see any purpose for studying a foreign language and rebel against any attempt by the teachers or the 'system' to force them to do so, we may need to invest considerable energy into creating the vision (Chapter 2), making it plausible (Chapter 4) and keeping it alive (Chapter 6). If, on the other hand, the learners seem to accept the value of a foreign language in general and yet this positive attitude does not translate into observable learning behaviours, we may want to place more emphasis on strengthening the vision (Chapter 3), operationalising it through concrete language tasks (Chapter 5) and perhaps even counterbalancing it with images of negative consequences (Chapter 7).

A final caveat before we move on to the practical content of Part II is related to our interim summary of Part I in Section 1.6 concerning the research basis of the framework itself. As shown in the previous theoretical discussion and also throughout the following chapters, our framework has emerged from a synthesis of extensive theoretical and research activity across a range of disciplines. On the other hand, empirical research that would attest to the overall validity of the vision principles outlined in Part II for the domain of language education is only now beginning to emerge in applied linguistics. With this caveat, therefore, comes an open invitation to the teachers to adopt an 'attitude of inquiry' (Larsen-Freeman 2000a) as they explore the plausibility and relevance of these new ideas in their own practice and then (it is hoped) contribute to the knowledge construction in this novel domain of applied linguistics.

2 Creating the language learner's vision

> We are limited, not by our abilities, but by our vision.
> *Attributed to Jonathan Swift (1667–1745)*

As will be clear by now, the (obvious) prerequisite for the motivational capacity of any desired future self – or future self-guide – is that it needs to exist. It has also been mentioned that people differ in how easily they can generate a successful possible self, which suggests that one of the main sources of the absence of motivation in some learners is likely to be the lack of a properly developed desired self-image in general, and an ideal language self component of this image in particular. For instance, even if a foreign language has been made a compulsory subject in the school curriculum for a good reason, many students sitting in our classrooms will not have a clear idea of what that reason might be or how knowing that language could enrich their personal lives. Therefore, the logical first step in a motivational intervention programme that follows the self-approach is to help learners create their desired future selves, that is, to *construct their vision* of who they could become as L2 users and what knowing an L2 could add to their lives.

What do we mean by 'constructing' a vision?

Before we discuss specific approaches for constructing desired future self-images, some reflection is needed on what we mean by the verb *construct* in this context. It is highly unlikely that any motivational intervention will lead a student to create a brand new ideal self out of nothing; the realistic process is more likely to be one of *awareness raising* and *guided selection* from the multiple aspirations, dreams and desires that the student has already entertained in the past. Dunkel, Kelts and Coon (2006) explain that during the formation of their identities, adolescents produce a wide variety of possible selves as potential identity alternatives to explore and 'try on' without full commitment. The origins of these tentative possible selves often go back to views held by others, most notably to the ideals that parents hold for themselves and for their children (Zentner and Renaud 2007). In countries where several languages coexist – for example, English or French is used as an official language besides the local vernacular – these views are often affected by language attitudes. Alternatively, the various possible selves can also stem from the students' peer community, which acts as a powerful reference group exerting strong social pressure (Boyatzis and Akrivou 2006). The fourth common route is related to the impact of role models that the students have seen in films, on TV or in real life: the term *celebrity culture* that is so often mentioned in the media nowadays refers exactly to the increased impact of such external models to serve as behavioural templates for the wider population.

Whatever the source may be, the fact is that most adolescents encounter a number of ideological and occupational options available in society, and experiment with a wide range of social roles and possible identities in an attempt to consolidate their beliefs and values into a more or less personal ideology which will, in turn, allow them to make provisional commitments to life plans and projects (McAdams 2001). Put simply, they search widely to establish who they really are. Ideal self-images offer an optimal framework in their search for the integration of the disparate roles, talents, proclivities, hopes, desires and visions into a unified configuration that provides life with some semblance of sense and purpose. Thus, igniting the vision involves, in effect, increasing the students' mindfulness of the significance of desired self-images, guiding them through a number of possible selves that they have entertained in their minds in the past, and presenting powerful role models as templates for crafting their own ideal language selves. Dunkel *et al.* (2006) note in this respect that alternative possible selves can often be mutually exclusive or at least difficult to reconcile. Therefore, the construction of an ideal self also involves the process of making decisions about which possible selves to pursue and which to give up on. Finally, Oyserman, Terry and Bybee (2002) underline the importance of helping students to personalise the emerging preferred self-images, that is, to build into them as much as they can of what they know about themselves in order to capitalise on their own existing strengths and unique features.

Why is 'agency' important?

Taking Oyserman *et al.*'s (2002) recommendation to personalise the emerging self-images one step further, another reason for further reflection on the term *construct* stems from a specific view of education which places *learner agency* – that is, learners' proactive investment in the learning process – at the heart of the educational process. This emphasis is embedded in numerous approaches to language learning and teaching, including a focus on learner autonomy (e.g. Murray, Gao and Lamb 2011), learner identity (e.g. Norton 2000), action-based

Motivating Learners, Motivating Teachers

teaching (e.g. van Lier 2007) and self-regulatory learning (e.g. Cohen and Macaro 2007) as well as specific views of motivation, including motivational self-regulation (Ushioda 2008) and self-determination theory (Noels 2009). Central to these approaches is the belief that learners enjoy a fuller and more meaningful learning experience when they are in charge of their own learning, when their motivation is generated from within rather than through external rewards such as grades, and when they are given opportunities to make the learning material their own. In short, agency implies that learners are allowed to exercise their capacity to act in ways that are congruent with their own lived experiences and identities. Leo van Lier (2007: 47) describes the significance of this notion within language education well:

> our learners are people with their own lives, aspirations, needs, worries, dreams and identities. As I envisage an AB [action-based] approach to teaching and learning, treating the learners as persons in their own right is crucial. This means, quite simply, that they are listened to and respected as speakers in their own right, and as agents of their own educational destiny … Learning an L2 involves a struggle to forge a new identity that is true to the self. The core of identity is voice, and voice implies agency.

In keeping with this view, we see the 'construction' of ideal language selves ultimately as the outcome of the students' rather than the teachers' effort. The way teachers can help to facilitate the construction process is by orchestrating encounters for the learners with a variety of images of attractive possible selves and by supporting students in their pursuit of those self-images that are congruent with their own identities. In short, the teacher can listen and prompt, but the L2 vision must ultimately become the students' own.

Towards designing a 'visionary' programme

There are several examples of successful motivational intervention programmes focusing on possible self-enhancement, and we have listed some of the best-known ones in Toolbox 2.2. So far little work has been directed at specifically developing an ideal language self, although for interesting exceptions, see the motivational experiments conducted by Michael Magid and Letty Chan (Chan 2012; Magid 2011; Magid and Chan 2012), the self-enhancement projects by Fukada *et al.* (2011) and Sampson (2012), and the motivational programme described by Hadfield (2012). However, it seems to us that in an era when international

Creating the language learner's vision

holidays are becoming increasingly accessible and cross-cultural communication is a standard part of our existence in the 'global village', it is possible to devise creative ideal-self-generating activities that draw on the students' past adventures, the exotic nature of encounters with a foreign culture or on role models of successful L2 learning achievers. In the remainder of this chapter, we break down the broad process of generating language learning vision into five facets: (1) understanding students' current identity concerns and lived experiences, (2) providing regular tasters of desired future states, (3) using guided imagery, (4) using guided narratives and (5) ensuring ample exposure to role models.

🔧 Toolbox 2.2 Examples of possible selves intervention programmes

Oyserman, Terry and Bybee's (2002) School-to-Jobs programme

As part of what has been the highest-profile possible selves intervention programme to date, the researchers developed a nine-week after-school syllabus to enhance African American low-income teenagers' abilities to imagine themselves as successful adults and connect these future images to current school involvement. The intervention had positive effects on the participants' engagement and behaviour at school, as well as on their possible selves, providing evidence that the self-concept of adolescents can be shaped with a structured intervention.

Hock, Deshler and Schumaker's (2006) Possible Selves programme

This successful intervention programme was aimed at increasing the motivation of university and middle-school students with academic difficulties. After students explored their expectations, hopes and fears, and then identified words or phrases that described them in targeted areas (as a learner, a person, a worker and in a strength area) in an individual interview with an adviser, they were asked to draw a Possible Selves Tree: the limbs and branches of the tree represented the areas the students had talked about in the interview and the positive possible selves associated with those, while the feared possible selves were represented by dangerous conditions for the tree such as termites, poison in the soil and lightning. They were instructed to add the exact words they recorded in the interviews to the relevant parts of the tree, and afterwards they discussed with their tutors how to maintain the strength of the tree, provide it with nourishment, make it grow and protect it from harm.

Sheldon and Lyubomirsky's (2006) 'Best Possible Selves' writing project

In this project university students were asked to visualise themselves in the future and imagine that they have succeeded in accomplishing their life goals. Then, they were to prepare a written narrative that described their 'ideal future life' in as much detail as they could (for more information about such tasks, see Section 2.4). The task was found to produce a significant increase in positive emotions, leading the researchers to conclude that envisioning ideal future selves is inherently motivating and self-relevant.

Magid and Chan's (2012) pioneering training programmes in language education

Based on Dörnyei's (2005, 2009) L2 Motivational Self System, Michael Magid and Letty Chan designed and conducted two separate training programmes with Chinese university students of English (one in England, the other in Hong Kong) which were successful in enhancing their language vision. The programme in England consisted of activities asking the learners to list current concerns and goals regarding their future jobs, relationships and lifestyle as well as their ideal selves in each of those domains in order to help them create a vision of their ideal L2 self. This was followed by further tasks of drawing a timeline, developing action plans and considering feared selves. The intervention programme in Hong Kong was based on the 'Ideal Self Tree' activity adapted from the above-mentioned Possible Selves Tree (Hock *et al.*, 2006). In spite of the differences between the circumstances of the programmes, both were effective in motivating the participants to learn English and in increasing their linguistic self-confidence through strengthening their ideal L2 self-image. As a result of the motivational interventions, participants on both programmes reported exerting more effort towards learning English and motivation to work harder to achieve their ideal L2 selves.

2.1 Understanding students' current identity concerns and lived experiences

All the programmes outlined in Toolbox 2.2 start with considerations of the students' present state. This is, of course, logical and is supported by research findings which show that possible self-images are rooted in people's developmental and contextual concerns (Oyserman and James 2009). That is, these images of ideal (or dreaded) future states are anchored in the reality of our most immediate and pressing concerns in the present time. For example, occupational concerns tend to be more prominent for young adults, while family- and parenting-oriented future images usually come a bit later, followed by health-related and then pension-related concerns even later. With regard to the relevance of sociocultural issues, an extreme example is a study of imprisoned fathers by Meek (2007), which reveals that becoming like their own

Creating the language learner's vision

fathers was a common feared possible self for those men. Thus, a clear lesson for language educators is that a 'visionary' intervention cannot begin without first understanding the students' current identity concerns. This implies more than merely doing a needs analysis in order to try and make language tasks relevant to the particular characteristics of the learners. What is really involved is a conscious effort to gain an understanding of the persons that the students in the classrooms are and of the range of unique life experiences, dreams and worries that they bring into the learning environment with them.

Of course, such an emphasis is not new in our field – see, for example, Stevick's (1990) notion of *humanism*, Tudor's (1996) summary of *learner-centredness* or Richards's (2006) discussion of *teacher–student talk* – and it is certainly not restricted to language education. Echoing Bonny Norton's (2000) point in the quote below, the question is not whether students' current identity concerns are relevant to the learning process (they most certainly are), but rather *how* language teachers can gain a deeper understanding of them. In the following discussion, we present some practical illustrations and suggestions in this respect.

> But how does the teacher take seriously the lived experiences of language learners? How can the lives of language learners become an integral part of the second language curriculum when a teacher may have thirty students in the classroom, all with different histories, experiences and expectations? My position is that the identities and lived experiences of language learners are already part of the language learning / language teaching experience, whether or not this is formally recognised in the second language curriculum. What the language teacher needs to understand is how the identities of learners are engaged in the formal language classroom, and how this knowledge can help teachers facilitate the language learner's interaction with target language speakers in the wider community.
> (Norton 2000: 140)

2.1.1 Illustration: Transforming the 'unteachable'

Consider the following illustration from a fascinating memoir by Erin Gruwell (2007), an enthusiastic young teacher at a high school in Long Beach, California, whose story has been documented in the Hollywood movie *Freedom Writers* (starring Oscar-winner Hilary Swank). On the first day of her teaching career, Erin found herself in a classroom full of 'at-risk' inner-city youths, also known in that school as the 'unteachables', who had no vision, no hope for the future and, consequently,

Motivating Learners, Motivating Teachers

no motivation for academic work. Yet – and this is a true story! – by not having anything else to rely on but a range of creative educational strategies to raise the students' motivation and promote group dynamics in her classes, Erin was able to transform her students' learning experiences and, without exaggeration, their lives.

> ### ✏ Illustration 2.1 Ms G's first day in Room 203 (Gruwell 2007: 2–3)
>
> To gain my composure, I tried to sound authoritative while reading my supervising teacher's 'Guidelines for Student Behaviour.' I heard some students snickering. I stopped reading to see what they were laughing about.
>
> 'You got chalk on your ass,' yelled a student from the back.
>
> 'Daaamn, girl! Can I have some fries with that shake?' said another.
>
> Somehow the 'Guidelines' weren't sticking, because the class was completely out of control. Even though I had studied classroom management, it was obvious that my students were the ones managing me. I just wanted to make it to the end of the hour.
>
> Right before the bell rang, one of my students, Melvin, leaned back in his seat and announced, 'I give her five days!'
>
> 'You're on,' said Manny.
>
> 'I'm gonna make this lady cry in front of the whole class,' Sharaud bragged as he walked out the door.
>
> ...
>
> I felt like a failure. It was obvious that I didn't know what I was doing. I had no idea how to engage these apathetic teenagers who hated reading, hated writing, and apparently hated me.
>
> ...
>
> Once the students left, I picked up the paper airplane off the floor. I circled the room, collecting handouts that had been left behind, and saw ESL scribbled in black marker on several desks on the left side of the room. In educational jargon, ESL stands for English as a Second Language. Earlier, when I'd seen ESL etched on my door, I'd foolishly thought some Spanish-speaker was paying homage to my classroom. I soon realised this ESL had nothing to do with education – it was the acronym for East Side Longos – the largest Latino gang in Long Beach.
>
> Similar gang insignias were on other desks. These defaced desks marked my students' territory. The Asian students hit up the desks with the name of their respective gang affiliation, as did the African Americans. My multicultural classes in college had conveniently left out the chapter on gangs and turf warfare.

Creating the language learner's vision

> In lieu of a seating chart, I naively let the students pick their own seats. What struck me now was that they chose comfort zones determined by race. This realization gave me pause. I had imagined my students filing into my class and forming a melting pot of colors as they chose their seats, but the pot must have been pretty cold, because there was absolutely no melting. The Latinos had staked out the left side, while the Asian students occupied the right. The back row was occupied by all the African American students, and a couple of Caucasians sheepishly huddled together in the front.

The context is likely to be (luckily) too extreme for most of us, but the key to our discussion here is what Ms G – as Erin Gruwell came to be called by her students – did in response to the frustrating experience of her first day (and no doubt many other days that followed). Through a careful observation of her classroom and a determination to meet the students where they were – 'I was determined to find a way to reach my students. If I was going to survive the semester, I knew that I'd have to learn to speak their language' (Gruwell 2007: 15) – she was gradually able to uncover the carefully hidden yet vitally important identity concerns with which the students came to school every day, but which had remained totally unacknowledged throughout their education prior to Ms G's arrival. We would like to argue that this emerging understanding was the single most important step in allowing this teacher to initiate the future vision-construction process with the students, because it allowed her to build on what mattered most in the students' present lives. Talking about visionary leadership in general, Kouzes and Posner (2009: 21) confirm the significance of such observation as follows:

> the best way to lead people into the future is to connect with them deeply in the present. The only visions that take hold are shared visions – and you will create them only when you listen very, very closely to others, appreciate their hopes, and attend to their needs. The best leaders are able to bring their people into the future because they engage in the oldest form of research: They observe the human condition.

2.1.2 How can we find out more about our students?

How can teachers gain an understanding of their students' identity concerns in language classroom practice? We have come to believe that most regular language learning activities have the potential to shed light on the students' real lives if we choose to exploit this potential, and in the following pages we present some instructive research studies whose data collection methods can inspire the development of relevant pedagogical strategies.

In her study of language learner self-concept, Sarah Mercer (2011) has drawn on data from multiple sources, including interviews and written elicitation tasks. While interviews with the students may not always be a tool available or practical for a busy practitioner, some of the writing tasks used by Mercer lend themselves to be incorporated within the existing curriculum to help the teachers understand the students' current self-concept beliefs and concerns. For example, the activity entitled 'Your Language Learning Life History' requires students to relate their experiences chronologically from the point when they first developed an interest in L2 (or started to learn it) to where they are now. Interestingly, Mercer encouraged the learners to also include in their account experiences that they thought had played a role in their language learning life history even if they were not directly related to language learning. As she argued (2011: 168):

> learners often refer to other domains, which they perceive as being relevant and related, maybe in unexpected ways, when describing themselves as EFL learners. Thus, in terms of understanding how a learner may view themselves in a specific FL [foreign language] domain, a teacher may need to take a holistic view of the learner, in order to gain an insight into a learner's self-beliefs in other domains which the learner perceives as connected.

In another, well-documented, project, Bonny Norton (2000) explicitly extended her research approach to propose a useful framework for classroom pedagogy. She defined her practice – which she called *classroom-based social research* – as 'collaborative research that is carried out by language learners in their local communities with the active guidance and support of the language teacher' (p. 152). The approach places an emphasis on the goal of enabling the learners themselves to investigate systematically with the use of diaries, observation charts or log books their own experiences of learning and using the L2 in a variety of settings, a practice which is also highlighted in Allwright and Hanks's (2009) summary of exploratory classroom pedagogy. What is important for our present discussion is that such an approach can also become an invaluable tool for deepening both the teacher's and the students' understanding of the students' current identity concerns and lived experiences.

Creating the language learner's vision

🔧 Illustration 2.2 Diary study as 'pedagogy of possibility' (adapted from Norton 2000: 146)

The diary study in Norton's research on the L2 learning experiences of five immigrant women from Poland, Vietnam, Czechoslovakia and Peru was originally framed as a project about the learning of English as a second language in Canada. Through the participants' documentation of their lived experiences in a diary format, a very different picture of the complex landscape of living and being in a second language began to form, which eventually led Norton to propose this format as pedagogy that can link the classroom with the lived identities of its members. As she summed up the emerging shift:

> The way that it [the project] proceeded, however, was a project about the complexities of living as a woman in a new and sometimes threatening society, coping with the daily demands of family, work, schooling, housing, unemployment – much of which was conducted in a language that was only just beginning to make sense. It took place at a time when the women were beginning to question the usefulness of formal ESL classes and were confronting the lack of congruence between their understanding of the world and their experience of it in Canada. It took place at a time when they saw the need for practice in the target language, but also a time when they were beginning to understand that their access to Anglophone social networks was compromised by their position as immigrants in Canadian society.

Another useful research approach to understanding student identities that can be adapted for language classroom use is a *photovoice* (Wang and Burris 1997). This technique requires the students to capture their experiences through photos and talk about what these mean for them personally in an interview or written narrative. This has been successfully used in research on emotional experiences of learners of Italian in a study-abroad context (Gallucci 2011) and in the study of students' willingness to communicate in an L2 within the setting of Chinese university education (Zhen, in preparation), and it can serve as an interesting model for the development of language teaching materials and tasks. TOOLBOX 2.3 presents a summary of these and additional techniques.

🔧 Toolbox 2.3 Techniques for understanding the students' stories

Language learning histories, autobiographies and narratives

Students' narratives are elicited via specifically designed, typically one-off, writing tasks (for more details, see Section 2.4).

Photovoice

A visual approach to learner ethnography. Students are asked to take pictures of situations, events, people that matter to them as persons and L2 learners/users. They then make a selection of the most important images and describe why they matter to them in an oral or written narrative.

Diaries

Students document in a diary the complexities of learning an L2 in their specific setting. This can be an especially effective technique in study abroad and ESL contexts in which the L2 learning and use blend with the daily demands of study, work, housing or relationships.

Reflective journals

Students regularly reflect on their learning in the classroom in relation to their own experiences and aspirations (for more details, see Section 3.3).

Becoming an ethnographer of your own classroom

Teachers become ethnographers and carefully observe (and record, if possible) the dynamics of their own classrooms for what these can tell them about the students' identities and lived experiences.

To reiterate, acquiring an understanding of who our students are in a way that goes beyond the somewhat superficial level of interpersonal familiarity that characterises so many language classrooms worldwide is an important initial step in creating the foundations for a vision-building motivational programme. Let us close this section with a recent example of how a teacher-researcher gradually incorporated a focus on vision into his programme by carefully orchestrating various channels of communication, such as interviews, songs and poems, to tackle the participants' dreams and worries (ILLUSTRATION 2.3).

Illustration 2.3 Experience from an intervention programme (adapted from Magid 2011: 153)

I shared the poem, 'The Road Not Taken' by Robert Frost (1916) and the song, 'Father and Son' by Cat Stevens (1983) with the participants in order to encourage them to try to make their dreams come true and follow their heart. I believe that even if people have a clear vision of their ideal L2 self, they need to have the courage to attain it, especially if it clashes with their ought-to L2 self. I have often used that poem and that song when

Creating the language learner's vision

teaching Chinese learners of English. Many of my former Chinese students told me that they were inspired by both of them to follow their dreams. Therefore, I chose to use them during my intervention programme. After discussing the poem and listening to the song, I asked the participants to tell me about the three things that they value most in order to get a better sense of them as individuals and have them think about themselves in more detail in order to help them think about their ideal selves. Then, I read a scripted imagery situation to the participants in order to help them start to create a vision of their ideal L2 self. The scripted imagery situations were all based on the interviews about the students' ideal and feared L2 selves that I had conducted with them prior to the intervention programme.

2.2 Providing regular tasters of desired future states

We have pointed out above that the teacher's role is not so much to actually 'construct' a specific future image for the students as to create opportunities that will allow them to 'taste', explore and try out various versions of their possible selves. One way of doing this is to help students to experience a range of situations involving the L2. Depending on the resources available, this can include participating in intercultural encounters, meetings or campaigns either face to face or online, inviting L2 speakers to the language class, having a video conference with students from another country, working on a class project involving communication with other L2 speakers around the world, visiting an international company or university locally or abroad and, if possible, organising school exchanges, study-abroad trips and field visits. These experiences are important because they can sow the seeds of future images. An image-seed in this sense is a remembered moment from our history or an encounter that imprints itself in our memory, and it is these pictures that can later aid the construction of fully-fledged desired language selves by serving as useful building blocks.

The significance of creating such experience-based images explains, for example, why renowned Michelin-star chef Michel Roux, Jr, who decided to train eight young apprentices from disadvantaged backgrounds to become world-class waiters, started his unique training programme – documented in the BBC television series *Michel Roux's Service* – by taking his trainees to one of the finest restaurants in London to let them experience the best of the world that they could one day become part of. A further illustration of how tasters of future possible selves are utilised to motivate us is offered by tourism advertisements.

While some of the beautiful scenes in magazines or in the travel agents' windows describe attractive destinations (e.g. happy camels in front of pyramids in the sunset), others show less exotic scenes, for example a family having a meal on a sunny veranda or a couple walking hand in hand on a quiet road. These images serve a purpose that is very different from showing the Taj Mahal: they are there to help the viewers to create their ideal 'holiday self', made up of familiar scenarios that are cleverly fused with holiday fantasy. These images obviously work – that is, motivate us to spend money – or travel agents would not use them.

In sum, in order to build up a vivid image of a desired future self, we first need 'tasters', that is, sensory glimpses of the bigger picture to which our efforts could eventually lead us. Such short 'vision-immersion' opportunities offer a kind of foretaste of the future, which is exactly what Michel Roux's trainees were allowed to experience on their first day or what travel agents would like to provide us with. The lesson is this: *we need to taste the future in order to desire it.* ILLUSTRATION 2.4 presents an example from Maggie's early encounters with an L2 – English in her case – which demonstrates well just how powerful such tasters can be in motivating action.

> **Illustration 2.4 From our own experience (Maggie)**
>
> I still have a very vivid image in my mind's eye from the early days of my learning English. For the first time in my life, I am outside my country, taking part in a large international conference. I am wowed by the atmosphere: all the interesting people, some from countries I had not even heard of ... a whole new big and exciting world is opening up before my eyes ... But I can also feel the frustration of not being able to make the most of this 'once-in-a-lifetime' opportunity – I am unable to put together a single coherent sentence in English!
>
> I am convinced today that this was a significant turning point in my English language learning history; this was the critical encounter when the seed of my L2 vision was sown and grew almost instantly with immediate consequence for action. While friends of mine were enjoying the rest of that summer swimming and doing hiking trips, I spent mine cramming irregular verbs and lexical chunks!

It is difficult, if not impossible, to consciously orchestrate such significant 'chance encounters' that will have a profound and lasting influence, but what teachers can do in order to inspire and facilitate

Creating the language learner's vision

the construction of ideal L2 self-images is to create a rich menu of 'future-self-immersion' opportunities both in the classroom and outside it. Modern language teaching methodologies such as project-based instruction or task-based language teaching lend themselves to simulating intercultural situations in order to experience what it would be like to be a successful user of the L2; to illustrate an imagery-based approach that might also work for this purpose, TOOLBOX 2.4 presents an example of utilising the students' own imagination for creating tasters of possible desired L2 end states.

🔧 Toolbox 2.4 How to create a 'vision board' of one's ideal L2 self

You will need: lots of different types of old magazines (e.g. travel magazines, college prospectuses, etc.), a flipchart or cardboard paper for each student to create their treasure maps on and glue. You can ask the students to bring their own supply.

Step 1: Ask students to think about who they would ideally want to become and how the L2 features in that vision.

Step 2: Ask them to go through the magazines and cut out interesting bits from them. No gluing yet! Just let them have fun looking through magazines and pulling out pictures or words or headlines that strike their fancy. They should end up with a big pile of images and phrases.

Step 3: Then they should go through the images and begin to lay their favourites on the board and eliminate any that no longer feel right. You should encourage the students to design their board creatively, in any way they want. Once they have finalised the design, they can start gluing everything onto the board, also adding writing if they want or even some further painting/colouring to complete the composition.

Step 4: Students should leave space in the very centre of the vision board for a fantastic photo of themselves and paste it there. Alternatively, they can display a picture (or several pictures) of themselves being, doing or having their desired objective (travelling around the world, having a high-profile international job, studying at a university/college abroad, etc.). They should show themselves in a realistic setting and insert a corresponding caption (e.g. 'Here I am graduating from Harvard').

Step 5: Hang their vision boards in the classroom where they will see them often. You could revisit them every once in a while and refer to them from time to time during the class, perhaps when you feel that a boost in motivation is needed.

2.3 Applying guided imagery

The motivating power of mental imagery has been well documented in psychology, and in Chapter 1 we saw various illustrations of it, including Paivio's (1985) influential model of imagery functions in human performance. In sport psychology, it has been generally concluded that imagery is an effective performance enhancement technique (see Weinberg 2008 for a review) and, as a result, virtually every successful athlete in the world applies some sort of imagery enhancement technique during training. A good illustration of this is the 'Future history' technique of world heavyweight champion boxer Muhammad Ali, which he developed to mentally rehearse winning. During the days before a fight, he would picture himself in the ring and experience all the sensations of exchanging punches, the roaring crowds, the flashes of the cameras and, at the end, his arm being lifted up by the referee to proclaim him the champion. He used to rehearse the details of each fight in a mental routine, going through the experience graphically in his mind until it had become history, even though it was yet to happen.

Although mental imagery may be a relatively new idea in relation to language learning, ILLUSTRATION 2.5 below demonstrates that it is not a wholly unfamiliar concept for the students who tend to apply visualisation in their daily lives. In this section, we examine how imagery can be used as a tool for *establishing* new desired future selves, while in Chapter 3 (Section 3.1) we look at ways of *strengthening* the already existing vision. Here we first discuss the nature and the role of guided imagery in education in some detail, and then survey the conditions that need to be in place for guided imagery to have real motivational capacity. Finally, we offer some practical suggestions on how to initiate guided imagery and how to write tailor-made imagery scripts.

> **Illustration 2.5 Visualisation: some students already know it ...** (from Letty Chan's research journal; personal communication, 2011)
>
> I started asking whether students know what visualisation is. I asked them whether they daydream and most said they could see motion pictures or images as they recall past events. Some could also hear the sounds. I suddenly realised that this was not new to everyone – quite a number of them were already using it in different areas of their life. A student who played sport said he would visualise how other teams in a different league played. A student studying food and nutritional science said she had tried to imagine what she would be like in an interview. She said imagining that the

interviewers were pleased with her performance and visualising herself talking helped her to gain confidence before the actual meeting. Another student said he would see how he had done in a previous presentation and see what he could achieve next time. A student studying chemistry said he visualised how the experiments would be performed. It helped him to memorise the procedures instead of going through the written notes ...

2.3.1 What is 'guided imagery'?

Guided imagery in the classroom can be understood as directing students in controlled daydreaming, that is, helping them to consciously generate images of desired (language) selves in their own minds. This procedure has a considerable history in various applied psychological domains, and we can distinguish three main types of practice. The first and the most common type – often termed *scripted fantasy* (but sometimes also referred to as 'Socratic imagery' because of the open-ended questions; see Stopa 2009: 79–80) – involves guiding students into the imaginary world by means of a scripted scenario that includes several suggestions and open-ended questions. The purpose is to let the students explore their own visions, which will be unique to each student, and to encourage them to communicate their visions in some form of a follow-up activity, either orally or in writing (see TOOLBOX 2.5 for an example).

> **Toolbox 2.5 Scripted fantasy of the future language self (adapted from Hadfield and Dörnyei 2013: 27)**
>
> Imagine the one that is most important to you: work, study, friends, travel ... now imagine yourself in that situation ... where are you? ... in an office, at a meeting, on the phone, with friends, in a university, in the foreign country? ... in a cafe? ... in a shop? ... in the street? ... at a station? ... choose one ... where are you? ... what does the place look like? ... what can you see around you? ... how many people are there? ... what do they look like? ... what are they wearing? ... what can you hear? ... what are you doing? ... what are you wearing? ... you are speaking (*L2*) to someone ... who is it? ... what do they look like? ... imagine that you are speaking (*L2*) very well ... what are you talking about? ... what kind of things can you say? ... how do you feel talking (*L2*)? ... how do people react to you?

The second type of guided imagery, which we can refer to as *scripted imagery*, is similar to scripted fantasy in that it also involves a ready-made script, but in this case the script is more detailed and specific, and thus the guided imagery experience closely resembles the situation of reading a novel or listening to a story: the characters are described in vivid detail, the story line is carefully delineated, and yet different individuals may still end up seeing, hearing and feeling different things because of their unique life experiences, personalities and desires. With effectively tailored scripts that are based on the students' current identity concerns and lived experiences (see Section 2.1), this type of imagery can be just as effective as scripted fantasy for helping students to try out a range of personally relevant visions of their future language selves. TOOLBOX 2.6 contains a script used by Michael Magid in a successful imagery-based motivational programme (cf. Magid and Chan 2012).

> **Toolbox 2.6 Scripted imagery: the perfect job interview (Magid and Chan 2012: 117)**
>
> Close your eyes and imagine that today is the day of a very important job interview in a large, famous, international company that you have been dreaming of working in for a long time. This job could be in any part of the world where you would like to live. You have prepared very well for the interview and as you get dressed, you are feeling really confident that you will do well. As you look at yourself in the mirror, you are happy with how professional and mature you look. You arrive at the company a few minutes before the interview and are feeling very calm as you wait to be called into the boss's office. When you step into his or her office, you can see that the boss is impressed by your businesslike appearance, your friendly, confident smile and your firm handshake. He or she asks you to sit down and starts to ask you questions. Although some of the questions are quite difficult, you are able to use your excellent English to answer all of them extremely well. You can see that the boss is pleased and very satisfied with all of your answers. The boss is also impressed by your fluency, grammar, vocabulary and pronunciation in English. You show him or her that you have so much knowledge, so many skills and are highly qualified for this job of your dreams. As the interview ends, there is no doubt in your mind that you will get this job. Stay with this feeling of complete confidence as you open your eyes and come back to this room.

Finally, a third version of guided imagery is a technique called *image streaming* (cf. Wenger and Poe 1996), which refers to a self-reinforcing imagery whereby individuals generate images through their own observation and description rather than someone else's script. The brief given to the students is no more than an initial prompt, and while

Creating the language learner's vision

the teacher or the students' peers may act as 'listeners' to stimulate the image streaming process, the principal outcome of this technique is a self-generated picture; the illustration in TOOLBOX 2.7 involves an image of being in the main square of a foreign city that can start an image streaming activity.

> 🔧 **Toolbox 2.7 Initial prompt for imagery streaming: in the main square of a foreign city...** (adapted from Hall *et al.* 2006: 34)
>
> I'd like you to summon up an image of being in the main square of a foreign city. It doesn't have to be a city you know or that you have visited. Just go along with the first image that comes into your mind and as the image becomes more real to you. Actually see yourself in the square. Now describe aloud to me what you can see. Be in the square. And now if you can, don't just see yourself in the image. Be there, looking through your own eyes at what you can see around you.

Following the initial imagery prompt, the essence of the image streaming activity is to get students to provide descriptions of objects, scenes or people in increasingly elaborate detail in the *present tense*. The assumption is – and once you have tried it, you will know that it is by and large true – that through perfecting a description, one is actually perfecting both one's mental imaging ability and the vividness of the particular image itself. This means that describing an image to an audience can become part of a feedback loop which both tracks the images and helps to generate them at the same time. This is a versatile task and by using this process students can, for example, 'word paint' the images of their desired future selves or 'talk themselves into' their future language vision. A sample vision-construction activity which can be usefully combined with image streaming is presented in TOOLBOX 2.8.

> 🔧 **Toolbox 2.8 Image streaming of a 'future history'**
>
> One interesting way of engaging students in constructing their future visions is to ask them to narrate their *future histories*. There are many variations of this simple technique, but the key is to ask the students to talk about their future plans involving an L2 as if they have already experienced the outcomes (i.e. they have to use the present tense to describe their projected state and the past tense to recount their future

plans as if these have already materialised). Some examples of elicitation questions include: *Imagine that it is two years ahead in time and you are looking back at those two years. Where are you now? What are you doing? Where have you been on holiday? Where are you working? What have you achieved in L2 learning that you are most proud of and why?*

To make the most of the image streaming technique, students should be asked to describe orally everything they see in as much detail as possible. This can be done, for example, as homework: students audio record themselves as they are describing their future history images. As a second step, they can then write up their descriptions in a narrative, which they should be allowed to edit as much as they want to (partly to further improve it and partly because they may not want to share with other students everything they have envisaged). Alternatively, the task can be performed as a pair-work activity in the classroom, with one student acting as the 'image streamer' and the other as the 'listener', who listens and encourages even more detailed descriptions.

2.3.2 Conditions for effective guided imagery

As exhibited throughout this book, there is ample evidence for the value of visualisation across several fields in the social sciences, and guided imagery techniques have also gained widespread acceptance in sports, health care and business domains. However, because many teachers, students and parents may not have been exposed to guided imagery in the language classroom, some apprehension about – and even resistance to – adopting this technique as a motivational tool may be inevitable (and in the context of the many competing pressures in the educational system, quite understandable). While imagery may appear fascinating because it seems mysterious, it can also strike some students as nothing more than hocus-pocus. It is therefore important for teachers to address any possible misconceptions and to generate some 'street cred' for the method by citing examples of language learners who have used the technique successfully and by explaining, for example, that virtually all the celebrity athletes use it or that laboratory research has consistently found measureable improvement in performance as a function of visualisation. Of course, imagery is not a substitute for language practice but acts rather as a 'vitamin supplement' or a 'language-building steroid'. ILLUSTRATION 2.6 offers some tips from Maureen Murdock, a teacher who has been using guided imagery with schoolchildren for many years, on how to deal with possible resistance either from the students or their parents.

Creating the language learner's vision

> **Illustration 2.6 How Maureen Murdock (1987: 15) deals with students' resistance to imagery**
>
> I suggest to my students that they close their eyes or look down at the floor with 'soft' or half-closed eyes. I state two rules before we begin: no talking or whispering during the exercise and no interfering with anyone else. I understand that because of the unfamiliarity of the technique not all students will participate at first, but they all must learn to respect others' choice to relax and focus. It may take several weeks before teacher and students become comfortable with the process. I advise teachers to give themselves six weeks before expecting positive results. Expect giggling at first. Students may be embarrassed, be worried about others looking at them, or view the idea of having time in school to exercise their brain as silly. I find that the giggling disappears if the students receive no attention for it. The most surprising thing to me is that students themselves ask those who are disruptive to stop. They don't want their imagery time interrupted. When I taught third grade, my students asked latecomers to wait outside the classroom until our quiet time was over. Before long there were no latecomers! Sometimes there is resistance from the parents of students. In my class, some parents were sceptical at first, so I invited them to join our morning quiet time. Without exception they enjoyed it, and several parents made it a regular part of their day to join us for quiet time when they brought their child to school. They enjoyed beginning their work or other daily activities relaxed and centred.

An important element in making imagery work in the classroom is to conclude the visualisation task with some sort of a follow-up, thereby integrating it into the flow of the lesson purposefully. As Arnold *et al.* (2007) summarise, this follow-up can involve either some feedback, that is, simply talking about what students have experienced, or setting a more demanding written or oral language assignment. We conclude this section with Magid and Chan's (2012) summary of three essential conditions for the effectiveness of imagery tasks, which can serve as useful signposts for teachers who wish to integrate imagery into their language teaching:

- *Condition 1: Learners are aware of the benefits of visualisation.* Learners who understand and agree with the rationale behind visualisation tend to find it both enjoyable and motivating. Therefore, it is important for teachers to explain that visualisation is an effective L2 motivational strategy in order for L2 learners to take it seriously.

53

- **Condition 2: *Learners know how to visualise*.** The L2 learners' ability to visualise will affect the vividness of their vision of their desired language selves and the intensity of the arousal caused by the visualisation process. Therefore, appropriate knowledge of how to visualise situations is a prerequisite for students to participate fully in the visualisation activities in our programmes. If L2 learners lack the skills to use their imagination to visualise situations, they can be helped to develop this skill (see Arnold *et al.* 2007 and Hadfield and Dörnyei 2013 for practical resources).
- **Condition 3: *Learners are sufficiently fresh to visualise*.** The participants in Letty Chan's Hong Kong projects mentioned that they were less able to visualise elaborate and vivid situations when they felt tired, for example after attending lectures for the entire day. Therefore, it is important to choose a time of day for such tasks when the L2 learners are feeling energetic, so that they can focus their attention on visualisation.

2.3.3 Introductory imagery exercises

In order to 'sell' the idea of imagery to the students, it might be worth introducing the technique through a few simple but powerful visualisation tasks to help them hone their imagery skills. However, first, even before these tasks (and indeed any guided imagery task), students need to go through a breathing routine. Deep, slow breathing quietens the internal organs (lowers the metabolic rate and decreases the heart rate), increases the alertness of the mind (by increasing the supply of oxygen), relaxes the students and clears their minds of possible distractions, thereby setting the appropriate emotional climate for the images to readily come up. Slow breathing has been traditionally utilised in relaxation exercises of various sorts, and there is also medical evidence confirming its beneficial effects, as it lowers the blood pressure (e.g. Kaushik *et al.* 2006). TOOLBOX 2.9 contains a typical breathing exercise script and a short script to bring students back to their normal awareness gently.

Toolbox 2.9 Sample scripts for beginning and ending an imagery exercise (adapted from Fugitt 1983: 51 and Arnold *et al.* 2007: 27)

Using a quiet, serene voice say:
Please sit quietly with your feet on the floor, legs uncrossed. Keep the back straight so that the lungs can function at their very best. Hold the head straight and quietly close your eyes if you wish ... Now slowly take a deep breath, so silently that no one can hear you. Feel the breath going

deeply into your chest, feel the chest expanding as the breath fills the chest cavity. Slowly and quietly let the breath go. Take another deep breath, again experience it, become aware of what is happening in your body as the ribs expand. Release it now, quietly and slowly, at your own pace. Take one more breath, and simply enjoy the quiet feeling inside you.

When you end an imagery task that students have been very involved in, you might say:
When I count from one to five, return to this room, feeling relaxed and alert. One ... two ... three ... four ... five.

Alternatively, simply say in a quiet voice:
When you are ready, open your eyes, *or* Very good.

At an early stage, the imagery exercise should start out with some basic scenes such as the participants' home (e.g. bedroom), the sound of their alarm clock, their best friend or even a simple object such as a red apple. For example, Arnold *et al.* (2007: 27) suggest the following super-quick visualisation in a lesson on means of transportation: 'You have only three seconds. Close your eyes and see a car and afterwards tell me what colour it is. Ready, get set, go. (3 seconds). Open your eyes.' This process can be adapted to many different situations and can serve a variety of purposes, such as vocabulary memorisation. The point is to gradually add visual and kinaesthetic details to the scene and get students to start interacting with it, for example by walking around in their home, turning on and off the alarm clock, interacting with their best friend or biting into the red apple, followed up by an awareness-raising discussion about the imagery experience (see TOOLBOX 2.10 for an awareness-raising exercise).

> Toolbox 2.10 Awareness raising about mental imagery (adapted from Arnold *et al.* 2007: 54–5)

Tell your students that you are going to ask them a series of questions. In a quiet voice ask these questions, and give the students about half a minute's silent time after each question.

Can you imagine holding a red apple in your right hand?
Can you see it now?
Close your eyes for a minute.
Can you see it better when you close your eyes?
Can you feel it too? What does it feel like if you touch it?
Can you imagine taking a big bite from it?

Motivating Learners, Motivating Teachers

> Can you hear a sound while doing so?
> Are you aware of the taste?
>
> Have a discussion about your students' experiences. Usually students respond very positively to this activity because it involves several main sensory areas (seeing + feeling + hearing + tasting). Then explain to your class that you want to do a daydream-like activity with them. Inform them that they don't need to try hard to see things in their mind's eye. Tell them that they should become aware also of any smells, tastes, sounds and feelings in their daydreams.

TOOLBOX 2.11 offers an example of a visualisation scene that can be used as an introductory imagery exercise for constructing the L2 self. Short, 3 to 5-minute practice exercises of this type will make the procedure familiar without losing the interest factor, allowing the students to get vivid and controllable images consistently. If the scripts are in the L2, they can also be useful as listening comprehension tasks. (See 'Imagery workout' in Section 3.1.2 for more suggestions.)

> **Toolbox 2.11 Sample introductory imagery exercise involving L2 self**
>
> A fairly straightforward L2-related scene would be sitting in a nice café in the host environment with an L2-speaking friend, surrounded by local people and you placing an order with the waiter in the L2. Get students to try to see all the sights, eavesdrop into other people's conversation, taste the nice food that is arriving and notice how they are feeling. Then discuss with the students how clearly they could see the image, how clearly they could hear the sounds, how well they were able to control the imagery, and in general, how they experienced their feelings. Finally, ask them to reflect on how they felt as competent L2 users.

2.3.4 Creating your own imagery scripts

Guided imagery requires a script and the difficulty of finding appropriate scripts might be a deterrent for busy teachers. However, writing an imagery script is not difficult if we follow a simple template of six components:

- *Initial breathing routine* (see previous section).
- *Set the scene*: Where are you? What can you see? What can you hear? What can you smell? Incorporate vivid details into multi-sensory imagery, such as colours, fragrant smells, music coming through

Creating the language learner's vision

the window, etc. Arnold *et al.* (2007: 27) also recommend giving students clues to help them to get clearer pictures; for example, if you ask them to visualise a tree, ask: *What kind of tree is it? Is it big or little? Does it have leaves or not?*
- *Describe how you feel*: What sensations do you have? How does your body feel? Describe any contact between your body and objects in the environment.
- *Describe your thoughts and emotions*: What are your emotions? What thoughts come to mind? What are your reactions? How do your thoughts change as the imagery progresses?
- *Describe the main purpose of the imagery*: This is the point when the scenario unfolds according to the purpose of the imagery: some action starts; an encounter takes place; you do/say something, etc. Make sure that you include all the components of the action that are important in taking the scenario forward. Whatever the actual content of the scene is, there should be some positive outcome: achieving success, accomplishing a goal, carrying out a task, obtaining a result, etc. Conclude the imagery with a feeling of pride, satisfaction and happiness.
- *Exercise ending prompt* (see previous section).

2.4 Applying guided narratives

In a seminal paper that has foregrounded the role of narratives in the social sciences, American psychologist Jerome Bruner (1987: 12) presents the thesis that people 'seem to have no other way of describing "lived time" save in the form of a narrative'. Therefore, he argues, a life is not 'how it was' but how it is interpreted, told and retold; in short: 'a life as led is inseparable from a life as told' (p. 31). Accordingly, Bruner concludes, 'In the end, we *become* the autobiographical narratives by which we "tell about" our lives' (p. 15). This thesis has resonated with a lot of researchers and practitioners within a wide range of academic disciplines, because it does indeed seem to be the case that we organise and understand our experiences and memories of human happenings in the form of various narratives, such as stories, excuses, myths, explanations, etc. In this way, our autobiographical stories become the foundations of our selves so much so that we could almost say that we *narrate ourselves into the person we become*. As Kenyon and Randall (1997: 1) maintain, 'To be a person is to have a story. More than that, it is to be a story.'

Are narratives really that important? Along with many scholars, Clark and Rossiter (2008) give an affirmative answer. As they summarise, personal or autobiographical narratives are the tools we use to deal with the dizzying complexity of the world around us; we respond to and manage our experiences through describing them in narratives that make sense. In this way we can create coherence in what often appears to be chaos. There is no such thing as an objective narrative that simply copies reality – every narrative is a subjective interpretation, or reading, of the events. Indeed, cognitive psychologists have found that we recall autobiographical memories selectively, in accordance with how we see ourselves in our current lives (e.g. Conway and Pleydell-Pearce 2000). This is how Dan McAdams, a well-known narrative psychologist, has introduced his theory of human identity, which is built around the idea that we come to understand who we are by creating heroic stories about ourselves:

> We are all tellers of tales. We each seek to provide our scattered and often confusing experiences with a sense of coherence by arranging the episodes of our lives into stories. This is not the stuff of delusion or self-deception. We are not telling ourselves lies. Rather, through our personal myths, each of us discovers what is true and what is meaningful in life. In order to live well, with unity and purpose, we compose a heroic narrative of the self that illustrates essential truths about ourselves. Enduring human truths still reside primarily in myth, as they have done for centuries.
>
> (1993: 5)

Thus, narratives are powerful tools for crafting our identities; they engage our thoughts and imaginations in an unparalleled manner both when we listen to a story and when we construct one. In a comprehensive model of personality, McAdams and Pals (2006) go as far as to propose that 'integrative life narratives' are one of the five main pillars of human personality, as the narratives by which we reconstruct the past and imagine the future 'provide a person's life with identity (unity, purpose, meaning)' (p. 212). We make these personal life stories distinctly ours by adding to them characteristic images, tones, themes, plots and endings, thereby reflecting who we are. Personality development will be manifest in changes in our narratives, and because of the dynamic link between our narratives and our lives, changes in our personal narratives will also bring about changes in our self-images: because human beings construe their lives as ongoing stories, the way these stories are constructed will 'help to shape behaviour, establish identity, and integrate individuals into modern social life' (p. 209). It is against this background that we can understand Erikson's (2007) claim that a possible future self is, in effect, a narrative, that is, 'a story we tell (primarily to ourselves) about our selves in hypothetical future situations' (p. 355).

The close link between autobiographical narratives and future self-images offers an avenue for constructing desired future selves through

Creating the language learner's vision

getting the students to write various forms of guided autobiographies. To illustrate the pedagogical implications of this link, let us have a look at three ways of engaging students in generating real or imaginary guided biographies: (1) by asking learners to write about the future as if it were the past, (2) by reshaping life stories and (3) by identifying crucial, 'self-defining' turning points in autobiographies.

2.4.1 Writing an autobiographical story about the future

According to the saying, 'To teach something is to learn twice.' This is because if we want to teach any material, we must first make sense of it ourselves and then internalise this meaning thoroughly. Writing is similar to this in the sense that to record something in a visible and permanent form also requires clarity and coherence in our thinking, and the product will become 'our story', that is, a part of us in a more permanent way than what we say. In order to help students construct a personalised future language self, ask them to engage in what experts call 'concept-focused autobiographical writing'. They should imagine themselves a few years into the future as competent L2 users and recount their language learning story, starting with the present situation and leading up to successful mastery in the future – all written in the past tense as a recollection! TOOLBOX 2.8 in Section 2.3 ('Image streaming of a future history') can be easily used for this purpose, and TOOLBOX 2.12 offers sample instructions for writing a 'back-to-the-future' language learning history.

> **Toolbox 2.12 Instructions for writing your 'back-to-the-future' language learning history**
>
> Imagine that you are in the future when you have finally succeeded in mastering the L2. You are a competent L2 speaker! Write an autobiographical story about how you have managed to achieve this. Start with the present situation and narrate the progress towards the successful future state as realistically as possible, also describing how you overcame obstacles and how you found the energy to persist. Remember, this story is about you, and the more convincing it sounds, the better! Write the account in a retrospective manner (i.e. in the past tense) as a personal history and include as much detail as possible.

Whitty (2002: 226) reports that a (non-language-specific) project in which students were asked to describe how their dreams had come true 'was very successful at elucidating the complexity of the dream.

This study found that the strengths of the story-writing method were its ability to generate themes and to uncover "ideal" or "hoped for selves".' Such an exercise allows students to select from and experiment with possible story lines, and adjust those to fit their own unique personality features and life circumstances. In this way they can start appropriating a successful language learner identity.

Interestingly, using future-centred narratives is also recommended by Levin (2000) to produce effective visions for commercial organisations. In an insightful paper she describes how she produced such a vision statement for a medical institution following a parsimonious template consisting of the following four main steps:

- *Becoming informed*, that is, complementing the initial creative passion (which is indispensable for vision creation) with insights derived from relevant knowledge and experience, obtained through an extensive site visit to get to know the company.
- *Visiting the future and recording the experience*, which involved asking several managers and employees to project themselves five years into the future through various structured exercises and then recording their ideas.
- *Creating the story*, that is, writing up the 'vision story' in a narrative form – about 1,500 to 2,000 words long, written in the present tense – describing the future world in lucid detail but also with sufficiently strong links to current situational realities to convey familiarity and help people translate the future to their present experiences.
- *Deploying the vision*, which involved refining the vision story by eliciting feedback from beyond the core cadre who helped to develop it and then making amendments accordingly.

According to Levin (2000), then, a vision without disciplined and focused execution is nothing more than a dream that will not ensure organisation success. However, if this dream is transformed into a 'vision story' through adding vivid imagery and dynamic narration of experiences, it can become a compelling mechanism as it 'provides people with a lifelike glimpse into the future of possibilities and directly answers the fundamental question: What will this future mean for me?' (p. 106).

2.4.2 Retelling a story in a different light

We have seen above that autobiographical stories are far from being objective accounts of facts but reflect in many ways the storyteller's present disposition. The same reality can be processed in very different ways, similar to the 'glass is half full/empty' perceptions. Students will probably identify with the experience that even periods that appear to be

Creating the language learner's vision

bleak and hopeless can have the seeds of something positive and forward-pointing, and later retrospection might show that 'everything started then even though I didn't know it'.

Toolbox 2.13 below offers a sample exercise which can help the students to retell their negative experiences as opportunities for future success. Potentially, such an activity can become a transformative learning experience, because as people externalise their own stories by recounting them to others, they have a more empowered perspective on their own lives, one which may show them where constructive changes or alternative story lines are desirable and feasible.

Toolbox 2.13 'Restorying' the past in a positive light

Ask students to write a composition by putting a 'positive spin' on the negative events in their past language learning history, showing how it contained the foundations of spectacular future success. This interpretation – entitled 'Who Would Have Believed It …?' – should sum up the roots of their powerful motivation to continue to study the L2 and make a success of it. A successful story of this kind does not avoid past failures, disappointments or traumatic experiences, but addresses these head-on while also offering interpretations that translate these difficult life moments into fully elaborated stories with a constructive, positive edge (e.g. the way by which a salutary experience works).

The point of such a 'restorying' exercise is that by shedding a positive light on their autobiographical memories, students reshape their present disposition and create a positive mental environment for progress. Kenyon and Randall (1997: 120) recommend that such a guided autobiography exercise can be further developed in small groups when students can 'restory their lives together', perhaps as part of a PR team.

2.4.3 Identifying 'self-defining moments' in language learning histories

Conway and Pleydell-Pearce (2000) explain that autobiographies often describe highly specific events that acted as turning points or 'self-defining moments' for the individual, leading to the adoption of a life goal – and thus to the generation of a possible self – that then determined much of the individual's later activities. Such self-defining moments can involve interactions with a significant person, such as a teacher, parent of a friend; something the person has heard/seen through media channels; or a specific event with a profound lesson. By saying that such events are 'turning points', we mean exactly that: they 'turn' people round or away from the course of action or a mindset that has characterised their behaviour and thoughts so far.

The activity described in Toolbox 2.14 is a creative example of an 'instructional case study', which involves the story of some kind of a professional practice, in which a problem is presented and needs to be solved or addressed in the form of a story. As Clark and Rossiter (2008) explain, the open-endedness of the story draws in the students as they become authors in a problem-solving task, but at the same time they also start learning to think like practitioners, engaging with theoretical concepts and practical insights into the specific realities of the imaginary person. If there are successful role models around (see below in the next section), their initial situation can also serve as a starting point for a similar activity, and learners must then try and guess how these real people reached what they have.

> **Toolbox 2.14 Creating a Hollywood-style success story for 'Lingo Star'**
>
> In this task of imagination, students have to create a Hollywood-style (L2) success story for 'Lingo Star', who used to be a student with no motivation whatsoever to master a second language, and who consequently acquired virtually no L2 proficiency. However, a series of life-changing episodes and encounters have made Lingo what he/she is now: a triumphant polyglot!
>
> Ask students to describe in vivid details and images Lingo's journey from abject language poverty (total disinterest and lethargy, accompanied by a lack of social support, unhelpful attitudes and a firm belief that he/she was not good enough at languages) to multilingual success. How did he/she overcome difficult life experiences in his/her language history, and how did he/she manage to excel above his/her peers with similar opportunities?
>
> Special attention should be paid to the psychological turning points – self-defining moments – that have formed the attitudes of the present Lingo, transforming the language-basher into a language-lover.

2.5 Ensuring ample exposure to role models

> Setting an example is not the main means of influencing another, it is the only means.
> *Albert Einstein (1879–1955)*

Influential role models play an important part in several areas of social life, and 'observational learning', that is, the process whereby learners observe and imitate others' behaviour, is a much researched topic in educational psychology. The important aspect of role models for this book is that modelling is known to be highly effective in changing people's

Creating the language learner's vision

attitudes and outlook; this has been expressed very clearly by one of the principal originators of the theory, Canadian psychologist Albert Bandura, when he concluded: 'Seeing or visualising people similar to oneself perform successfully typically raises efficacy beliefs in observers that they themselves possess the capabilities to master comparable activities' (1997: 87). In other words, a positive role model – that is, an individual who has achieved outstanding success – can raise the observers' hopes for the future and thus motivate them to pursue similar excellence. In their theorising, Markus and Nurius (1986: 954–5) explicitly foreground the role of salient others in the construction of individuals' possible selves – their thoughts about the 1984 Olympic Games in the United States no doubt apply equally in the UK after the 2012 London Olympics:

> Many of these possible selves are the direct result of previous social comparisons in which the individual's own thoughts, feelings, characteristics, and behaviours have been contrasted to those of salient others. What others are now, I could become … The 1984 Olympic Games probably created powerful possible selves for some young runners.

Celebrities are obvious role models for young people; for example, the world-famous Chinese pianist Lang Lang has inspired a real craze of 'I-want-to-be-like-him' followers in his home country; it is estimated that over 30 million children play the piano in China today and much of this can be attributed to Lang Lang's inspiration: through his mass piano concerts where he invites children on stage and his autobiography with a special edition for children, he has been making his success a desired and vivid possibility for a whole new generation. Research in social psychology has confirmed that showcasing the talents of a star can indeed boost the aspirations and self-images of people, and this motivating impact is particularly strong if the modelled behaviour or skill is seen as *attainable* and *relevant* (Lockwood and Kunda 1997). This makes sense: students are likely to be more inspired by an outstanding individual who excels in their own area of interest and who is close to their social background or age level, because in this way they can more easily use this model for generating a possible future image for themselves.

The potentially huge impact of these 'near peer role models' – as Tim Murphey has called them (see Dörnyei and Murphey 2003; Murphey and Arao 2001) – can be best illustrated by comparing it to the often life-changing influence that a sibling can have on a younger brother or sister who is desperate to emulate his/her behaviour. ILLUSTRATION 2.7, an extract from an interview with a Chinese university student studying in Nottingham (UK), presents a fascinating example of the significance of role models in general and of 'near peer role models' in particular: the interviewee explains that a less famous model, who was more similar to

Motivating Learners, Motivating Teachers

her and who had actually studied at the same university, had gradually replaced the previous source of her motivation, a TV celebrity.

> **Illustration 2.7 Role models and 'near peer role models' (from Xin 2012)**
>
> Extract from an interview with a Chinese student studying in Nottingham, UK:
>
> > My idol has been Lan Yang since my secondary school. While in China, I watched her Talk-show programmes, with so many celebrities from all over the world. She is so wise, elegant, and her English, her knowledge impressed me so much; I access her blog for her latest news – I have got lots of information related to my future career. Now, Xiaojun Ji is playing an even more important role in my career plan. We are so similar to each other. He is an MBA in Nottingham and now a host of CCTV 9 Culture Express. His career is just taking off, not that successful and famous as Lan Yang – if he can do it, then I can.

Besides inviting attractive near peer role models to his classes, Murphey has also experimented with a variety of ways of modelling language learning success, such as *newslettering* (compiling a regular classroom newsletter containing a selection of inspirational extracts from the students' action logs, reflective journals or language learning histories) and recording special topic videos portraying, for example, successful older students speaking about an aspect of their language learning experience for use in other classes. TOOLBOX 2.15 summarises some useful techniques that can be used in language classrooms to harness the motivating capacity of role models.

> **Toolbox 2.15 Techniques for utilising the motivational power of near peer role modelling**
>
> - Create a platform for sharing students' successful language learning strategies and experiences (newsletters, classroom online blogs, wikis, special topic videos and podcasts, classroom displays, etc.).
> - Gather stories of successful L2 speakers and use them as teaching materials.
> - Ask students to collect biographies of famous language learners and incorporate the material into your teaching.
> - Invite successful L2 learners to your class from the same school, town, region.
> - Tell students about your own successes with L2 learning/use.

3 Strengthening the vision through imagery enhancement

> The very essence of leadership is that you have to have vision. It's got to be a vision you articulate clearly and forcefully on every occasion. You can't blow an uncertain trumpet.
>
> *Theodore Hesburgh*

Section 2.3 has introduced visualisation and guided imagery as a tool for creating L2 vision, and many of the strategies and techniques which we consider in this section could in fact also be used for that purpose. Yet, we have also seen that the mere existence of a desired self-image may not be an effective motivator of action if it does not have a sufficient degree of elaborateness and vividness. Indeed, the more intense the imagery accompanying the vision, the more powerful the vision. Markus and Ruvolo (1989) also point out that the clarity and elaborateness of a future vision offer greater access to cues for achieving it and, consequently, a greater likelihood that the future visions will translate into action. ILLUSTRATION 3.1 presents an example of just such an elaboration in which a student paints a detailed and vivid picture of what her life will look like in ten years' time and how L2 competence will be integral to her career, readily elaborating on the details of the future place of work, the type of job, and even specific tasks that she would ideally like to perform. Therefore, in this section we explore avenues for strengthening student vision, that is, helping students to see their desired language selves with more clarity and, consequently, with more urgency for action.

Illustration 3.1 The vision of a highly motivated Chinese learner of English (from Xin 2012)

Interviewer: What will your career and life be like in 10 years' time?

Student: (No hesitation) Middle class, cosy, colourful life in America or Hong Kong, more western style. I hate routine work. I cannot imagine myself translating files as an office clerk, you know. I want a job with surprise and challenge from time to time. A lot of challenges, very busy, working with international colleagues and even go abroad on business frequently. I may start in the Beijing or Shanghai branches and then work in the

> headquarters of OGILVY [an international advertising, marketing and PR agency] in Washington. I like this kind of job, seeing new things and facing new challenges. Mainly deal with product promotion, advertisement design. I hate routine jobs. English will be important for me and I will keep improving it. You can never reach the highest standard, you know. But my [original] dream as a hostess of a TV program will still be alive. I know I will succeed in the field, I am sure.

3.1 Training imagery skills

Methods of imagery enhancement have been explored in several areas of psychological, educational and sports research in the past, and the techniques of guided imagery can be utilised to promote ideal L2 self-images and thus to strengthen the students' vision (for reviews and resources, see e.g. Berkovits 2005; Fezler 1989; Gould, Damarjian and Greenleaf 2002; Hall *et al.* 2006; Horowitz 1983; Leuner, Horn and Klessmann 1983; Singer 2006; Taylor *et al.* 1998). Gould *et al.* (2002) describe how imagery training for athletes is designed to enhance the vividness and controllability of an athlete's imagery. These can involve a variety of exercises, starting from very simple ones (e.g. imagining one's home and gradually adding details) to complex ones that include controlling and manipulating the content of elaborate image sequences (see the next section for specific details). In psychotherapy, too, there are a number of different approaches, from the *positive imagery approach* (which involves the use of highly pleasurable, relaxing images to counteract anxiety), to behaviourists' systematic desensitisation or to guided imagery in the treatment of conditions as diverse as anorexia or childhood phobias (see Leuner *et al.* 1983; Singer 2006). Finally, imagery also has definite educational potential. Taylor *et al.* (1998), for example, present evidence that mental simulation was beneficial for university students preparing for an exam, and Berkovits (2005: xvii–xviii) argues passionately that imagery is the ideal way to work with children:

> When a child uses imagery to find solutions to problems in her current life or from the past, she obtains a sense of autonomy and confidence in her ability to resolve situations she may have felt controlled her. These situations run the gamut of the child's experience, pertaining to her relationship with herself, her peers, her parents, siblings, teachers, authority figures, and learning situations in school, to name a few. Using imagination to find solutions to these situations has the added

advantage of improving the child's verbal ability, because the images are clear and precise, and they lend themselves to clarity and precision of expression.

3.1.1 Imagery training in sport

Conscious imagery enhancement has been used in several fields sporadically, but there is one area where the stakes (and potential financial implications) are so high that the training of mental imagery skills has become a featured area: professional sports. Therefore, sport psychology offers detailed and very practical guidelines for imagery training, and due to the nature of the domain – specific sporting behaviours in real life – these guidelines have stood the test of time in actual competitive environments.

A special book called *Imagery Training* (Hale 2005), published in the UK by the National Coaching Foundation, highlights in its introduction the fact that sport involves more than a physical performance – it is also a 'mind game' because mental factors greatly affect achievement. Indeed, as discussed in Section 1.3.2 when we reviewed Paivio's theory of imagery functions in performance, visualisation can promote motor skills and psychological readiness for competitions, and it also has long-term motivational power. However, Gould *et al.* (2002: 70) stress that, regardless of which area an athlete is working on, 'imagery is a skill like any other, requiring consistent effort to attain a high level of proficiency'. This gradual learning curve is evident in the following account by an Olympic champion springboard diver:

> It took me a long time to control my images and perfect my imagery, maybe a year, doing it every day. At first I couldn't see myself, I always saw everyone else, or I would see my dives wrong all the time. I would get an image of hurting myself, or tripping on the board, or I would 'see' something done really bad. As I continued to work at it, I got to the point where I could feel myself doing a perfect dive and hear the crowd yelling at the Olympics. But it took me a long time. (p. 70)

Thus, it is an established fact in sport psychology and coaching practice that imagery, like any other skill, needs to be developed and practised systematically. A collection of key principles in this area that would also be useful to follow in language learning is the '4Rs' (Hale 2005): *relaxation*, *realism*, *regularity* and *reinforcement*:

- *Relaxation* is the necessary condition for virtually any mental practice, and it is particularly relevant to imagery exercises. Therefore, as we saw in Section 2.3, guided imagery usually starts with a relaxation technique, typically a breathing exercise.

- *Realism* refers to the need for the imagery to be completely realistic, mirroring the experience that is simulated as closely as possible. Crucial elements of the realistic visualisation are clarity, vividness (incorporating all senses), emotional content and a positive focus, in the sense that only positive outcomes should be visualised (ILLUSTRATION 3.2 shows some of these elements of realism in action). Interestingly, this latter point – the avoidance of debilitative imagery – has been refined by MacIntyre and Moran (2007), who have found that experienced athletes do sometimes imagine errors in order to prepare for worst-case scenarios in competition by using sophisticated meta-imagery control skills to restructure the negative imagery. We consider a related idea of counterbalancing the positive vision through considering failure in language learning in Chapter 7.
- *Regularity* concerns consistency in training; similar to practising playing a musical instrument, maximum benefit can be gained through frequent (e.g. daily) practice. Furthermore, Hale (2005) concludes that optimal effects can be reached if one spends three to five minutes of uninterrupted imagery concentration on each image scene. The recommendation to coaches is that mental rehearsal should be a regular part of every training session, alternating actual physical practice with imagery practice, and the same advice is relevant for incorporating imagery into the language classroom.
- *Reinforcement* means that visual aids such as pictures and video recordings can enhance the quality and control of the imagery, resulting in the initially often hazy mental pictures acquiring improved clarity and vividness. Rymal and Ste-Marie (2009) present evidence that imagery vividness of the self could be improved following a 'self-modelling' intervention, that is, observing oneself repeatedly on videotape while performing the target behaviour successfully. This finding has interesting implications for the strengthening of desired future self-images (for more detail, see TOOLBOX 3.2, on p. 71, describing a video self-modelling project).

Illustration 3.2 From the autobiography of Jack Nicklaus, widely regarded as the most accomplished professional golfer of all time (Taylor *et al.* 1998: 431)

I never hit a shot, not even in practice, without having a very sharp in-focus picture of it in my head. It's like a color movie. First I see the ball where I want it to finish, nice and white, sitting up high on bright green grass. Then the scene quickly changes and I 'see' the ball going there; its path, trajectory and shape, even its behavior on landing. Then there is sort of a fade out, and the next scene shows me making the kind of swing that will turn the images into reality on landing. Finally, I see myself making the kind of swing that that will turn the first two images into reality. These 'home movies' are a key to my concentration.

3.1.2 Imagery workout

Similar to a training session in the gym, teachers can lead their students to do short, intensive imagery workouts to strengthen their imagery muscles, that is, to enhance the vividness and controllability of the imagery. Such regular workouts (e.g. 5 to 10 minutes once a week) can help learners to be more sensually aware of the environment – the principle of 'practice makes perfect' also applies to imagery skills. Reports of such training programmes are consistent in that participants do experience an increase in their imaging ability, but it is important to remind students to be patient with themselves and not to expect too much too soon.

The shortest and yet still effective workout sequence described in the sports literature is the 'Quick Set Routine' (Simons 1996) that was originally developed for athletes for the purpose of a fast, last-minute preparation immediately before a performance. It is a useful tool for quickly focusing or refocusing under diverse circumstances – in under 20 or even 10 seconds – made up of three simple steps that can be adapted for language learners:

- A *physical cue* for body awareness/control (e.g. close your eyes, clear your mind and maintain deep rhythmical breathing, in through your nose and out through your mouth).
- An *emotional cue* for confidence and positive energy (e.g. imagine a pleasant scene or remember some success).
- A *performance focus cue* to prime the actual performance (e.g. focus on the image of the desired action or task).

Longer workout routines can take many forms; TOOLBOX 3.1 presents a sequence with various options depending on the stage the students are at. These general techniques for training imagery skills form a good basis for introducing more specialised workouts involving students' ideal L2 selves. Starting out with broad L2 communication situations, such as restaurant scenes or service encounters, more focused workouts can target specific L2 skills that the students may struggle with, such as public speech, oral interviewing or conversational fluency, preparing for a particular event (e.g. a job interview) or overcoming stress in specific communication settings.

🔧 Toolbox 3.1 The components of imagery workout

Beginning

- Sitting comfortably, with their eyes closed, participants first go through a short relaxation exercise (e.g. slow, deep breathing; see Section 2.3).
- An initial scene is presented and learners are asked to introduce details using all their senses throughout the workout, and applying both internal and external perspectives (see Section 1.3.5 on imagery perspective).

Intermediate

- While students are still in the process of mastering the basics of imagery skills, they are likely to benefit more from high-quality images presented for shorter periods of time, after which the imaging time can be gradually increased.

Advanced

- More advanced tasks can involve controlling and manipulating the content of elaborate image sequences (e.g. moving the furniture in one's bedroom or peeling an apple).
- A further important step is to include some movement in the imagery which requires pronounced body experience to match what is being imagined. This, then, can be expanded into a communicative situation by adding some L2 interaction. Ultimately, we would like the learners' language visions to involve a whole-body experience, similar to the objectives of Asher's classic method of Total Physical Response (see e.g. Larsen-Freeman 2000b).

Concluding

- Imagery workouts might be concluded with a feedback session in which participants are asked to report back various details about their imagery (e.g. the fastest movement, the most vivid colour or the most unusual object they saw; the most pleasant smell or most intense feeling they experienced, etc.).

Some students are bound to experience debilitating language anxiety: research findings from sport psychology indicate that guided imagery is particularly suitable for 'immunising' them, that is, helping them to cope with this condition and hold their nerves. This is consistent with desensitisation procedures in clinical psychology, whereby patients are helped to overcome phobias through a series of systematic

Strengthening the vision through imagery enhancement

imagery approximations to the fearful stimuli. In a detailed analysis of how desensitisation procedures can be applied to reducing language learning anxiety, MacIntyre and Gregersen (2012: 207) emphasise that for desensitisation to be complete, 'the image needs to be repeatedly imagined until language learners are able to imagine it without feeling anxiety or worry'.

Finally, a technique that many students are likely to find motivating and useful is *video self-modelling* (cf. Dowrick 2012). This method involves first producing a 'success video montage' made up of clips of a student performing well in the L2, and then asking the student to regularly watch these images of him/herself performing desired L2 behaviours. TOOLBOX 3.2 offers guidelines for using this technique in the language classroom.

Toolbox 3.2 Video self-modelling project

Video self-modelling (VSM) is an innovative technique using video creation technology that is becoming increasingly accessible to everybody (see Collier-Meek *et al.* 2012 for a detailed overview of the procedure). It involves preparing a video recording of a student, performing a target behaviour, and then editing the video (cutting out any mistakes or other indications of a lack of mastery, compiling a collection of the best trials) so that the final version – typically a 2 to 4-minute vignette – contains optimal examples of the desired behaviour. This model video is then viewed repeatedly by the student, and because the footage portrays the highly skilled future self, it is effective in feeding visually the student's vision. In effect, the participant serves as his/her own role model.

One way of utilising this technique for the purpose of increasing L2-related imagery is to get students to work in small groups for a few days (e.g. a week) and to video record each other as they are using L2 in a variety of relevant settings, including pair/group interactions, communications with other L2 speakers outside of the classroom and class presentations (the precise focus, instructions and timing will depend on the L2 skill you want them to practise/acquire). Then, in the next phase of the project, students work individually with the support of the teacher or peers and use the footage to create a short compilation of their best language performance by editing out anything less than perfect (the teacher or other group members can provide feedback to identify the best performance). The completed videos can be presented to the class or posted on an internet class blog. Finally, students are asked to watch their own video daily for two weeks and record their reflections in a journal or action log. Of course, students should be encouraged to practise the specific behaviours/skills alongside the repeated self-observation.

3.2 Building creative visual and narrative tasks into the teaching routine

Guided imagery is an effective way of tapping into our vision in order to further develop and strengthen it, but we can also achieve this purpose by building into our teaching practice creative visual and narrative tasks that do not have an explicit mental imagery element. Arnold *et al.* (2007) and Hadfield and Dörnyei (2013) offer a range of easy-to-apply classroom activities of this sort, and there is also a rich collection of language teaching materials available that utilise visual aids and stories creatively for diverse purposes (e.g. Goldstein 2008; Keddie 2009; Maley, Duff and Grellet 1981; Morgan and Rinvolucri 1983; Spiro 2007; Stevick 1986; Wajnryb 2003; Wright 1989, 2009; Wright and Hill 2008). We cannot summarise the broad spectrum of these applications here, but in order to illustrate the relevance of using such media, TOOLBOX 3.3 offers sample activities that utilise visual aids and narrative elements to strengthen the students' language vision. To conclude this section, we describe an intriguing theoretical proposal, the psychological theory of *transportation* (Green and Brock 2000), that offers a compelling link between narratives and imagery.

> **Toolbox 3.3 Sample visual and narrative tasks to strengthen the students' language vision**
>
> **Start an 'image portfolio'**
>
> After doing some vision-formation exercises with the students (or simply invite them to list up to five wishes by completing this sentence stem: *If I could speak English really well, I would ...*), ask them to be on the lookout for images of their L2-related desires over the following week. When they spot some good ones, they should get hold of copies of them somehow (e.g. by cutting them out, downloading them, printing them, buying them, photographing them, drawing them, etc.) so that beginning with these, they can build a portfolio of dreams that resonate with them, adding to this collection continually throughout the course.
>
> **Write a 'vision journal'**
>
> Another option is to ask students to get a large sketch book and keep an ongoing 'vision journal'. In it they should record as much detail as possible about what their vision looks like. Encourage them to write regularly about important events related to their vision. This can be combined with regular class writing tasks.

Strengthening the vision through imagery enhancement

Conduct a 'creative visual survey'

This technique is based on the idea of *photovoice* mentioned in Section 2.1 (TOOLBOX 2.3), in which students were asked to take pictures of situations, events and people that matter to them. Here they are invited to participate in a creative visual survey which involves taking photographs of the 'imagined L2 community' they have become part of through their command of the L2 and including themselves in these images as if they were already fully participating in these communities.

Telling your future story creatively

Ask the students to narrate their future story by designing a comic (either by drawing it themselves or using some software, such as Comic Life or Photo Story), writing a poem or even making a short video diary portraying themselves in the future.

Embroidering the learners' 'back-to-the-future' language learning history

In Section 2.4 we presented a task (TOOLBOX 2.12) in which learners were asked to imagine that they are in the future and have successfully mastered the L2; their task then was to write up their imaginary language learning history. An effective way of strengthening their vision is to revisit this narrative from time to time in order to embroider it further, that is, to extend it by adding various details through additional tasks, such as writing a letter to themselves from the future. There is a variety of things they might want to share with their past selves: what it is like to have made it; how they got there; some useful advice; things they have learnt during the journey; or simply some small stories and personal bits and pieces that often make up letters. In this way the students can gradually build a 'back-to-the-future' portfolio while at the same time developing some relevant language skills.

3.2.1 Transporting students into the narrative world of their future vision

We have seen in Section 2.4 that narratives constitute a powerful tool for people to understand themselves and the complexity of the world around them, to the extent that in the end the narratives we generate start shaping our own lives – as Bruner (1987: 15) concluded, 'we *become* the autobiographical narratives by which we "tell about" our lives'. We can observe a similarly powerful effect when we encounter other people's compelling narratives, and the enticing nature of stories – whether fictional or real – is well reflected by the popularity of novels and soap operas, for example. *Transportation theory* (Green and Brock 2000; see Green and Donahue 2009 for a recent review) grew out of the recognition of the distinctive strength and persuasive power of narrative worlds, and its primary focus is on exploring the unique human condition – termed *transportation experience* – when people become so immersed in a story that they temporarily leave their own realities behind. This is the experience we feel when we are enraptured by a book which is a real page-turner, or when we could watch an exciting film for hours and hours. In this sense, a transportation experience can be seen as the imaginary counterpart of the *flow experience* (Csikszentmihalyi 1988), which involves such an intense involvement in an actual activity that people lose self-consciousness and track of time amidst their absorption. This is how Green and Donahue (2009: 241) explain what is involved in a proper transportation experience:

> Imagine a person immersed in a favourite mystery novel. This person may not hear others enter or leave a room while she is reading. She may stay up late into the night because she does not realise how much time has gone by. Her heart may start beating faster during tense moments in the plot, or she may laugh or cry along with the main characters in the story. She may have a vivid mental image of the appearance of these characters. Being lost in a book, or what we call being transported into a narrative world, can have all of these effects and more.

Listening to stories and following their narrative trails can be, then, an immersive, imaginative experience, and it lends itself to be utilised within our teaching practice for the purpose of strengthening the students' future language visions: once we are engrossed in a story, we are more readily able to align ourselves with the lessons and principles offered by the story; therefore, being transported into the narrative world associated with our desired future selves increases the motivational 'pulling power' of vision. The nature of this alignment is further explained by the Transportation-Imagery Model (see Green and Donahue 2009): according to the model, compelling narratives create transportation experience, which, in turn, generates mental imagery in the reader/listener. The transportation experience links these images with the beliefs or new perspectives implied by the story. These 'loaded' images, then, have particular power that often exceeds the strength of reasoning-based arguments, which explains the potency of narrative-based persuasion. Furthermore, subsequent recalling of the image evokes the whole set of story-relevant beliefs and thus reinforces the vision.

Although most of the past research on transportation has used written narratives, the mental processes involved in transportation experiences are assumed to take place across a variety of media, including written, spoken and filmed narratives (Green and Donahue 2009). The transportational power of stories is partly a function of their literary and

Strengthening the vision through imagery enhancement

stylistic qualities (e.g. interesting characters, intricate plots and vivid descriptions), but a crucial condition for a text to transport is its association with the readers' prior experiences. This makes intuitive sense, because pre-existing familiarity with aspects of the particular experience or situation as well as some common ground with some of the main characters are expected to create an easier access into the imaginary world (this recognition is, in fact, consistent with the established principles of teaching extensive reading in the language classroom; see e.g. Day and Bamford 2002). At this point let us return to Ms G, the novice teacher introduced in Chapter 2 (see Section 2.1.1 on transforming the 'unteachable'), because as ILLUSTRATION 3.3 shows, she consciously harnessed the power of transportation in order to raise her students' hopes for the future. In fact, it was this transportation experience that provided the first real breakthrough in her attempts to create a positive vision in her students and to engage in positive ways with their learning and the world around them.

> **Illustration 3.3 Ms G's students' recollection of transportation (from the Freedom Writers Foundation's official website)**
>
> She gave us books written by teenagers that we could relate to, and it was through these books that we began to realise that if we could relate to a little girl who lived on the other side the world, fifty years before we did, we could certainly relate to each other.
>
> We felt like Anne Frank, trapped in a cage, and identified with the violence in Zlata Filipovic's life. We were so inspired by the stories of Anne and Zlata, that we wrote letters to Miep Gies, and to Zlata, in hopes that they would come to Long Beach and share their stories with us. When Miep visited us, she challenged us to keep Anne's memory alive and 'passed the baton' to us. It was then that we decided to begin chronicling our lives.
>
> We began writing anonymous journal entries about the adversities that we faced in our everyday lives. We wrote about gangs, immigration, drugs, violence, abuse, death, anorexia, dyslexia, teenage love, weight issues, divorce, suicide, and all the other issues we never had the chance to express before. We discovered that writing is a powerful form of self expression that could help us deal with our past and move forward. Room 203 was like Anne's attic or Zlata's basement, it was our safe haven, where we could cry, laugh, and share our stories without being judged … When we began writing these entries as a simple English assignment, we had no idea that they would one day be collected and published in a book, The Freedom Writers Diary.
>
> (http://www.freedomwritersfoundation.org/our-story)
> (last accessed on 23/9/2013)

Motivating Learners, Motivating Teachers

There is a wide variety of narratives that can be used with language learners for creating a transportation experience, including memoirs, inspirational literature (some of these are also available in the form of graded readers) and stimulating films that portray the human experience of pursuing one's vision – for example, Alice Kaplan's (1993) *French Lessons* and Eva Hoffman's (1989) *Lost in Translation* are two well-known autobiographical narratives of what it is like to learn, speak and live in a foreign language. As we saw above, the key issue in selecting works that will transport the students to the worlds of who they could become as language users most effectively is their links with the students' life experiences, a notion we discussed in Section 2.1. For those teachers who would like to examine the transportation value of narratives to particular groups of students, there is even a short questionnaire, originally developed by Green and Brock (2000), which can be used to gauge the students' level of transportation evoked by a specific narrative (see TOOLBOX 3.4).

> **Toolbox 3.4 Gauge your students' level of transportation (adapted from Green and Brock 2000)**
>
> Students respond by using a numeric rating scale from 1 to 7 (with 7 meaning 'very much' and 1 'not at all') by writing the number that best expresses their reactions regarding a specific narrative they have covered in the space before each item. This means that the higher the score, the stronger the transportation experience, with the exception of items marked with 'R' in which the result is reversed (i.e. high scores represent poor transportation).
>
> **Part 1: General items**
>
> ___ 1. While I was reading the narrative, I could easily picture the events in it taking place.
>
> ___ 2. While I was reading the narrative, activity going on in the room around me was on my mind. (R)
>
> ___ 3. I could picture myself in the scene of the events described in the narrative.
>
> ___ 4. I was mentally involved in the narrative while reading it.
>
> ___ 5. After finishing the narrative, I found it easy to put it out of my mind. (R)
>
> ___ 6. I wanted to learn how the narrative ended.
>
> ___ 7. The narrative affected me emotionally.

___ 8. I found myself thinking of ways the narrative could have turned out differently.

___ 9. I found my mind wandering while reading the narrative. (R)

___ 10. The events in the narrative are relevant to my everyday life.

___ 11. The events in the narrative have changed my life.

Part 2: Items specific to the chosen narrative

Here the teacher can design a few questions that specifically relate to the narrative used in the classroom (e.g. 'while reading the narrative I had a vivid image of x (the specific character, situation, etc.)').

3.3 Encouraging students to keep learning journals

In a summary of *narrative learning* (see Section 2.4), Clark and Rossiter (2008) point out that getting students to keep a learning journal encompasses all the beneficial characteristics of this approach. Through reflecting on and articulating what they are learning in a course, students bring additional understanding to the process, which helps to integrate the learning experiences into their personal lives. Sustained journaling is, in effect, the creation of an ongoing personal narrative in which the students are interacting with the material, thereby shaping not only the instructional intake but also their own emerging academic and personal identity. An additional benefit of such journals is that they can then be used for furthering the whole learner group's language vision (see Section 3.5).

Ms G used student diaries as one of the primary tools for transforming her 'unteachable' students, and this is explicitly foregrounded in the subtitle of the collection of these journal entries, *The Freedom Writers Diary: How a Teacher and 150 Teens Used Writing to Change Themselves and the World Around Them* (The Freedom Writers and Gruwell 1999). The students started out with transportation experiences (Section 3.2.1), using books that reflected aspects of the ethnically segregated gang culture surrounding them, and particularly two diaries – Anne Frank's *The Diary of a Young Girl* and *Zlata's Diary: A Child's Life in Sarajevo* (written by Zlata Filipovic, an 11-year-old girl who wrote about her life in Sarajevo during the Bosnian civil war) – made an impact on them. When they were visited by Miep Gies, the person who helped to hide Anne Frank for two years from the Nazis and who retrieved Anne's diary after she and her family were arrested, she

Motivating Learners, Motivating Teachers

challenged the students to make sure that 'Anne's death is not in vain'. This message made them realise the potential power of writing and storytelling; ILLUSTRATION 3.4 describes Ms G's personal recollection on the journaling process.

> **Illustration 3.4 Ms G's recollection of journaling (Gruwell and The Freedom Writers Foundation 2007: 2)**
>
> When one of my students exclaimed, 'I feel like I live in an undeclared war zone,' I realised that these young people needed to be encouraged to pick up a pen rather than a gun. Tragically, this student had lost two dozen friends to gang violence. In an attempt to connect with my class, I gave my students journals in the hopes of giving them a voice. Before long, they began to pour out their stories openly, unburdened by the anxieties associated with spelling, grammar, and grades. Journals provided a safe place to become passionate writers communicating their own histories, their own insights. As they began to write down their thoughts and feelings, motivation blossomed. Suddenly, they had a forum for self-expression, and a place where they felt valued and validated ... Following in the footsteps of extraordinary teenagers like Anne and Zlata, my students used their own diaries to share their experiences of loss, hardship, and discrimination.

3.4 Harnessing the power of virtual worlds

When we talk about possible selves and vision, we are concerned with the sensory experiences of our future in the absence of any actual stimulus. In this respect the rapid development of virtual online spaces opens up exciting new opportunities, because they allow mental images of future selves to be 'embodied' by digital realities: virtual environments have the potential to act as powerful arenas for strengthening language learners' L2 selves by making the constituent images more vivid, elaborate and in some sense more 'real'.

Thorne, Black and Sykes (2009) divide virtual environments (VEs) into three broad categories of online spaces: (1) *Open social virtualities* (e.g. *Second Life*), which include various urban locations (e.g. a university campus or a night club) or fantasy settings for participants to move around and interact with each other. (2) *Online gaming spaces* featuring goal-directed activities in fantasy worlds (e.g. *World of Warcraft*, *The Lord of the Rings*), which differ from open social virtualities in that participants are presented with specific tasks in tiered orders of difficulty. (3) *Online environments specifically designed for educational*

Strengthening the vision through imagery enhancement

purposes (e.g. educational areas of *Second Life*). All these environments typically involve participants interacting with others through self-created or assigned avatars and feature text-based – and increasingly, voice-based – communication within the multiple-participant environment. Of interest to us in this section are the self-created avatars which are used to enact the users' alternate identities.

3.4.1 Avatars and virtual environments

VEs have been increasingly utilised as simulated environments for all kinds of purposes, from influencing people's exercise behaviours (Fox and Bailenson 2009) to raising students' awareness of social and cultural attitudes and stereotypes (Lee and Hoadley 2007), including those associated with L2 cultures (Buckingham 2009); most importantly from our point of view, they have also been used as spaces for language and literacy development (Thorne and Black 2007) and multilingual communication (Thorne 2008). Let us consider a highly instructive example of the power of VEs in linking individuals' ideal selves with self-regulatory action. As summarised in ILLUSTRATION 3.5, Fox and Bailenson (2009) demonstrated that shaping one's avatar to approximate one's ideal self-image (in this particular case in terms of body weight) had a direct impact on what the research participants exposed their actual selves to (in this particular case in terms of doing actual exercises).

The study by Fox and Bailenson (2009) as well as other investigations in a similar vein are relevant for language educators and materials writers, not simply because they open up alternative avenues for educating language learners, but also because they highlight the considerable motivational potential that virtual worlds can offer: VEs have the capability to become an effective platform for visualising students' ideal L2 selves and to witness the consequences of their actions played out before their eyes, which in turn seems to have a direct impact on offline behaviour.

Illustration 3.5 On the power of virtual environment technology in motivating people

Fox and Bailenson (2009) investigated the impact of research participants' use of avatars on their actual behaviour in real life. The participants were asked to perform exercise behaviours using their avatars in the VE and received either rewards for engaging in such exercises (i.e. their avatars visibly lost weight) or punishment for failing to do so (gaining weight). The findings of the study are fascinating: participants in the experimental group which observed their self-resembling avatars and the consequences of their actions were much more likely to repeat the physical exercise in the real world than members of various control groups. This result confirms the key premise of possible selves theory, namely that seeing a vivid, elaborate and plausible image of oneself in the future (a desired healthy self or, in contrast, its feared counterpart) has significant motivational consequences for the present. In addition, this research also demonstrated that VEs offer effective technologies which can help individuals to visualise an ideal version of their own future selves (i.e. their desired end states) and motivate them to invest effort to achieve such ideal future images outside of the virtual space.

In sum, VEs seem to be optimal spaces for harnessing the power of L2 vision in language learning and teaching. At the moment little relevant research exists in this domain of applied linguistics, but the process of integrating virtual realities into language teaching and learning materials design has already started (a good example is *Avatar English* – www.avatarlanguages.com/home.php – which is an innovative online language school that utilises avatars and the VE platform *Second Life* amongst other technological developments). Therefore, exploring the motivational potentials of virtual L2 selves in VEs is likely to become an exciting direction for future research.

3.4.2 Online gaming spaces

We cannot finish a discussion of virtual worlds without considering the potential of online gaming spaces for language learners' vision and motivation. The potential of games as 'clues to the future' is not a new concept. For example, Bernard Suits (1978: 176) noted over 30 years ago that

> it is games that give us something to do when there is nothing to do. We thus call games 'pastimes' and regard them as trifling fillers of the interstices of our lives. But they are much more important than that. They are clues to the future. And their serious cultivation now is perhaps our only salvation.

With the rapid developments of digital spaces, similar ideas to those of Suits are being explored with regard to online gaming. *Massively multiplayer online games* (MMOG) are multiplayer video games capable of supporting hundreds or thousands of players simultaneously via the Internet. They have seen unprecendented growth commercially and as many as half a billion people around the planet are believed to play online video games regularly (cf. McGonigal 2011). While there is still a widespread popular belief (expressed mainly by those who do not engage in such activities) that gaming is a waste of time, McGonigal sees online games as a 'primary platform for enabling the future' in the twenty-first century (p. 13), and there remains little doubt about the massive educational potential of engaging with this new technology. Yet, this potential has not been sufficiently exploited by educational games, because, as Lee and Hoadley (2007: 1) summarise, such games 'frequently consist of repetitive, superficial tasks with limited transfer or poorly disguised attempts to sugar coat learning, which can leave the student feeling patronised or deceived'. As the scholars argue, one of the main reasons for this failure has been insufficient recognition of the importance of the learners' identities and possible future selves in these games. Their research, which utilised VE platforms, shows that enacting a variety of possible selves allowed students to experience who they could become, including selves that are competent in the domain being taught, and through these experiences, they were motivated to learn associated skills. As Lee and Hoadley conclude (p. 5), while research in this vein is still in its early stage, the initial indications are promising:

> We are not yet at the point where we can always identify what types of environments would encourage learners to adopt the identity of an expert in some subject. However, allowing players to construct identity is an important way to keep activities engaging and ... good for learning as well. As educational tools, MMOGs can provide realistic scenarios and a safe space for learners to test and explore possible selves, including selves that are competent in the domain being taught. Identity thus may be the key to the balance between engagement and learning, allowing the two to support, rather than compete with, each other.

We cannot offer here a comprehensive discussion of the relevant developments in this exciting area of research (see Thorne *et al.* 2009 for a review), but we are confident that virtual realities, and online games in particular, are an important part of the language education future. On the other hand, we also agree with Zheng *et al.* (2009) that simply placing children in virtual spaces in the hope that they will make rapid progress in L2 learning is naïve: 'To fully take advantage of affordances of virtual space, the goals and intentions of students embedded within information-rich metaverse environments should be understood' (p. 505). This understanding will need to start with recognising how avatars in virtual realities are associated with ideal self-images. We conclude this section with an instructive 'insider account' by Dawid Krystowiak (2012), an English teacher from Poland (ILLUSTRATION 3.6). As a participant in a MMOG (*Lord of the Rings*), he describes in detail how the players' investment in a range of social identities ('guild' officer, language teacher, co-gamer) and desired future selves (successful player, would-be 'guild' member, etc.) had direct consequences for both their online and offline behaviours, including their language learning.

> **Illustration 3.6 Playing games or learning English? (adapted from Krystowiak 2012)**
>
> I met Frosty, a 24-year-old graduate of Pedagogy from Poland, and Sparky, a 32-year-old saxophonist from South Africa (both pseudonyms), online in different circumstances. Frosty was one of the first people I met in the game (*Lord of the Rings Online* – LotRO). He showed me the game mechanics and recruited me into his guild. Thanks to his help, I learnt a lot about how the social community works in LotRO and how the game is played. When I became an officer of the guild myself, I recruited Sparky into it – I used all the skills and information learnt from Frosty to scaffold Sparky's participation in the game. Through the gameplay we have had many conversations in which I used my professional background as a teacher to help her with her English.
>
> As for Sparky's journey into the LotRO world, it was a bit more difficult than in the case of her friend. Before she started playing the game, she only had a very limited range of English vocabulary. Unlike Frosty, who had received extensive education in English, Sparky had only learnt the language from games and her English-speaking friends. When she started playing LotRO, she was already an experienced player (she had been playing the *World of Warcraft* and other games for over a year), so she was able to figure out most controls and actions on her own thanks to her previous experience ... Quests, on the other hand, were a completely different 'ball game' for her. When Sparky joined Frosty's and my kinship, her education, both about the game and the English language, picked up pace. Sparky recalls that the officers in her kinship offered her a lot of support and patience with her English. She spent a great deal of time talking with one of them using the Ventrilo voice chat software. The officer, Tuck (pseudonym), helped her with quests as well as taught her some English every time they played. I have also spent a lot of time talking to Sparky, using my background as an English teacher in order to help her with vocabulary and grammar. After several months of playing, Sparky was able to communicate with others in a satisfactory way.

3.5 Strengthening the whole group's vision

So far, we have covered a variety of approaches – imagery, narratives, student journals and virtual realities – for strengthening the language

Strengthening the vision through imagery enhancement

learners' vision. However, because most language teachers work with class groups rather than individual learners, this last section considers the main principles for enhancing the whole group's vision.

The principal recognition underlying the field of group dynamics is that groups have a life of their own, that is, individuals in groups behave differently from the way they do outside the group. Therefore, concepts such as group development, group cohesiveness and group goals have been of interest to both researchers and practitioners in order to understand the impact of the various group properties on the individual students and on the quality learning that can take place within the group (see Dörnyei and Murphey 2003 and Senior 2006 for summaries). In keeping with these premises, an effective way of strengthening the learners' individual vision is to generate and strengthen the collective vision of the whole group they belong to.

We have seen earlier that the concept of vision subsumes goals, and in group dynamics the group's goal-orientedness – that is, the extent to which a group is attuned to pursuing a composite group goal – is seen as an important determinant of the group's productivity. In his summary of motivational strategies, Zoltán has formulated several goal-related recommendations (Dörnyei 2001), including the following three strategies:

- Get the students to negotiate their individual goals and outline a common purpose, and display the final outcome in public.
- Keep the class goals achievable by re-negotiating if necessary.
- Draw up a detailed written agreement with individual students, or whole groups, that specifies what they will learn and how, and the ways by which you will help and reward them.

While goal-setting strategies of this sort definitely help to focus learners on the tasks, we saw in Chapter 1 that a vision is more than a goal in that it also involves a multi-sensory (imaginary) experience to accompany the cognitive objectives. Can such an imagined reality be achieved at a group level? History shows us that it can: various groupings and political movements have successfully achieved collective visions throughout the centuries, uniting members under some vision-related banner, both in the artistic world and in the political and social arenas. Such a collective vision has two main facets: a shared vision about (1) the future for the group members (e.g. 'We all want to be multilingual because we believe in the significance of reaching across language boundaries') and (2) the future state of the whole group itself in relation to the goal (e.g. 'We want to become a task force that effectively promotes positive attitudes about multilingualism'). This latter aspect is often referred to as the 'mission' of the group. Promoting these two facets often goes hand

Motivating Learners, Motivating Teachers

in hand; for example, the California schoolteacher we have already met more than once in this book, Ms G, endorsed both aspects in a parallel manner: she placed emphasis on the learners' individual futures (i.e. that they should all graduate against the odds), while the group as a whole gradually turned into the Freedom Writer Foundation with its own collective vision (see ILLUSTRATION 3.7).

Illustration 3.7 The Freedom Writers Foundation's mission (adapted from the Freedom Writers Foundation's official website)

The mission of the Freedom Writers Foundation is to empower educators and students to positively impact their own lives and the world around them by:

- Training educators to teach every student through challenging, relevant, and project-driven activities
- Awarding scholarships to first-generation high school graduates
- Developing challenging, high-interest curriculum
- Leading empowering training seminars, student assemblies, classroom discussions, and professional development in-services through our Freedom Writers Outreach program

Through these strategies they hope to achieve the following results:

- Highly effective educators who love their jobs
- Empowered students who graduate prepared for college and career
- Classroom culture of tolerance and inclusion
- Reduced dropout rates
- Reduced instances of bullying

(http://www.freedomwritersfoundation.org/about.html)
(last accessed on 23/9/2013)

In the following we discuss three specific approaches to strengthening group vision: (1) *pooling individual narratives*, (2) *modelling group vision through transformational leadership* and (3) *communicating the vision effectively*.

3.5.1 Pooling individual narratives

We have seen in several places (most notably in Sections 2.4, 3.2 and 3.3) that getting the students to produce various forms of narratives (e.g. descriptions of imagined future states or personal journals) helps to create and then strengthen desired self-images in them and thus

Strengthening the vision through imagery enhancement

contributes to the formation of a powerful vision. Can such individual products be turned into group properties? We believe so and creative teachers will undoubtedly find several ways to achieve this; for illustration, here are three methods:

- *'Newslettering'*: Tim Murphey has developed a simple but highly effective method for sharing information from the students' personal journals (cf. Dörnyei and Murphey 2003). The essence of 'newslettering' (as he called the procedure) is to feed the students' views – gathered from their journals or some other forms of feedback such as questionnaires – back to the whole class anonymously by including them in a regular class newsletter. Since the entries come from 'near peer role models' (Section 2.5), they can provide persuasive models of positive attitudes, roles and self-images that students are implicitly invited to take on: as Dörnyei and Murphey (2003: 130) conclude, 'The proximal relationship of the writers and readers … invites identification and the realisation that it is possible for the readers to also do the things mentioned in the newsletters.' This is confirmed by some student feedback; for example: 'Everyone's storytelling is a brand-new impact to my thought and mind, exciting me very much' or 'Because of the newsletter, I realise what my classmates do after the classes. I hope that I can do as well as them!!' One student summed this process up so clearly that it is worth quoting the whole entry:

    > Every time I see the NL [Newsletter], I can see what my classmates' feeling, sometimes theirs are the same as mine. It gives me lots of encouragement. Also make me eager to learn more. Because they are a very good model for me. Show me what I should do to learn well. Hope one day I can also be a good model for them or someone else. (p. 130)

- *Story sharing session*: Clark and Rossiter (2008) report that when students in a course on adult learning shared stories of transformative learning experiences, the public positioning of the narrative enabled them to understand their experiences in a new way. Within applied linguistics contexts, it has been a well-known fact that one of the most inspiring and instructive parts of learning strategy training is the 'sharing session', where students are asked to share their learning discoveries and self-generated learning strategies as a regular part of class. As Zoltán has summarised (Dörnyei 2005), (a) students who are directly involved in the learning process often have fresh insights that they can share with fellow learners in simplified terms, and (b) personal learning strategies are often quite

Motivating Learners, Motivating Teachers

amusing and therefore students usually enjoy discussing them. The outcome of this potent combination is typically deeper-than-average, potentially transformational, engagement. In a similar manner, we can expect that the simple act of sharing the various focused narratives that the students have created will short-circuit individual creativity and contribute to generating an overarching vision.

- *Creating a 'group chronicle'*: Collective wisdom, vision and identity have traditionally been captured in 'chronicles', and Section 2.4 reported on a project by Ira Levin (2000), in which she constructed an elaborate 'vision story' for a commercial company by drawing on the collective fantasy, expertise and experience of a large number of employees. This shared-vision creation involved several structured data-gathering rounds such as initial fact-finding visits, recordings of people's projections for the future and circulating a first draft for structured feedback by a wide range of stake-holders. In a similar way, the class group could also be asked to produce a 'group chronicle', which would start in the past and end in the future. Initial ideas and drafts can be solicited from individuals, pairs or small groups (perhaps as part of a competition), followed by an organised editing process in which sub-editors would be in charge of compiling various sections of the chronicle, and a final editorial board would solicit feedback and then fine-tune the final text accordingly.

3.5.2 Modelling collective vision through transformational leadership

Whenever we talk about the behaviour of groups rather than individuals, we need to address the question of *leadership*, because the functioning of groups is inseparable from the behaviour of the officially most influential group member, the leader (in our case, the teacher). And if we talk about group vision, the most obvious area in leadership theory to turn to is *transformational leadership*. This term has been introduced in the literature to separate two fundamental leadership styles: *transactional* and *transformational*. Leaders belonging to the former category (making up the majority of leaders) treat their relationship with their groups as a transaction: they set goals and offer rewards for achievement or punishment for unsatisfactory performance. While transactional leaders can be very effective in a wide variety of settings most of the time, what they cannot do is provide members with vision and inspiration in order to empower them to transcend their ordinary achievement level and to 'go the extra mile' in the service of the collective interest – this is the function of transformational leaders. Bass and Riggio (2006: 4) summed up what transformational leaders do as follows:

> Transformational leaders motivate others to do more than they originally intended and often even more than they thought possible. They set more challenging expectations and typically achieve higher performances ... Transformational leadership involves inspiring followers to commit to a shared vision and goals for an organization or unit, challenging them to be innovative problem solvers, and developing followers' leadership capacity via coaching, mentoring, and provision of both challenge and support.

As is clear from the above description, transformational leaders do not simply want to manage things as they are; they want to *transform* things – hence the term – by producing shifts in their followers' beliefs and values and thus motivate them to perform beyond standard expectations of performance. This can be done only by building consensus and increasing the participants' commitment to a *collective* mission and vision. When successful, transformational leaders can indeed shape the culture of whole units or organisations. Peterson and Deal (1998: 29) list four specific ways school leaders achieve this purpose: (1) they communicate core values in what they say and do; (2) they recognise and celebrate the accomplishments and service of staff and students; (3) they observe rituals and traditions to support the school's heart and soul; and (4) they eloquently communicate the deeper mission of the school.

3.5.3 Communicating the collective vision effectively

Research on transformational leaders highlights the fact that in order for a whole social group to adopt a collective vision that transcends the individual members' self-interest, it needs to be articulated very clearly and communicated persuasively to the group members by the group leader (the teacher). This can be achieved in a number of ways:

- Articulating the vision precisely, framed within the 'big picture', outlining both the desired end state and the proposed route towards it.
- Expressing the vision in highly engaging terms – after all, effective visions 'describe a future that is more attractive than the present' (Levin 2000: 92) – and offering a vividly detailed description of a future that people can readily picture, thereby making a compelling case and an inspirational appeal for it.
- Displaying infectious enthusiasm in the group/organisation and the project.

Motivating Learners, Motivating Teachers

- Setting high performance expectations in combination with expressing confidence that the goals will be achieved.
- Offering encouragement to the group members and instilling pride in them for being associated with the project.
- 'Walking the talk', that is, communicating the vision in both words and deeds, and leading by example.
- Aligning fully all the main administrative, financial and personnel decisions within the group with the spirit of the vision.
- Emphasising the vision with symbolic actions such as establishing ceremonies to celebrate it and organising assemblies to honour any effort towards it.
- Preparing and displaying a mission statement that summarises the vision.
- Communicating key aspects of the vision visually in mottos, logos, letterheads, banners, posters, etc.

Thus, communicating the vision effectively goes beyond merely using eloquent words: aspects of the vision need to permeate every facet of the group's life in a salient manner. In Bolman and Deal's (2008: 370) words, transformational leaders need to tell 'mythical' stories of collective vision:

> Symbolic [i.e. transformational] leaders often embed their vision in a mythical story – a story about 'us' and about 'our' past, present, and future. 'Us' could be a school's faculty, a plant's employees, the people of Thailand, or any other audience a leader hopes to reach. The past is usually golden, a time of noble purposes, of great deeds, of legendary heroes and heroines. The present is troubled, a critical moment when we have to make fateful choices. The future is a dreamlike vision of hope and greatness, often tied to past glories.

TOOLBOX 3.5 offers a sample classroom activity aimed at strengthening collective language learning vision through putting students in the place of a transformational language teacher who needs to prepare and deliver a motivational speech – that is, a 'mythical story' – to his/her language class.

Toolbox 3.5 Preparing a motivational speech

Ask students to imagine that you – their current language teacher – are leaving and that they have just been appointed to be the new language teacher of the class. This is their long-awaited opportunity to transform language education by introducing new agendas and goals, and by turning

Strengthening the vision through imagery enhancement

the L2 lessons into an enjoyable learning process that leads to ultimate success! Therefore, the introductory speech the new teacher will need to make to the class will have special significance in trying to gain collective support for his/her vision. The students' task is to prepare and then to deliver this crucial motivational speech.

- In preparation, discuss with the students some key aspects of a motivational speech, using the material presented in this section.
- Ask students to model their speeches on the three-component template of Bolman and Deal's (2008) 'mythical story', describing (a) the glorious past, (b) the troubled present leading to a crossroads, and (c) a dreamlike vision of hope and greatness.
- Students prepare their speeches in pairs or small groups. Encourage them to consult a variety of resources (e.g. motivational speeches on *YouTube* or in famous books/films), potentially turning the task into a project that includes some home research.
- Each pair/group selects a spokesperson to deliver their speech to the rest of the class. A possible follow-up activity may be to collect the most attractive elements from the various speeches for the purpose of preparing a joint class video drawing on these.

4 Substantiating the vision by making it plausible

> All men dream: but not equally. Those who dream by night in the dusty recesses of their minds wake in the day to find that all was vanity: but the dreamers of the day are dangerous men, for they may act their dream with open eyes, to make it possible.
>
> T. E. Lawrence (alias 'Lawrence of Arabia'), 1922

We saw in the theoretical overview in Chapter 1 (Section 1.2) that possible selves are only effective insomuch as the learner perceives them as *plausible*, that is, conceivable within the person's particular circumstances. As Pizzolato (2006: 59) succinctly states, 'the relation between what students want to become and what students actually become may be mediated by what students feel they are able to become'. Thus, in order for ideal L2 self-images to energise sustained language learning behaviour, they must be anchored in a sense of realistic expectations, resulting in the curious mixed aura of imagination and reality that effective visions share. This requires honest and down-to-earth reality checks as well as considerations of any potential obstacles and difficulties that might stand in the way of realising students' ideal L2 visions.

If carefully managed, virtually all of the teaching interventions that we have proposed so far can work towards substantiating the vision. For instance, a 'taster' of L2 visions can function as convincing experiential evidence that the L2 vision is indeed within the students' reach. Similarly, inviting successful role models to class can send a powerful message to students that, although everybody faces certain hurdles in reaching their ideal selves, it can be – and has been! – done. In the same vein, the construction of avatars representing one's future images of self in virtual environments can work as a tool for making future visions realistic. In this section, we will complement these previous suggestions and insights by addressing three specific points: (1) *the importance of realistic learner beliefs,* (2) *methods of constructive reality self-checks* and (3) *approaches to eliminating obstacles.*

4.1 Cultivating realistic beliefs about language learning

In his book on motivational strategies, Zoltán starts the discussion of creating realistic learner beliefs by stating, 'Most learners will have certain

Substantiating the vision by making it plausible

beliefs about language learning and most of these beliefs are likely to be (at least partly) incorrect' (Dörnyei 2001: 66). This situation poses a real danger, because one of the worst-case scenarios in vision-formation is constructing a 'story of self-deception' (Polkinghorne 1988: 154), that is, a projection of unrealistic desires rather than a configuration of real actions. Optimal future selves that are indeed possible rather than merely the product of sheer fantasy require adding to one's imaginative creativity some realistic beliefs about the individual's own capabilities and also about the skills and strategies that are needed to become the hoped-for future self. It is therefore a central issue to sort out some of the most far-fetched expectations in our students and to get rid of the preconceived notions and prejudices that are likely to hinder L2 attainment. Without doing so, any visions developed might be unsubstantiated.

In his *New York Times* bestseller, *Outliers*, Malcolm Gladwell (2008) repeatedly talks about the '10,000-hour rule', claiming that it takes approximately 10,000 hours of practice to become virtuosos at anything regardless of how talented we are. He sees this therefore as a fundamental condition for success in any field. Even though it obviously varies across situations how competent we need to become to have a comfortable working knowledge of the L2, there is no doubt that successful language learning requires long hours of exercising conscious effort, which in turn requires a matching level of vision that is anchored in reality. Dörnyei and Ushioda (2011) argue that in order for language learners to rectify their erroneous assumptions, they need some clarity in at least two key areas: they need to develop an informed understanding of the nature of second language acquisition regarding (1) the reasonable criteria for progress, particularly in terms of time and ultimate level of L2 attainment, and (2) the existence of a number of alternative routes to success, which makes it necessary for learners to personalise their learning, that is, to discover for themselves the methods and techniques by which they learn best.

To illustrate the main point of this section, consider the true story of Steve (ILLUSTRATION 4.1), whose vision was not rooted in realistic beliefs about language learning. As a consequence, he soon became disillusioned, and he also failed to pursue the learning process strategically, which is the subject of the next chapter (Chapter 5: *Transforming the vision into action*).

Illustration 4.1 Steve's 'foolish dream'

Someone whom I (Maggie) knew well – let's call him Steve – decided to come to spend a year in the UK. He arrived with zero English but lots of enthusiasm and hope to make up for it, ready to embrace the 'brave new world'. On the first night, as he was watching a movie on TV, he said:

Motivating Learners, Motivating Teachers

'Wow, I've no idea what they're on about, but in a year's time I will understand every word of it!' It turned out that Steve eventually spent not one, but two years in the country and still left with little more than a few conversational gambits which allowed him to get by but which never really opened the doors for him to the English-speaking world. When asked about that first-night remark, he admitted: 'Oh, it was such a foolish dream. I had no idea then how impossible and unrealistic it actually was!' (We will look at several aspects of Steve's lack of progress in this and the next section.)

Looking back, it would have been useful at that point to bring Steve down to earth with a bit of straight talk, because sorting out misconceptions and prejudices about language learning is a key motivational issue: possible selves should not only *seem* possible but *be* possible, and language visions are effective only if they are grounded in realistic expectations of what learning a foreign language actually entails. To illustrate the practical implications of this principle, TOOLBOX 4.1 lists some suggestions of how to cultivate such realistic beliefs.

> **Toolbox 4.1 Techniques for cultivating realistic learner beliefs**
>
> - *Analyse with your students case studies of successful and unsuccessful learners for what they reveal about the language learning process.* This book contains numerous illustrations that can be used for this purpose, but even more instructive might be drawing on the students' autobiographical narratives or stories they collect about real people they know.
> - *Use questionnaires about language learning beliefs in the language class.* Examples include questionnaires published in Horwitz (1988) and Lightbown and Spada (2013); the items in these questionnaires highlight key areas to address in subsequent discussion.
> - *Integrate student-friendly summaries of SLA research into the language teaching materials.* This may sound like a tall order, but language learners are actually often quite curious to read research results about the process they are engaged in. Research on the 'good language learner' might be a good starting point (see e.g. Griffiths 2008; Norton and Toohey 2001).

4.2 Creating channels for constructive reality self-checks

Students will have formed the notion of what is possible for them very early on through their experiences in families, schools and friendship

Substantiating the vision by making it plausible

networks. Unfortunately, these conceptions of self-capabilities often tend to be inaccurate. In the previous section we already mentioned briefly one common type of learner with an unrealistic disposition, illustrated by Steve's case, the 'pie-in-the-sky' wishful thinker whose aspirations seem over-optimistic and out of touch with reality. There is also a second type of misjudgement, displayed by people who appear convinced that becoming a successful speaker of L2 is simply beyond their reach and therefore not worth the effort. Constructive reality self-checks are crucial in both cases: they enable the wishful thinkers to face reality and calibrate their expectations and action plans accordingly, and they also help the pessimists to see that, with appropriate strategies, achieving success in an L2 is within everybody's reach.

4.2.1 Empowering the 'pessimists'

Let us examine constructive reality self-checks for the 'pessimists' first, because this type of false belief seems to be the dominant one in L2 learning contexts. We can see pessimists within a possible selves framework as people who find it difficult to translate their hopes into realistic expectations and, as Carver, Reynolds and Scheier (1994) explain, because their hopes fail to evolve into expected selves, they are unlikely to engage the motivational control systems that govern behaviour. In other words, unlike optimists, who formulate their possible selves on the basis of positive experiences, pessimists are inclined to use negative experiences as the foundation for extrapolating possible selves formation; this may lead to no possible self – or even a feared self – and certainly no forward-pointing action.

Let us consider two techniques that can be used in language classes to counteract this negative tendency and provide the more sceptical language learners with constructive feedback on the plausibility of their L2 visions. The first (TOOLBOX 4.2) uses affirmations as a springboard for identifying and then counteracting any obstacles, negative thoughts or doubts the learners may struggle with – these can be further processed later through follow-up discussions of affirmation tasks.

🔧 Toolbox 4.2 Tackle the implausible through affirmations

This task, adapted from a creative visualisation text, is admittedly quirky, but it has the potential to tap into some basic underlying issues and offer self-generated constructive feedback. The repetitive (but far from mechanical) writing process enables the students to come to a fuller realisation of the consequences of their possible selves. It also allows them to articulate and, more importantly, to tackle any doubts and anxieties that they may have about their learning the L2.

1. Ask students to write on the top of a sheet of paper whom they would ideally like to become as an L2 speaker. This should be one relatively short L2 sentence, written in the present tense and should also include their first names (e.g. *I, Teresa, am a successful speaker of English.*). Provide any new words and corrective feedback if necessary in order to ensure that the students' affirmations are linguistically correct.
2. (Here comes the quirky bit.) Ask students to write the sentence 10 (or even 20) times in succession on the sheet, in the first, second and third persons (e.g. *I, Teresa, am a successful speaker of English. Teresa, you are a successful speaker of English. Teresa is a successful speaker of English.*).

   HOWEVER, explain to the students that you don't want them to write these sentences mechanically, but rather they should really think about the meaning of the words every time they are writing them. AND also ask them to notice any internal resistance, doubts or negative thoughts about what they are writing.
3. Whenever such negative thoughts occur, they should turn the paper over, and on the back write out the negative thought, that is, the reason why the affirmation cannot be true or cannot work (e.g. *I'm really not good enough. I'm too scared. I've never been good at languages. I will never be able to speak with other native speakers.*). This task works only if students are willing to give this reflection phase a serious go. Depending on their level of L2 proficiency, they can do this in either their L1 or their L2. Every time they have jotted down an 'issue', they should go back to the other side of the paper and carry on writing their affirmation.
4. When they are finished, ask them to take a look at the back of the paper. If they were honest, there will be a list of reasons why their L2 vision seems implausible, giving raw material for relevant discussion / follow-up activities to address the doubts and (wrong) assumptions about their language learning.
5. As a final task, ask students to pretend to be someone who disagrees with them and think of powerful affirmations that can counteract the negative issues (e.g. *I've never been good at languages* can be counteracted by the sentence *There are plenty of examples to prove that everyone can learn another language if they put their mind to it.*). Ask them to formulate these counterarguments in sentences and write them on the 'positive' side of the sheet.

This process of self-generating constructive feedback can be applied regularly in class or in the students' reflective journals.

The second technique (TOOLBOX 4.3) can be used as part of a project for outside the classroom or for material for the students' reflective journals. It involves a 'strength-based approach' to enhance the plausibility

Substantiating the vision by making it plausible

of possible selves; such approaches have a simple premise: 'identify what is going well, do more of it, and build on it'. This positive angle allows students to become aware of the relevant strengths that they can bring to the L2 learning experience in order to make their L2 dreams come true. In line with Boyatzis and Akrivou's (2006) argument, it is important to emphasise that any approach aiming to identify students' past successes and strengths (e.g. the current task in TOOLBOX 4.3) should be accompanied by the active construction of a vivid and elaborate *future self*. Without a clear future vision, the boost in self-confidence that may result from these 'strength-based' techniques might encourage learners simply to dwell on their past successes and feel good about themselves rather than prompt them to invest in the future.

Toolbox 4.3 A strength-based approach to develop plausible ideal selves (adapted from Boyatzis and Akrivou 2006)

This 'strength-based approach' to L2 learning seeks to help students first to identify strengths they have shown in the past. They are to interview 10 to 20 people who know them relatively well (e.g. those with whom they live, study or play), asking these people to recall 'a time when I was at my best' and then describe the student's actions at that time as well as the impact those actions had on others. The students then take all of these stories of themselves and conduct a thematic analysis, looking for themes and patterns. This should result in a list of ways by which they act when they were 'at their best', constituting an inventory of their strengths as observed, experienced and remembered by others.

This powerful exercise makes people feel a surge of self-confidence and often accompanying self-esteem. This burst of positive emotion and self-evaluation can, in turn, provide a boost to their hopes about the future, and the key to channelling this boost into formulating plausible language visions is to find meaningful links between the students' strengths and the behaviours, skills and attitudes needed for achieving their L2 future selves (which will be further discussed in Chapter 5).

4.2.2 Treading softly with 'over-optimists'

In this section we have looked at the 'pessimists' first, because when it comes to language learning, they seem to be the majority. Learners who are on the optimistic extreme of the plausibility continuum will need to be exposed to a different kind of reality check: rather than affirming their past and current strengths, teachers may need to gently shake them out of their comfort zone and provide an honest and down-to-earth reality check on their progress. However, the issue with wishful thinkers is not unambiguous. This was illustrated in a heated debate in one of Maggie's recent doctoral seminars comprising experienced educators. On the one hand, there was a strong opinion that the teacher has the responsibility to steer students away from images of future selves that are unrealistic, as, for example, in the case of a pupil aspiring to study at Cambridge University and yet barely achieving C grades. Agreeing to this pupil's vision, the group reasoned, would have amounted to no less than harmful deception. Another camp, however, argued with conviction that a teacher does not have the right to deflate students' hopes by telling them that they are aiming too high and that there is something that they simply cannot achieve.

So, what is the constructive thing to do when faced with such a dilemma? Research framed within positive psychology has addressed this question; for example, drawing on hope theory research, Snyder (2002) argues against active misleading and maintains that honest feedback actually engenders people's hope for the future. This is because high hopers tend to adjust their goal expectations in view of the relevant boundary conditions (i.e. in our case, Cambridge University entry requirements), and even if their hopes are momentarily dashed, the feedback enables them to refocus their energy and come up with an alternative strategy for achieving their goal. For this reason, our response to the dilemma would be to offer sensitive, respectful but honest feedback to people engaging in what has been termed in research as *unrealistic positivity*, that is, taking credit for successes but turning a blind eye to limitations and failures. In this way the student can create more plausible self-images by either revising the vision itself or reviewing the action pathways leading to its attainment.

Having said that, assessing the plausibility of our students' future visions and dreams is not at all straightforward because, apart from extreme cases (like C grades for Cambridge University acceptance), we usually cannot be 100% certain that our views are right. Our conceptions of what is realistic and what is not are a function not only of our knowledge and experiences but also of our subjectivity, our prejudices or even our lack of imagination. Therefore, given that our views can have serious consequences for the possible selves that our students construct for themselves and the career choices they make, caution is needed as we may easily cause damage. Yeats has expressed this concern beautifully when he wrote, 'I have spread my dreams under your feet; / Tread softly because you tread on my dreams.' Indeed, in order not to tread on our students' dreams we need to 'tread softly' and strive for a careful balance between restricting the students' vision and cultivating realistic beliefs and expectations through constructive feedback.

4.3 Eliminating obstacles and barriers

Some of the obstacles that stand in the way of realising a possible self are not internal to the students but exist as real external barriers. We can think of two main types of such barriers. First, there might be specific situational or social constraints that make a possible self unrealistic in a given situation: for example, there might be insufficient funding to do a required course, or gender restrictions may exist in a certain culture regarding some career paths. The second major obstacle type is related to the negative attitudes coming from the students' reference groups: some influential peers or significant authority figures around the students may object to, and sometimes even actively try to prevent, their plans, for example when parents have strong views on what career their child should pursue or when the students' friends harbour detrimental norms. In such cases students may feel that their desired plans do not stand a chance, which is referred to in psychology as a lack of *perceived control* over the attainment of possible selves. It is explained by Norman and Aron (2003: 501) as follows:

> In the context of possible selves, perceived control is the degree to which individuals believe their behaviours can influence the attainment or avoidance of a possible self. If individuals believe they have control over attaining or avoiding a possible self, they will be more inclined to take the necessary steps to do so.

In order to pre-empt the subversive role of real or imagined barriers, a visionary training programme must address the question of any potential obstacles head-on, as was done in both Oyserman *et al.*'s (2006) School-to-Jobs programme and Hock *et al.*'s (2006) Possible Selves programme (see TOOLBOX 2.2). In the former, students drew a timeline to depict their future and were asked to include any 'roadblocks' they thought they might encounter (e.g. obstacles placed by others or detrimental situations such as a lack of financial resources, racial and/or sexual discrimination) as well as strategies to overcome these obstacles. Then, towards the end of the nine-week programme, two sessions were specifically dedicated to 'solving everyday problems', aiming at providing participants with concrete experience in breaking down everyday school problems into more manageable tasks. By this time students were confident enough in one another to work together in small groups, and through discussing possible obstacles they developed strategies (which they recorded in writing) of how to cope with them. In the follow-up session, they worked together again developing a list of specific requirements for high school graduation and prerequisites/skills needed for entry into college or other training, linking these back to the outcomes of the earlier timeline session in order to make the process by which they can attain their vision more realistic.

In Hock *et al.*'s programme, students drew a 'Possible Selves Tree', also representing dangerous conditions for the tree, such as termites, poison in the soil and lightning, which stood for obstacles of various kinds. These were then discussed with their tutors in personal interviews. Thus, the lesson from these programmes is that bringing such worries to the open is a first step towards finding some solution to overcome the barriers or towards deciding on some modification in the desired possible self to make it more realistic. In such situations it might be particularly useful to present role models who have managed to succeed in the face of difficulties. Both programmes have emphasised the metamessage that some difficulties are inevitable but they are *not* insurmountable or self-defining. As George Bernard Shaw once said, 'People are always blaming circumstances for what they are. I don't believe in circumstances. The people who get on in this world are the people who get up and look for the circumstances that they want ... and if they can't find them, they make them.'

The second type of barrier, active opposition coming from the learners' environment, is in effect an example of a clash between the ideal selves (i.e. internal desires) and ought-to selves (external expectations). For future self-guides to be effective, a person's different possible selves need to be in harmony with each other, which is not easy when peer-group norms or other normative pressures (e.g. ethnic community expectations) actively block the desired visionary pathway. We do not pretend that we have a blanket answer to this age-old issue, but it is worth considering the fact that one reason why negative group images counter potential visions is their disproportionately high visibility and accessibility (cf. Oyserman *et al.* 2006): they are 'contextually cued', that is, modelled directly by the learner's immediate social context, which makes them unduly salient. Therefore, simply helping students to step back from the immediacy of these influences and take a more comprehensive and detached view of the situation might put detrimental peer-group norms into perspective, thereby empowering students to maintain their own integrity. Demonstrating with examples that many celebrities succeeded exactly because at one point they had the courage to ignore the opposition coming from their environment and stick to their dreams will be tremendously encouraging to many students.

5 Transforming the vision into action

> Vision without action is daydream. Action without vision is nightmare.
>
> *Japanese proverb*

In Section 4.1 we described Steve's 'foolish' dream: he spent an extended period in the UK hoping that he would learn English but, in fact, he never did (see ILLUSTRATION 4.1). We argued there that his vision was not rooted in realistic beliefs about language learning, which was true. However, there may be more to the story of Steve (and of others in similar situations). He had never studied a foreign language in his life and assumed that living in the country in which the language is spoken would somehow 'cause' his learning to happen automatically. Although he did initially entertain a future L2 vision (an image of himself as someone who can understand English movies), he was not able to grasp its practical implications and, as a result, did very little to actually make this vision come true – in fact, he never even watched an L2 movie again because, as he stated, 'I wouldn't understand a word, so what's the point?'

So, it seems that although Steve's actual vision itself was not unattainable, it would have needed Steve's active contribution to make it realistic. Yet, because he did not know how to go about mastering the L2, at a certain point his initial hope turned into defeatism: he came to assume that the vision was beyond his reach and eventually dismissed it as a foolish dream. Thus, Steve's story illustrates well the Japanese proverb cited as the motto of this chapter: 'vision without action is daydream'. Even when we have a clear idea about a desired end state, the vision is likely to remain ineffective if our notions about the ways to achieve it are fuzzy – future self-guides are productive only if they are accompanied by a set of concrete *action plans*, that is, a blueprint that maps out action pathways that will lead to them. The energy released by the vision needs to be channelled into constructive behaviour to make real progress, and this requires available action opportunities. Therefore, the ideal L2 self needs to come as part of a 'package' consisting of an imagery component *and* a repertoire of appropriate plans, scripts and self-regulatory strategies. Even the most galvanising self-image might fall flat without appropriate ways of operationalising or 'growing' the vision, which was the fifth key component in Hock *et al.*'s (2006) Possible Selves programme:

> The fifth component, GROWING, helps the student answer the question 'How do I get there?' It is utilised to get the student to start thinking about specific ways to nurture and 'grow' his or her tree and attain identified goals ... In short, during the Growing activities, a well-developed Action Plan is constructed by the student. The Action Plan will list a specific hope, a short-term goal underpinning the hope, the specific tasks that must be completed to reach the goal, and a timeline for completing all of the tasks. The action plan provides 'pathways' to support the attainment of long-term goals and hopes for the future. (p. 213)

How can a vision be operationalised? Hadfield and Dörnyei (2013) argue that the best way of doing so is through first identifying separate *ambitions* subsumed by the vision and then using this list as the basis for a set of *long-term goals*. These, then, need to be further broken down into specific *short-term goals* which are actionable. This narrowing process should eventually result in specifying concrete *language tasks* and accompanying task-execution *strategies*. Thus, the journey from vision to reality involves a process of brainstorming and analysing overall ambitions, aspects of the vision and possible options as well as identifying, evaluating, discussing and selecting goals, strategies and tasks specifically related to the mastery of the L2.

Hadfield and Dörnyei also emphasise that an important part of transforming the vision into action entails making the finalised study intentions public and charting progress towards the long-term goal systematically. The former concerns making some sort of a learning contract in which the intentions are written down and witnessed, while monitoring the process involves keeping a public or private record of any advancement, which in turn validates effort. The charting of progress can be done in a visual form, such as some kind of a 'contract wall' or 'contract tree', but it can also utilise the Internet through a 'progress blog', that is, through setting up and maintaining an online discussion board for the class that includes weekly entries.

It is clear that operationalising the vision is an area where L2 motivation research and language teaching methodology overlap: an effective action plan will contain a goal-setting dimension, which is a motivational issue, as well as individualised study plans and concrete instructional avenues, which are methodological in nature. In fact, providing a roadmap and a variety of tools for operationalising language learning goals is a basic requirement for any good teaching – which is exactly the reason why good teaching is inherently motivating. We will not be able to summarise the main features of effective language instruction in this chapter – there are excellent books offering such

Transforming the vision into action

summaries (e.g. Celce-Murcia, Brinton and Snow 2013; Hadfield and Hadfield 2008; Lightbown and Spada 2013) – and the idiosyncratic circumstances of different learning environments would not allow us, in any case, to offer very specific advice here on how to operationalise the students' language learning vision. Instead, in the following we discuss three generic approaches to transforming vision into action and executing desired future selves: (1) *providing students with self-relevant roadmaps*, (2) *mapping out pathways to success through visualisation* and (3) *providing individual guidance*.

5.1 Providing students with models of self-relevant roadmaps

In order to construct their own action plans, language learners, especially inexperienced ones or those who have never learnt an L2 before, will need relevant roadmaps to achieving their desired language selves. In the same way that students may come to the classroom with unrealistic beliefs and expectations about language learning and have therefore unsubstantiated L2 selves (see Section 4.1), they may equally lack models of appropriate learning techniques and strategies that one needs to adopt in order to attain an L2 vision. To paraphrase Tessa Souter in ILLUSTRATION 5.1, many learners may not know how to take their vision one step in the right direction, an essential condition for operationalising a future self.

> Illustration 5.1 Taking it one step in the right direction (from Souter 2006: 19)
>
> It was a really lucky break ... [but] if Michael hadn't been taking photographs in the first place; if he hadn't made it his business to learn all the technical stuff; if he hadn't decided (at forty, mind you) to do something completely new; in other words if he hadn't started, no amount of luck in the world would have got him that job. The point is, your beginnings don't need to be huge. They just need to be one step in the direction of where you want to end up.

A study by Oyserman, Johnson and James (2011), whose title says it all – 'Seeing the Destination but Not the Path' – has generated powerful evidence that the 'step-in-the-right-direction' principle applies to learners in general. The researchers found that, contrary to popular belief, it was not merely the lack of aspiration that contributed to

Motivating Learners, Motivating Teachers

low school attainment of pupils from disadvantaged socioeconomic backgrounds; many of the students who participated in their study did possess school-related aspirations and images of their successful future selves. What they lacked, however, was an understanding of the strategies for achieving them. In other words, the pupils saw the destination, but not the path, and according to Oyserman *et al.*, this was the major factor contributing to their low school attainment: 'What children need is help seeing the path. Interventions that link a child's possible selves with specific strategies hold promise of doing just that' (p. 489).

It appears, therefore, that exposing language learners to realistic models of roadmaps to their L2 selves is a critical step in enabling them to construct and execute their L2 visions. In TOOLBOX 5.1 we offer some ideas on how to provide students with relevant roadmaps.

> **Toolbox 5.1 Providing students with models of appropriate roadmaps to attaining their L2 selves**
>
> - As part of a classroom project (group or individual), ask students to interview a few successful learners/speakers of L2. They should focus on the steps these individuals took to achieve their proficiency and on any piece of advice they would want to give to beginning learners of L2. As a follow-up to the interviews, students should construct their own realistic action plans, incorporating the steps that are relevant to their own circumstances (see also the specific techniques described in the next section).
> - As part of a classroom project, ask students to identify and study 'success recipes' of high-achieving individuals in areas other than language learning. Ask them to identify the steps that they think also apply to language learning and then to devise their L2 vision roadmaps modelled on the identified success recipes.
> - Ask students to perform a dialogue – in their imagination or orally or in writing; on their own or in pairs – in which they are talking to their future L2 self. They should ask their future self how they have achieved what they have achieved. Follow up with the construction of individualised pathways.
> - Tell stories/anecdotes about how you (the teacher) started, what worked for you and what didn't, and how you dealt with any obstacles.

ILLUSTRATION 5.2 presents some tips taken from Tessa Souter's (2006) book, which carries a suitably encouraging title: *Anything I Can Do, You Can Do Better: How to Unlock Your Creative Dreams and Change Your Lives.*

Transforming the vision into action

Illustration 5.2 Tessa Souter's roadmap to success (adapted from Souter 2006: 19–21)

1. Dare to dream and believe in your dream.
2. Having identified your dream, identify how to make a start. DO it every day, even if it's just for an hour. To quote the Nike ad – just *do* it.
3. Study. Study. Study. Know your subject.
4. Surround yourself as much as possible with people who are doing what you are doing.
5. Take it 'bird by bird'. If you need to do a specific task that you've been putting off, make it as small as possible by not imagining the big picture.
6. Don't give up before you even begin. Treat failures and setbacks as lessons, and soldier on.

5.2 Mapping out pathways to success through visualisation

As we have seen throughout this book, mental imagery is a basic self-regulatory process that humans can engage in order to make sense of or reconstruct the past, to monitor the present and to rehearse future events. Taylor and Pham (1996) explain that in terms of the target of the visualisation, there are two different approaches to mental imagery. The first can be called *outcome simulation*, as it involves envisioning the desired future end state. When we talked about mental imagery in the previous chapters, this type of visualisation has usually been our primary concern. The second approach to imagery is to focus on the *process* rather than the outcome, that is, on the sequence of events that lead up to the future goal. Thus, the emphasis here is not on visualising the 'what/who' of the future vision but rather on the 'how' element, the actions that are necessary to achieve one's desired L2 self. Taylor and Pham provide convincing empirical support for the value of such *process-oriented imagery*; they explain its conducive impact by the fact that while envisioning a positive outcome in one's future can instil a sense of general motivation in the individual, in order to translate this 'hype' into actual hard work, one also needs a plan of action laid down and diligently pursued.

The difference between focusing on the goal and focusing on the journey to the goal has been acknowledged in motivational psychology through the distinction made between *goal intentions* and *implementation intentions*. The former involves the decision to try to achieve a goal (e.g. a New Year's resolution), while the latter refers to concrete plans that help to bridge the gap between the desired goal and human action towards the goal along the lines of 'Whenever situation X arises, I will initiate the goal-directed response Y!' (Gollwitzer 1999: 493). Thus, implementation intentions refer to action plans that will get us going; for example, a student might decide that if there is homework to do, no matter how he/she feels about it he/she will always at least sit down at his/her desk, open his/her exercise book or task sheet and read the instructions (and often such an initial routine is enough to set things in motion). This approach, then, can be combined with mental imagery to good effect by getting students to visualise their actions in such critical points of task engagement (for a concrete example, see ILLUSTRATION 5.3). As Knäuper *et al.* (2009) argue, strategically adding mental imagery to implementation intentions can compound the latter's effectiveness, because the sensory information enriches the mental representations of the action plan and thereby strengthens the situational cue–response link.

Illustration 5.3 On visualising short-term and long-term goals

In a visualisation intervention study with British learners of German, Jones (2012) addressed the research question, 'Does visualising the Ideal L2 Self increase motivation more or less than visualising the steps needed to reach the long-term goal?' Based on a series of interviews with one of her participants, Greg, she found, 'Greg used his own spontaneous short-term visualisations to motivate him to complete homework tasks or speak German in Turkey ... which can be taken as evidence that learners need a long-term vision, but must also visualise the "path" to keep them on track to reach their ultimate Ideal L2 Self' (pp. 48–9). Therefore, she concluded, 'There is clear evidence in this study of the undeniable usefulness of creating action plans as part of an intervention programme. Many people have a goal or vision, but lack the understanding of the process needed to reach it, and setting out clear action plans certainly helped the learners in the current study to focus their attention on the steps they could take to reduce the gap between their current and ideal selves. I believe that the action plans were made all the more effective by the addition of visualisations, as being able to "experience" how it feels to achieve the goals made them seem more tangible and plausible to the participants, thus increasing their belief in their ability to achieve them' (p. 49).

Thus, using mental imagery when forming implementation intentions results in higher rates of goal achievement. In Sections 2.3 and 3.1 we discussed various methods of guided imagery, and the visualisation of action plans can be seen as a special subset of this procedure whereby we direct the students' attention to the journey rather than merely to the destination. TOOLBOX 5.2 presents some illustrations of how to map out visually pathways to success.

Transforming the vision into action

> **Toolbox 5.2 Techniques for visually mapping out pathways to L2 success**
>
> **'Strategy boards' adapted from Oyserman *et al.*'s (2002) School-to-Jobs programme**
>
> In order to practise articulating specific strategies to approach their vision and to concretise the connection between current behaviour and future outcomes, students are asked to use a poster board and coloured stickers to map out their next-year and adult possible selves: they are to post stickers describing their short-term (next year) and long-term (adult) desired identities in the middle and right third of the poster board, and stickers denoting the strategies they are currently employing or thinking of introducing in the left third. Then they are asked to link the strategies with lines to the future identities that they are expected to lead to.
>
> This activity can easily be turned into a 'strategy sharing session': participants using particular strategies have a chance to explain what they are currently doing and how it helps them, and even guide those participants not currently using these strategies through obstacles that prevent their use.
>
> **Other forms of visual representations of pathways to success**
>
> Students can be asked (individually or in pairs/groups) to produce a *visual landscape* (drawing, painting, collage) of their L2 vision that includes various pathways that may lead to them, or they could produce other forms of visual representations such as mapping out their pathways to L2 success in diagrams, mindmaps, timelines or decision trees for the same purpose. Alternatively, they could be invited to create a collaborative graphic adventure story about approaching their L2 visions, and all these tasks could be concluded by a class discussion in which their peers evaluate the reality of the proposed pathways.

5.3 Providing students with individual guidance

Hock *et al.*'s (2006) Possible Selves programme (described in TOOLBOX 2.2 at the beginning of Chapter 2) contained dedicated sessions for the participants to round up the process of generating an action plan by discussing with their tutors on an individual basis their envisaged pathways (in their specific case, how to maintain their Possible Selves Tree, how to provide it with nourishment and how to protect it from harm). We can see the significance of offering students such one-to-one time given the massive potential impact these action plans might have on their personal development. Making these tutorials salient also gives purpose and closure to the students' previous preparations and a successful advisory session can be seen as 'sealing' the prepared roadmap. After the discussion session, students can finalise the plan of action and prepare a decorative summary of some sort (e.g. a pledge, a contract, a drawing or a Magna Carta-style resolution on a scroll, etc.).

Oyserman *et al.*'s (2002) School-to-Jobs programme (mentioned above) even included a concluding session when parents (or other important adults) were invited to learn about the programme and, specifically, about their children's emerging plans. In school settings where parents meetings are regularly scheduled, one of these sessions can relatively easily be turned into a 'Career Meeting'; this would not only allow for bringing parents on board but could also offer an opportunity for parents to share the experiences of their own career journeys, thereby enabling the youth to explore the similarities and differences between those and their own current circumstances.

6 Keeping the vision alive

> You've got to think about big things while you're doing small things, so that all the small things go in the right direction.
> *Alvin Toffler*

Everybody has several distinct possible selves stored in their memory, related to different aspects of that person's life. For example, we may accommodate diverse ideal self-images concerning various career options, social ambitions or family dreams. These self-guides cannot all be contained in our 'working self-concept' at the same time: while some are active, other possible selves inevitably remain dormant. For this reason, in order to keep our vision alive, we need to activate it regularly so that it does not get squeezed out by other life concerns or does not fade into oblivion amidst the day-to-day business of doing grammar exercises and writing essays in the language classroom. Accordingly, the various methods described in this chapter are all aimed, in one way or another, at keeping the vision online in the working memory.

Very little is said in the literature about activating and re-activating desired future selves, but this is an area where language teachers have, perhaps unknowingly, a great deal of experience. Classroom activities such as warmers and ice-breakers as well as various communicative tasks – especially ones that concern L2 films, music, food, traditions, other cultural aspects, etc. – can all be used as potent 'vision-reminders' because they offer cues that enable students to make links between what they do in the classroom and what they will be required to do to fulfil their future L2 visions. Indeed, good teachers often have an instinctive talent for providing an engaging framework that keeps the enthusiasts going and the less-than-enthusiasts thinking. In the following we briefly highlight a number of routes that lend themselves to achieving this goal.

6.1 Including regular reminders and 'priming stimuli' in the teaching content

Zoltán used to use a short warm-up activity in his language classes in which he wrote the names of a number of famous British, American and Australian cities on the board (about ten in all), and students were

107

asked to read out these names in various ways, for example making them question–answer pairs (*Los Angeles? – Chicago!*) or reading them in a surprised, happy or sad manner. This kind of warm-up activity is quite common in acting studios, and Zoltán found it a good way to bring the class together and make them focus on the English language. He soon realised, however, that they also offered an extra benefit: not only did the reading out of the city names serve as a dynamic speaking exercise, but the mention of the various exotic locations also created an Anglophone spirit in the students. What happened in effect was that the names *primed* a positive affective state.

Priming is a well-known technique in psychological research; it refers to activating certain mental mechanisms indirectly, without the participants of an experiment being aware of what is being examined. For example, if the first task is to read a long list of words which includes *window*, and the second task requires the participants to complete a word stem that starts with *win...*, the probability of producing the word *window* rather than something like *winter* or *winner* is significantly higher than without having had the initial reading task, even if the participants cannot consciously recall that the first list contained *window*. This priming effect also works with semantic areas: it has been repeatedly shown in perception experiments, for example, that after hearing the word *black*, people are quicker to perceive the word *white* than without hearing *black* first. In *cross-modal priming*, two sensory modes are activated at the same time – for example, someone watching something and listening to something else through earphones – and even though the subject's attention is intentionally kept on one of the tasks (e.g. they have to concentrate on a text appearing on a computer screen because they need to answer comprehension questions), the stimulus they receive through the other sensory channel will still affect their responses.

In a similar manner, one way of offering vision-reminders is to include regular 'priming stimuli' in the teaching content that are related to the vision and that help to evoke it, causing a kind of déjà vu of the future. This can involve simply changing some of the details of communicative tasks – or what is even more effective: to ask the students themselves to change these details – in order to include vision-related elements (see TOOLBOX 6.1 for an example). Alternatively, more complex virtual or simulated scenarios can also be designed and enacted that make the language and the L2 culture come alive for the students. Establishing some vision-relevant rituals may also work well for this purpose; for example, each student has to discover one attractive thing about other cultures through internet research each week and students vote on what's the 'best of the best' of the week.

Keeping the vision alive

> 🔧 **Toolbox 6.1 Personalising communicative tasks**
>
> Contemporary coursebooks often include suggestions for communicative activities such as role-play situations. Students could engage in a challenging imagery task by taking one of the made-up coursebook scenarios and visualising what the scene would be like if it *really* happened to them. Remind them that very often it is the small personal details that bring a situation to life; so their task is to make the scenario *real* by recreating it in such a way that their classmates would recognise that it is about *them* even if their name was not mentioned.

A particularly powerful way of linking classroom learning to the visionary realm of language beyond the classroom is to extend the class beyond the classroom walls by organising relevant out-of-class projects and extracurricular activities. For example, for a class of students learning Japanese a once-a-term visit to the local sushi bar might be appropriate to keep their language appetite whetted, and the prospect of a study-abroad trip to Japan can offer vitalising power for several academic years. It is often said that we live in a 'global village', and therefore it is often the case that with a bit of resourcefulness teachers can find some form of an authentic L2 experience for their learners in many contexts.

6.2 Engaging learners' transportable identities

We saw in Chapter 3 that narratives, stories, fantasy worlds and virtual realities all have the power to draw people in – that is, to get people to be 'transported' out of their ordinary realities into an imaginary world. This 'transportation experience' (see Section 3.2) can cause people to be totally immersed in the reality of the stimulus they encounter and, therefore, being transported into the realm of one's vision is a potent way of increasing the motivational pulling power of the vision. Indeed, priming through vision-reminders (discussed in the previous section) can be seen as small-scale transportational initiatives.

However, the 'transporting' potential of such activities becomes alive in the language classroom only when we are connected to our central personal characteristics (sex, age, race, likes, dislikes, political inclinations) and lived experiences, rather than those which are solely determined by a specific situation (e.g. teacher/student). Zimmerman (1998) has termed these real-world identities 'transportable' (see ILLUSTRATION 6.1 for a fuller explanation of his three-level framework of identities in social interaction), because their features are not determined by the specific situation the person is in but instead '"tag along" with individuals as they move through their daily routines' (p. 90). These transportable identities therefore profoundly define us in the present and also, inevitably, in how we imagine ourselves in our future visions, and this has important implications for the language classroom: only when we are connected to our genuine transportable identities can we experience transportation to our future vision.

> **Illustration 6.1 Three levels of identity in social interaction (Zimmerman 1998)**
>
> In a paper analysing social interactions, Zimmerman makes a useful distinction between three levels of identity: (a) *discourse (or interactional) identity*, which relates to the person's communicative role (e.g. 'storyteller', 'questioner', 'lecturer'); (b) *situated (or institutional) identity*, which relates to the person's social position/role (e.g. 'teacher', 'student'); and (c) *'transportable' identity*, which refers to the person's core or master identity that subsumes such fundamental features as one's sex, age, race as key components as well as other central personal characteristics that the individual transports from one situation to the other (e.g. art enthusiasm, conservative worldview, high-tech geek).

If students are engaged in the kind of pseudo-communication that is so typical of language classrooms when they perform various roles – most often that of the 'student', but in some communicative activities also some other ones such as the 'waiter' or the 'tourist' – the strong discourse or situated identities that they adopt will block their transportation channel and they will not be able to envision themselves projected into the future as competent L2 users. Of course, we are not suggesting here that the various kinds of popular classroom interaction tasks, such as role plays or drama, do not have potential to activate students' desired future selves. Quite the opposite. This, however, is likely to happen only if such tasks offer students opportunities to invest their real experiences, opinions and imagination. Put differently, students need to be 'themselves' to be able to link their current activity to their personal future visions. As Ushioda (2011: 20) explains, only when we allow learners to speak and behave as themselves, that is when they can engage their 'transportable identities' during language practice, do we stand a chance of keeping the students' desired language selves alive:

> Thus, to the extent that language learners engage (or are enabled to engage) their current selves in their L2 interactions in the classroom now and to 'speak as themselves' with their 'transportable identities',

Keeping the vision alive

one can argue that they are also enabled to engage directly with their future possible selves as users of the target language, but within the scope and security of their current communicative abilities.

Illustration 6.2 On 'learning modes'

In a classroom study investigating the relationship between the students' motivation and their participation in a communicative language task, Dörnyei and Kormos (2000) found that when learners were asked to perform the same task in both their L1 and their L2, they behaved very differently. In the L2 version it was – predictably – the 'motivated' learners who excelled, whereas when the task was performed in the students' mother tongue these learners lost their edge and, in fact, their less-motivated peers overtook them provided they were paired up with someone they were friendly with. Surprisingly, it was found that this friendship aspect did not play any role in determining performance in the L2 task.

This curious situation can be explained by the fact that in the L2 task, students adopted a proper 'learning mode': they suspended their normal identities and relational preferences and performed 'student roles', with the good students naturally doing better than their less-motivated peers. In contrast, when the task was an L1 communicative activity – that is, something that is not normally part of standard language practice – students suspended their 'learning mode' and engaged their normal, 'transportable' identities. This powerful effect illustrates well how 'being a student' can create an artificial reality for the participants that does not allow them to link their engagement to their natural selves.

What does this mean in practical terms? The main lesson is that while asking learners to do 'studenty' things in class in a rather meaningless way might result in effective language drilling or test preparation, without personalising the language tasks we cannot engage the students' identities to the extent that would allow them to link the language practice to their language visions. Language learning is, ideally, a lifelong activity and only by engaging the students' transportable identities can we allow them to keep their language vision alive in the long run. A powerful example of how the short-term 'efficiency' of L2 teaching can go at the expense of long-term engagement was documented by Norton's (2000) case study research of two Canadian immigrant language learners, Katarina and Felicia. These motivated learners were preparing for a life in a new country, and therefore the realm of their community (or rather, their 'imagined community') extended beyond the four walls of the classroom: they were operating at the interface of

111

Motivating Learners, Motivating Teachers

reality and imagination. However, because the teacher failed to give room to practices of imagination but only focused on the pragmatic aspects of the curriculum and the classroom reality, which were miles away from the real identity concerns of Katarina and Felicia, both of them ultimately withdrew from their English language classes.

6.3 Helping to re-envisage 'broken' visions

Even the most treasured and desired possible self-images can become outdated, impossible or simply 'out of sync' as time goes on. Consider the autobiographical extract from Tra Mi Do's (2012) Master's level research project, in ILLUSTRATION 6.3, in which she investigated international students' encounters with the realities of their future visions upon their arrival in the UK. Beginning with her own example, she makes it clear that the vivid and elaborate L2 vision that she had so relentlessly pursued as an English language learner in Vietnam *did* fuel her motivational engine in very significant ways. Yet, it turned out that while the future image had the power to ignite Do's L2 self in her initial language learning setting, it could no longer work as a source of motivational energy when she entered the 'real' world which that vision was supposed to represent.

> **Illustration 6.3 I dreamed my life too far ... (adapted from Do 2012)**
>
> There was never to me anything comparable to a dream being eventually lived. Studying in England means more to me than just going places and benefiting from another learning style; it also means having an opportunity to practise the British English I have spent more than 10 years studying. I used to draw imaginary images of myself being surrounded by and living with English. I envisioned myself accidentally bumping into people on the street and hearing them say 'Sorry', or talking over tea with British people about their culture, or seeing friendly faces offering me help with my first days there, and making friends with my fellow British students.
>
> But I dreamed my life too far. I was surrounded by the language, because it was almost everywhere, only I had little chance to 'live' with it. I was disheartened to see there were only three British names among the 80-student class list, and was disappointed to say only 'Thank you' at the counter after receiving my goods. As if that was not enough, the first friendly British face I saw on my way home from school shouted a 'Ni hao!' to me.

This illustration shows that students may end up with 'wrong' visions either because the world as they imagined it simply does not exist, or

Keeping the vision alive

because, with time and more experience, they discover that the L2 visions that they had entertained were unproductive or were not really theirs. Therefore, an important part of keeping the vision alive is to nurture the students' ability and willingness to re-imagine their future selves if the original ones turn out to be 'broken'. This can be done, for example, as part of a 'vision review' exercise when students appraise – either with their tutor or in peer groups – not so much their progress towards the vision as the development or necessary modification of the vision itself. Stock-taking is usually a motivating task, and therefore we would expect that some sort of a 'vision-inspection' activity would be relatively easy to implement.

7 Counterbalancing the vision by considering failure

> Fear is nature's warning signal to get busy.
> Henry C. Link (1889–1952)

A classic principle in possible selves theory – first proposed by Oyserman and Markus (1990) – is that for maximum effectiveness as a motivational resource, a desired future self should be offset by a corresponding feared self. For example, using a fitness illustration, if our ideal self-image is a person many pounds lighter than our current self, this image will motivate us more to go on a diet and do exercises if we also have an accompanying feared self-image of ourselves becoming fat and flabby and not fitting into our clothes. That is, future self-guides are most potent if they utilise the cumulative impact of both approach and avoid tendencies – we do something because we want to do it but also because not doing it would lead to undesired results. This dichotomy is reminiscent of the age-old 'carrot and stick' contrast, referring to the effectiveness of both rewards and punishment as tools for motivating learners (with the desired self acting as carrot and the feared one as the stick).

Thus, 'counterbalancing the vision' means that the vision of the ideal self should be balanced against a consideration of what would happen if the desired self were not realised. The key issue here is balance: the vision should be matched by an equally elaborated corresponding negative self-image of what one might become if the expected aspiration does not come to fruition. What does 'equally elaborated' mean in this context? It refers to the need for the negative consequences of not achieving the vision to be cognitively available, articulated, conceptually grasped and immediately accessible to the individual.

> Illustration 7.1 Which is more motivating: the desired or the feared self? (adapted from Magid 2011: 223–5)
>
> *When interviewed about the impact of positive and negative scenarios used in an imagery study, three university students summed up their feelings as follows:*
>
> I think that both of them played an equally important role. I need both of them to create a balance! Imagining the positive situations makes me feel

Counterbalancing the vision by considering failure

> excited to study English. When I feel very satisfied with my English, I need some pressure from negative situations to motivate me to study English.
>
> The positive ones gave me confidence in my English and helped me set my goals for learning English. The negative ones reminded me that if I don't study English hard, I won't succeed.
>
> I need both situations because if I only listen to the positive ones, it will make me feel too confident to work hard. The negative situations make me feel that time is limited and that I should study English hard. That feeling that it's very urgent for me to achieve the goals in a limited time motivates me.

Thus, a fourth student's summary seemed to reflect well the general perception:

> When you feel diffident, the positive situations make you study English harder, but if you feel over-confident, the negative situations may pull you back from a dangerous area. They may both work well in different situations and according to your confidence level.

Oyserman and Markus (1990) emphasise that the balance between a goal to be achieved and a corresponding goal to be avoided is particularly important in situations when learners are faced with a number of alternative potential visions. The danger here is that they can wander from the pursuit of one desired self to another, without committing themselves sufficiently to any single goal to work towards. In other words, the pressure coming from the negative counterbalance is needed to nail down a particular positive vision and to initiate a course of action towards it. This is illustrated well in academia, where scholars usually have more writing commitments than they can achieve, and of those they often prioritise the deadlines that would be most embarrassing or problematic to miss.

In the following we describe three approaches to offset the vision with an adequate negative dimension: (1) *offering regular reminders of the negative consequences of not succeeding*, (2) *foregrounding the ought-to self* and (3) the complex issue of *integrating images of feared selves into visualisations*.

7.1 Offering regular reminders of the negative consequences of not succeeding

In an interesting study, Carver, Lawrence and Scheier (1999) found that the perceived negative consequences of a feared future self-image decrease with the person's distance from the feared state: among people who were farther from the feared state, the motivating impact of the feared self faded away, while in cases when the feared value was perceived as more imminent, the 'getting away' urge was stronger, thereby motivating action. This indicates that for the negative counterbalance to be effective, it needs to be made – and kept – salient through reminders of the consequences of failing to achieve one's language learning goals. This is exactly why language examinations are so powerful in soliciting effort: they represent immediate and high-profile pressure. Indeed, Magid (2011) cites several students attesting to the need for some pressure in their own learning; for example, a Chinese learner of English stated that he does not study English hard when 'there is no pressure from English examinations' (p. 191), and another Chinese participant was particularly explicit in her honest summary:

> I am a lazy person. When I am in an environment where there is no pressure, I just take it easy. The environment always influences me. I got used to the pressure from my parents. I think I need pressure to study English hard. (p. 191)

Thus, there is a case for priming the negative consequences of not succeeding in one's language studies, not unlike the need to offer vision-reminders in the teaching content – as discussed in Section 6.1 – to help to evoke hoped-for positive images and thereby cause a kind of déjà vu of the future. However, some caution is in order here because not everybody responds well to negativity and people differ greatly in the extent to which they thrive under pressure. We will address this question in Section 7.3 below.

7.2 Foregrounding the ought-to self

We defined the ought-to self in Chapter 1 (Section 1.2) as a future self-guide generated by a sense of duty, responsibility or obligation – this is the self that one feels compelled to become rather than naturally desires to become. While the ought-to self is a positive force in the sense that it acts as a future self-guide that learners want to conform to, Higgins *et al.* (1994) explain that ultimately it is driven by an avoidance tendency: the wish not to disappoint people and to avoid disapproval or even actual punishment. That is, this dimension of one's vision is strongly linked to the avoidance of an undesired value and, accordingly, one way of counterbalancing the vision is to foreground the ought-to L2 self. This will prime the duties and obligations the learners have committed themselves to along with the undesired end

Counterbalancing the vision by considering failure

state that would follow if these commitments were to be broken. In practical terms, learners can be asked, from time to time, to summarise the various 'should' aspects of their language studies: they could produce narrative descriptions or even role-play sketches to act out situations in which duties/obligations are set and enforced (e.g. by the learners' parents).

> **Illustration 7.2 The importance of family and 'face' in China (Magid 2011: 183–4)**
>
> Extracts from interviews with two university students:
>
> When I was a middle school student, my only concern was not to disappoint my parents by failing my English exams. When I entered university, my parents also expected me to study English hard to get a high position in the future, which I did mainly because I didn't want to lose face by disappointing them.
>
> Face is the feeling of others toward you. In China, people value face and consider it to be extremely important. Once you lose face, you will feel very disappointed and if you are very successful, people will consider your face as being golden. I think I should try not to lose face and do my job well so that people will have a good image of me.

It is relatively straightforward to define prominent ought-to components of student motivation with regard to the study of high-prestige languages (e.g. Global English) and in cultures where social pressures such as family expectations are strong or where losing face is a primary concern (see ILLUSTRATION 7.2). For example, English can be seen throughout the whole world as the doorway to the 'global village', with concrete implications for travelling and career options, and in Asian cultures bringing honour to the family name is a more salient motive than in many western societies. However, in some other learning environments it is rather difficult to identify powerful external incentives for L2 learning, with a prime example being the English-speaking countries such as the UK, where the world language coincides with the population's mother tongue and therefore there is no real societal interest in L2 studies. How can we find an ought-to dimension of the learners' vision in such contexts? Illustration 7.3 describes a teacher-researcher's specific difficulty in this respect when investigating two students of German in Britain. Because they were studying the L2 out of a genuine intrinsic interest, a discussion of the negative consequences of failing to learn German would have had little impact on their motivation.

> ✎ **Illustration 7.3 When there is no obvious ought-to L2 self**
>
> Katherine Jones (2012) has conducted a longitudinal study to examine how the main principles of a visionary motivational approach worked with two learners of German in the UK. While she was by and large successful in validating the key components of the motivational framework described in this book, she ran into trouble when she tried to find ways of counterbalancing the learners' vision by foregrounding their ought-to language selves:
>
>> Although I tried to push the participants in the interviews to define their Ought-to L2 Self, they proved conspicuous by their absence. Both participants were adamant that they were learning German because they wanted to, that they felt no external pressure to become fluent and neither had a feared self in that they could not envisage negative consequences of failing to become fluent. This evidently made the counterbalancing part of the intervention difficult to design. (pp. 49–50)

One way of getting around the problem of the absence of a salient ought-to L2 self might involve focusing on the learners' own expectations as the normative standards to meet (e.g. being the sort of person who persists at and ultimately succeeds in a task) or, alternatively, to link the ought-to L2 self to more general social motives such as wanting to be seen as intelligent and educated (Jones 2012).

7.3 Integrating images of feared selves into visualisations?

In Markus and Nurius's (1986) original conceptualisation, the feared self is seen as a proper possible self with an imagery dimension: one can visualise the dreaded possibility. But is this something that we would want to encourage? We saw earlier that Oyserman and Markus (1990) believed that it was, as long as the negative image was properly balanced by a positive one, and Markus and Ruvolo (1989: 219) explicitly state that a representation of a feared self motivates the person to act to ensure that the feared images never materialise:

> In general, the more elaborated the possible self in terms of semantic, imaginal, or enactive representations, the more motivationally effective it can be expected to be … The sense of one's self in a feared or undesired state (e.g. 'me as incompetent' or 'me as failing') also can be motivationally significant. It can provide vivid images or conceptions of an end state that must be rejected or avoided.

Counterbalancing the vision by considering failure

This issue, however, is far from straightforward, because generating realistic images of dreaded states is a rather intensive and potentially unsafe process. In the discussion of his motivational intervention programme, Magid (2011) analyses three learner accounts about this issue, and even though on balance all three learners supported the usefulness of negative visualisation scenarios in an imagery training programme, the intensity of this practice comes across through the language they use ('I was really scared', 'they made me feel so afraid', 'I would pay any price to avoid', 'they gave me a huge pressure'). Indeed, the main affective power behind negative visualisation is emotions like guilt, shame, anxiety, fear and remorse. Do we really want to generate such fearful stimuli? A case in point is described in ILLUSTRATION 7.4, which presents an interview extract from a British learner of German (one of Jones's subjects, whom we met in the previous section) and which highlights the main role of visualisation as keeping any negative thoughts at bay.

> **Illustration 7.4 Positive visualisation and confidence (from Jones 2012: 68)**
>
> A British learner of German:
>
> > I think it [visualisation] definitely helps because it's not letting negative thoughts into your mind, because you're only visualising a really positive outcome and you're not letting the negative stuff infiltrate, whereas I think if I hadn't done visualisation, I think I would have been like 'ohhh I don't know if I can do this'. I think it's the confidence thing. I think I always had the motivation to do it, but it's the confidence, definitely.

In sports research, experts have been equally divided. *Imagery direction* (as they refer to this question) has been a much researched issue, and it was traditionally assumed that only positive imagery led to positive outcomes, while negative imagery impaired performance. However, in the same way that anxiety can be both facilitating and debilitating in learning depending on the particular context, more nuanced studies have revealed that some athletes can utilise imagining errors to good effect (e.g. MacIntyre and Moran 2007): they sometimes deliberately imagine errors in order to prepare for 'worst-case' scenarios in competition by using sophisticated meta-imagery control skills to restructure the negative imagery (e.g. by correcting the imagined error) or to practice reacting to these difficult situations optimally when they occur (see ILLUSTRATION 7.5 for an example taken from professional skiing). Furthermore, negative imagery might also be suitable for 'immunising' individuals, that is, helping them to cope with difficult tasks such as holding one's nerve in stressful conditions. We argued in Section 3.1 that this practice is consistent with desensitisation procedures in clinical psychology, whereby patients are helped to overcome phobias through a series of systematic imagery approximations to the fearful stimuli. In sum, negative imagery can potentially play an adaptive role for some individuals if they can minimise any detrimental effects that such imagery may have on their performance.

> **Illustration 7.5 Imagery in professional skiing: 'If I make a mistake ...'** (from Hale 2005: 4)
>
> Former World Cup Downhill ski champion Steve Podborski describes the use of imagery by elite skiers:
>
> > Another thing that gets you to the point where you are one of the elite is the ability to visualise not only the way it looks when you are going down, but how it feels ... the muscle tension that you actually go through when you make the turns, and to experience what attitude your body is in ... I feel what things will feel like and see everything run through my head. I have a moving picture with feelings and sensations. When I'm doing these mental runs ... if I make a mistake, I'll stop the picture and back it up. Then I run through it and usually get it right the second time. I run through the entire course like that.

Because of the potential dangers of encouraging mental visualisations of feared selves – even if it is fully within the spirit of being 'cruel to be kind' – it might be sensible to err on the side of caution. This is why in their teachers' resource book Hadfield and Dörnyei (2013: 48) make the following recommendation concerning undesired self-images such as possible failures:

> It seems that this subject is best dealt with cognitively rather than affectively, through discussion and analysis rather than visualisation or other affective and imaginative activities. 'Failure' is an emotive subject and powerful affective activities such as visualisation may have a negative effect on self-esteem and may thus 'counterbalance' the ideal self a little too far!

The authors then explain that contemporary methodology, in general, tends to focus on the positive – that is, on the carrot rather than on the stick – and, therefore, both teachers and students may feel hesitant about confronting the subject of failure in the classroom altogether. For such cases their recommendation is included in TOOLBOX 7.1.

Counterbalancing the vision by considering failure

> **Toolbox 7.1 Practical recommendation to teachers on how to deal with possible student failure (adapted from Hadfield and Dörnyei 2013: 48–9)**

If you feel very hesitant about embarking on the subject of possible failure, it may be best to avoid it altogether. However, it may be worth trying to approach the subject in a calm and unemotional manner at the beginning of the course, when perhaps some strategies could be put in place for avoiding failure rather than possibly resorting to crisis management at a later stage of the course. Reminding students of the work they need to do in order not to fail a course can have a counter-productive effect. No one likes to be nagged! For this reason, the reminder should be kept light and brief and move towards positive strategies for avoiding failure.

With these caveats in mind, it seems that a framework for counterbalancing the vision would involve:

- a brief consideration of the possibility of failure,
- a diagnosis of what could lead to failure,
- an analysis of how it could be put right (or what strategies would be helpful),
- an expression of confidence in the students' ability to persevere and triumph in the end.

Part III
Motivation and vision for language teachers

> Who shall kindle others must himself glow.
> *Italian proverb*

We have seen in Part II that viewing motivation to learn a second language through the lens of desired language selves has allowed us to generate a variety of promising motivational techniques for the language classroom. However, as we have stated in Chapter 1, transforming classrooms into engaging environments for language learning demands more than a repertoire of innovative principles and techniques – it requires teachers who will be motivated to put the knowledge into practice. To do it well necessitates a vision of what we would like to achieve and – similar to making the vision of our students effective – specific action plans that map out the pathway towards the vision. That is, in order to be able to have something worthwhile to give to our students, we need to look after ourselves and nurture our own motivational basis. This is expressed eloquently by Ronald Barth (1990: 42) who compares typical teachers to airline passengers in an emergency who try to give oxygen masks to the children without taking oxygen themselves: 'In schools we spend a great deal of time placing oxygen masks on other people's faces while we ourselves are suffocating.'

In the next two chapters, we follow the approach taken in Part II regarding students in that we will not cover every aspect of motivation comprehensively but focus on what we see as its highest-level dimension: vision. Teacher motivation is a complex and multi-faceted construct, and relevant theories need to address at least four key aspects of it (for an overview, see Dörnyei and Ushioda 2011): (1) a prominent intrinsic component (as few people go into teaching for extrinsic rewards such as high social recognition or salary); (2) a strong interrelationship with contextual factors associated with the affordances and constraints of the workplace; (3) a featured temporal dimension highlighting its role as career motivation (involving issues such as career structures and promotion possibilities); and (4) a particularly fragile nature of teacher motivation, resulting from its exposure to several powerful negative influences (some being inherent in the profession). While we will be touching upon all four of these dimensions, our chief concern in this book is transforming language classrooms, and therefore Part III concentrates on what is at the heart of the transformational capacity of teachers: their teaching vision, conceived of as the sensory experience of their desired future teaching selves. We strongly believe – because we ourselves have experienced it – that seeing, hearing and feeling the energy of motivating language classrooms through our visionary eyes and imagining ourselves as teachers operating in new ways can have transformational consequences for our everyday classroom practice.

In Chapter 1 we discussed the broad principles for creating the right conditions for language teacher conceptual change (Section 1.5); TOOLBOX 8.1 below summarises the two key points in this respect and, accordingly, Part III of this book is organised into two chapters. First, we examine several strategies for (re-)igniting the flame of language teachers' vision, including the prerequisite for such a transformation: the need to notice some dissonance between the desired and actual selves. Then, Chapter 9 concerns ways of guarding the vision against the many threats that can (and typically do) emerge in teaching environments in the real world.

Toolbox 8.1 A framework for motivating teachers through vision

Motivational conditions for desired future teacher selves	Key facets of motivating teachers through vision
The teacher has a well-developed and vivid desired future self-image (vision) based on his/her passions, purposes and philosophies and is aware of a discrepancy between the vision and reality, thereby experiencing 'creative tension' which motivates development.	*(Re-)igniting the flame of teacher vision*
The teacher protects his/her vision and shields it against adversity by building resilience and sustaining hope.	*Guarding the flame of vision*

8 (Re-)igniting the flame of teacher vision

> Good teaching comes from identity, not technique, but if I allow my identity to guide me toward an integral technique, that technique can help me express my identity more fully.
> *Palmer (2007: 66)*

The primary condition for the motivational capacity of possible selves is (obviously) that they have to exist, and the same is true for teacher vision. Igniting, or if necessary re-igniting, the flame of teacher vision is therefore the single most important step in any motivational agenda for language teachers. Developing a teaching vision is not dissimilar to the processes we have described in Part II of this book regarding student vision. In order to 'see' with clarity and conviction the future person one wants to become, language teachers, like learners, need to probe into their past and present experiences as potential sources of their vision and examine a range of images of good teaching which come from theories, teachers' own intuitions or real-life role models. The purpose of this exercise, however, is not to identify some kind of idealised fantasy image of a language classroom that may never exist, but, rather, to develop a personally meaningful *possible* vision that is integral to who the teacher is and that is sensitive to the context in which his/her work is located. We will argue in this chapter that in order to create such ideal language teacher selves, teachers need to engage with at least three processes:

- a deeper understanding of the person they have become through their gifts, passions and past experiences (*who*);
- a reflection on the bigger purposes guiding their work as language teachers (*why*);
- a construction of a visual representation of their desired teaching selves (*image*).

8.1 Understanding who we are for insights into who we want to become

We saw at the beginning of Chapter 2 that it is highly unlikely that any motivational intervention will lead a student to create a brand new ideal self out of nothing; the realistic process of constructing a vision is more likely to be one of awareness raising and guided selection from the multiple aspirations, dreams and desires that the individual has already entertained in the past. In a similar fashion, the seeds of any future teaching vision that wait to be grown and nurtured are contained in the teachers' past experiences as learners, teachers and parents. Therefore, some of the most fruitful vision-generating processes can start with self-reflection on our gifts, on the internal images we store of our past learning experiences and on the influential encounters that originally brought us into teaching.

8.1.1 Recognising our gifts

A well-grounded teaching vision needs to be congruent with the unique gifts, talents and passions that have shaped us into who we are. In an essay on inspiring ideas that influenced his own thinking about language teaching, Adrian Palmer (1999) reflects on the work of American mythologist Joseph Campbell (1904–1987), who has reached widespread popular recognition through his powerful formula, 'Follow your bliss'. These three words resonated deeply with the public as it was seen as a shorthand for following one's dreams and deep-seated desires, or in other (more complicated) words, the personal track inherent to the individual that has the potential to lead to the self-actualisation of one's core personal meaning. Thus, to follow one's bliss is to be congruent with one's heart and inner capabilities, and this maxim captures the essence of the current section: identifying the manifestations of any gifts in one's past history (both personal and professional) is a prerequisite for constructing an ideal teacher self-image. While this tenet makes a lot of sense, it is a curious fact that the role of teachers' unique personal talents and passions hardly ever features in L2 teacher education research or practice. Yet, if Campbell is right in suggesting that living an authentic life means 'following one's own bliss', a failure to build on such foundations might be a real waste of opportunities.

In Section 4.2 we presented an activity, 'A strength-based approach to develop plausible ideal selves' (TOOLBOX 4.3), in which students were asked first to identify the strengths they had shown in the past by interviewing 10 to 20 people, asking them to recall 'a time when I was at my best', and then to conduct a thematic analysis of the responses in order to uncover recurring themes and patterns. This activity can also be used by teachers to examine their own creative talents, keen interests and interpersonal skills, and subsequently to recognise them as important cues to their future visions. A further task to facilitate such an exploration of one's strengths, which can be built on, is offered in TOOLBOX 8.2.

(Re-)igniting the flame of teacher vision

🔧 Toolbox 8.2 Finding your 'bliss'

This task may work well in a teacher development course or some kind of in-service training context. On a piece of paper, brainstorm your gifts and passions, drawing on your current interests, childhood memories or interactions with family and friends, reflecting on questions such as:

- What are you good at? What kinds of achievements in the past have earned you positive feedback? What would be the characteristics that colleagues or friends would mention when they praise you? If you were allowed to highlight only three of your strengths, what would these be? When in the past did you feel you were doing yourself real justice?
- What do you really enjoy? When did you feel in the past that you were genuinely 'in your element'? What activities cause you a 'flow' experience (i.e. total blissful absorption)? What complex tasks do you find (perhaps surprisingly) easy to complete?
- What are your passions? What makes you unique? What do people remember you for? What can you get enthusiastic about? If you were allowed to be the member of only one club, what would it be?

Process your list by sharing it with your peer group or selected colleagues/friends, and by reflecting on it in a journal. Then, think about a time when you were able to bring some of your gifts and passions to your language teaching. Share the stories with the group.

8.1.2 Revisiting images of past learning experiences

It is a well-established fact that what teachers learn in teacher education programmes, in teacher development workshops or even from a book like ours is ultimately filtered through their prior experiences as learners, accumulated over the years of the 'apprenticeship of observation' (Lortie 1975). Focusing on SLA specifically, the set of language learning experiences in an L2 teacher's past is transformed, largely subconsciously, into fairly stable beliefs about how languages are learnt and how they should or should not be taught. There is a general consensus that if these beliefs are not made explicit so that they can be consciously processed and challenged if necessary, the teachers' pre-training cognitions might play a covert role, impacting their whole career regardless of any new stimulus and training input they might receive.

Language teacher educators and researchers have developed a number of methods whereby teachers can identify the deep-seated beliefs that they have acquired through the earlier periods of 'apprenticeship of observation' at a conscious level, such as *language learning autobiographies* (Bailey *et al.* 1996) and *narratives* (Golombek and Johnson

Motivating Learners, Motivating Teachers

2004; Johnson and Golombek 2002). Similar tools can be used to (re-)ignite teachers' visions. TOOLBOX 8.3 outlines a sample visualisation task which can be used by teachers to reflect on their language learning autobiographies and gain insights into their future language teacher selves by reliving their past.

🔧 Toolbox 8.3 Replay images of your past experiences

Alone or with a colleague, think back on your experience as a learner (in any learning context) and make a list of episodes and moments in your learning history that touched you, positively or negatively. Now construct images of these experiences and replay them in your mind's eye as movies. How do they make you feel? What do they tell you about who you are today? What do they tell you about the kind of teacher you want to become or fear of becoming? Write about this in a journal or talk about it with your colleague. Below is a list of significant episodes that Maggie came up with as she was revisiting her own images of past experiences as a learner of various subjects and at various institutions.

Maggie's significant moments as a learner

- The time my geometry teacher yelled at me and humiliated me in front of the whole class when I mistakenly highlighted a wrong angle in a triangle on the blackboard.
- The time in our German conversation class when instead of 'food' and 'clothing', our teacher told us about his grandparents' experiences from Nazi Germany.
- The time my biology teacher went red with rage because a group of us were amused by what she said.
- The time when our always formal and distant teacher of German first told us an anecdote from her personal life.
- The time my Russian teacher told us stories about the great Russian writers with such passion that made us believe she must have known them personally.
- The time our professor of philosophy encouraged us to question his theories and engaged in a genuine intellectual debate with us.
- The time when my English teacher let us borrow English books from his own library.
- The time a professor of education told me I would never make a good teacher.

As Maggie discovered through this exercise, many of her present practices are rooted in these past learning experiences. They impacted her teaching because they shaped the image as a teacher that she aspired to become or avoid.

(Re-)igniting the flame of teacher vision

Past learning experiences, both positive and negative, often leave an imprint on teachers' practices not simply because of their powerful emotional charge but because they are linked to the images of the teacher they would ideally like to become or avoid becoming. Revisiting images of past learning experiences can give teachers insights into what they deeply care about and thus uncover the foundations of their desired future visions. This will help them see more clearly whom they would ideally like to become (e.g. someone who facilitates genuine engagement of students' intellect as well as heart in the learning process) or avoid becoming (e.g. someone who hurts students' self-worth).

8.1.3 Remembering encounters that brought us into teaching

Understanding what brings teachers into the profession can shed important light on the nature of their engagement in their students' learning (Kubanyiova 2009) as well as on their persistence and commitment to stay in the teaching career (Watt and Richardson 2008). Having said that, we know all too well that however passionate people may have been about choosing teaching as a career, their initial enthusiasm is often stifled by endless external pressures, bureaucratic demands, an unsupportive school culture and imposed visions that are, more often than not, in stark contrast with the teachers' original aspirations and ideals (see e.g. Crookes 2009; Horn *et al.* 2008). As a result, teachers might begin to 'dismember' who they are (Palmer 2007), and it may be difficult for them to rekindle their passion, reconnect with their vision for teaching and 're-member' who they are if they have suffered the pain of dismemberment for too long. It is this backdrop that gives significance to Palmer's (2007) argument that remembering encounters that brought us into teaching in the first place can be useful: recalling the initial flame of vision can sometimes help us to re-ignite it.

> Academics often suffer the pain of dismemberment. On the surface, this is the pain of people who thought they were joining a community of scholars but find themselves in distant, competitive, and uncaring relationships with colleagues and students. Deeper down, this pain is more spiritual than sociological: it comes from being disconnected from our own truth, from the passions that took us into teaching, from the heart that is the source of all good work. If we have lost the heart to teach, how can we take heart again? How can we re-member who we are, for our own sake and the sake of those we serve? (p. 21)

One of the primary initial drives for pursuing a career in language teaching is the love of languages and a powerfully emerging L2 self in the would-be teachers. Many of us started with an intrinsic passion for the L2 and the worlds/cultures that its knowledge opened up for us. Reconnecting to these early images of L2 selves that once fuelled our own motivation and the desire to share these worlds with others can be a powerful way of getting back in touch with our ideal language teacher selves. Virtually all the techniques we have mentioned in Part II can be applied for this purpose.

A second, equally potent, method for re-energising our vision is to remember the teachers who inspired us. More often than not, it is not their specific teaching style or expertise that made the real impact – in fact, they may not even have represented exemplary models of teaching to be emulated. Rather, the power of these role models lay in their capacity to 'awaken a truth within us, a truth we can reclaim years later by recalling their impact on our lives' (Palmer 2007: 22). Therefore, the main purpose of remembering these teachers is to take us back to the seeds of our own vision.

8.2 Engaging with the 'whys': values, moral purposes and teaching philosophies

An essential part of how we imagine ourselves as teachers rests on the answers to the following questions: Why do we want to become a teacher? What do we believe teaching and teachers are for? and Why and how do languages matter? In her book *Teacher Development in Action* (Kubanyiova 2012), Maggie discusses in detail the different reasons why specific language teachers did not undergo any real conceptual change in spite of attending a teacher development course on motivation, and the quote from one of the participants in ILLUSTRATION 8.1 sums up perfectly the issue we are concerned with in this section. This teacher simply did not believe that the job description of an L2 instructor included being responsible for student motivation, which is a clear illustration of the fact that if the act of 'motivating learners' is not rooted in the educational philosophy of deeper values and purposes that underpin a language teacher's vision of whom he/she wishes to become, then any effort to radically alter his/her motivational practices is doomed to failure. Engaging with the moral fabric of the teacher's vision is therefore a crucial step in facilitating a transformational change in this respect.

> **Illustration 8.1 Why should I 'motivate'? (from Kubanyiova 2012: 112)**
>
> A practising teacher participating in an in-service training course:
>
> > I don't know … I haven't really thought that it's necessary to motivate learners. As I see it – they either want or don't want to learn.

(Re-)igniting the flame of teacher vision

In his compelling reflection on inspirational leadership in general, Simon Sinek (2009) outlines the idea of a 'Golden Circle', which consists of three concentric circles with 'why' in the centre, followed by 'how' and 'what' in the respective outer layers (see TOOLBOX 8.5 on pp. 133–4). He ascribes the success of countless leaders and businesses to the fact that they all started with the 'why' (the wider cause) and moved on to defining the 'how' and 'what' of their specific area through this lens. Among countless examples of inspirational leaders and successful companies, he gives an example of Apple, a globally renowned computer company, and concludes that the company's success was not so much due to what it does and how – after all, there were many similar companies around with similar products and resources when Apple was starting out – but in constantly thinking about, acting upon and communicating why it did it. And that, Sinek maintains, is how people get inspired: not by *what* leaders do, but *why they do it*. In short, within the Golden Circle, inspirational leaders live and communicate their ideas inside out, which Sinek (p. 38) sees as the hallmark of effective and inspirational leadership:

> The Golden Circle is an alternative perspective to existing assumptions about why some leaders and organizations have achieved such a disproportionate degree of influence. It offers clear insight as to how Apple is able to innovate in so many diverse industries and never lose its ability to do so. It explains why people tattoo Harley-Davidson logos on their bodies. It provides a clearer understanding not just of how Southwest Airlines created the most profitable airline in history but why the things it did worked. It even gives some clarity as to why people followed Dr. Martin Luther King Jr. in a movement that changed a nation and why we took up John F. Kennedy's challenge to put a man on the moon even after he died. The Golden Circle shows how these leaders were able to inspire action instead of manipulating people to act.

In stark contrast, many (if not most) L2 teacher education and development programmes start precisely from the opposite direction, focusing on *what* to teach (subject matter) and then *how* (methods, techniques), often leaving little or no space for any consideration of, let alone deeper reflection on, the *why*. And while the mainstream teacher education literature abounds with evidence of values underpinning teachers' work – for example, Borrero's (2011) examination of pre-service teachers of urban youth, whose visions centred around the desire to promote social justice and bring about positive change in their communities – there is very little trace in the language teacher cognition literature of teachers' concerns with purposes that go beyond the objectives of

Motivating Learners, Motivating Teachers

their lesson plans, instructional techniques or methods. Yet, evidence from research outside the applied linguistics domain clearly shows that teachers visualise their own teaching, and while more technical knowledge may partly contribute to the construction of these images, it is first and foremost the teachers' sense of purpose that forms the foundation of these visions (Kennedy 2006). Zoltán's personal account in ILLUSTRATION 8.2 offers some confirmation for this.

> **Illustration 8.2 How I became a language teacher ... (Zoltán)**
>
> My story as a language teacher starts at the beginning of the 1980s when as a hard-up university student of English and History of Art in Hungary, I realised that I could make very good money by teaching English as a foreign language in the evenings. So, one day I found myself walking into my first English class as the instructor rather than a student, and I soon discovered that I genuinely enjoyed the teaching process. Yet, it is probable that neither this enjoyment nor the generous remuneration would have been enough for the profession to completely hook me without a further element: the subversive nature of teaching English in a Communist country. For me and my friends, English represented the free world, and teaching it meant, to some extent, that we became the agents of freedom. I remember how much I enjoyed permeating the syllabus with everything I found valuable about the English-speaking culture at that time, ranging from the feminist songs of Dory Previn to Monty Python sketches. I was on a mission, and looking back now I can see that I have never ceased to be on this mission: although the content of my mission has evolved over the years, the desire to relate language education to a broader transformation of how we engage with the day-to-day reality of the language classroom has become a permanent part of my vision.

How can we start engaging with the wider purposes of language education? There have been a number of valuable works published in the language teaching literature, and these can be used as a starting point for initiating a conversation about the values, moral purposes and teaching philosophies guiding language teachers' work (for an annotated list of relevant readings, see TOOLBOX 8.4).

> **Toolbox 8.4 Resources on values, purposes and teaching philosophies**
>
> - *Bill Johnston's (2003) Values in English Language Teaching.* Analyses of anecdotes from real-life language classrooms encourage teachers to articulate and engage with the values that guide what they do while also uncovering the difficult moral dilemmas that can arise when different values clash.

(Re-)igniting the flame of teacher vision

- *Graham Crookes's (2009) Values, Philosophies, and Beliefs in TESOL.* This book-length discussion is the only material currently available in the TESOL domain that guides teachers through a range of philosophies of education as a source for constructing their own statement of purpose.
- *David Mendelsohn's (1999) Expanding Our Vision.* A collection of essays in which ten well-known TESOL authors, teachers and researchers discuss role models from outside of TESOL who have had a profound influence on the philosophies and values underpinning the authors' own visions for language teaching.
- *Judy Sharkey and Karen Johnson's (2003) The TESOL Quarterly Dialogues.* A collection of chapters in which teachers engage in a dialogue on values concerning language, culture and power with authors of research articles published in the *TESOL Quarterly* journal.
- *Mary Wong and Suresh Canagarajah's (2009) Christian and Critical English Language Educators in Dialogue: Pedagogical and Ethical Dilemmas.* A collection of 30 papers exploring the interrelationship of faith identities and teaching philosophies from both a Christian and a secular perspective.

TOOLBOX 8.5 presents a sample elicitation task to prompt a discussion in a teacher development course which is based on the concept of the Golden Circle mentioned above. In the remainder of this section, we consider a number of practical ideas which complement these sources in helping language teachers to become more aware of and, if necessary, to challenge the 'big ideas' that currently guide their visions and practices.

Toolbox 8.5 Constructing the Language Teacher's 'Golden Circle'

This is a teacher educator-led task, but it can be adapted for work in small, self-initiated teacher development groups or for teachers working individually.

Engage the teacher trainees in reflection on the Language Teacher's 'Golden Circle' without initially revealing its three layers. Instead, start by drawing a large circle with 'What' at the bottom and filling the space that will later become the outer layer with ideas elicited from the course participants on 'what' good/inspirational language teachers teach/do. Next draw an inner circle inside the existing one and write the word 'How?' at the bottom of this new circle. Again, fill it with ideas from the course participants about 'how' good language teachers teach, but remember to leave sufficient space for the centre, which will contain the last circle. When the discussion has come to an end, draw the central circle. Elicit suggestions about the label that should be applied to this circle and initiate a discussion on the importance of thinking about the 'why' of language teaching. This can be followed up by a similar elicitation process as was done with the other two layers or some other similar task. At this point the teacher educators should clearly communicate that the 'why' is at the core of the diagram and at the core of the teacher; without it, the 'what' and the 'how' are rendered rather meaningless. It is important that after the whole-group experience, the teacher trainees have the opportunity to reflect on their own personally meaningful philosophies individually (e.g. give a blank copy of the Golden Circle to each teacher and ask them to fill in the empty layers, or write a piece of reflective writing / seminar paper, etc.).

The Language Teacher's 'Golden Circle'

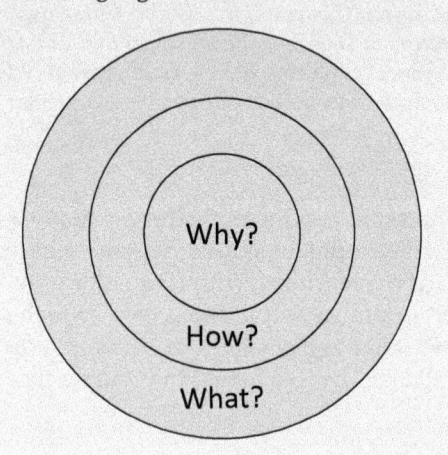

8.2.1 Unearthing the values that guide our teaching

Although we cannot always implement our ideals in the way we wish, we still enact, albeit often subconsciously, values and philosophies in subtle but significant ways: in how we treat our students in the classroom and outside of it; what we tell them; how we make decisions; what upsets us; what makes us feel good about the job well done; what we include in our lesson plans and syllabuses; and what we exclude, avoid or fear. In fact, because we cannot *not* live our 'whys', it is crucial to keep them under close scrutiny through reflection-on-action (Schön 1983) to see if they really epitomise the kind of teacher we wish to become. Sometimes we may be shocked at what we find (although, as we shall see in Section 8.4, this may not necessarily be a negative outcome); at other times we might come out with a renewed sense of commitment and a clearer vision, just like the teacher of auto mechanics (of all subjects!) in a vocational school, cited in ILLUSTRATION 8.3, who reflects on his experience of a teacher development course.

> **Illustration 8.3 What can be gained by reflecting on the whys?** (from Hermanson 2009: 10)
>
> An experienced teacher's reflection on an in-service training course:
>
>> I have gained much from reflection upon what I stand for and why I do what I do. I realise that I teach with the whole of my being, both lessons that are articulated and some that are not ... I have always felt to a degree that students could sound the depths of my knowledge and commitment regardless of my physical actions. It is more than just body language, but communication on a much different level. I know that they know. How many times have you attended a seminar, only to leave unfulfilled, knowing that the facilitator was full of BS? Was it his mannerisms, his body language or the light of his aura? No matter how you knew, the fact is that you knew. Critical reflection has flowered my awareness. We teach who we are, with continuity, vision and purpose to what we are doing. If nothing else, I can shine my spirit, and teach with all the illumination and clarity that is within me. This is the most treasured lesson I will carry from this class.

In order to facilitate an exploration of the values that guide language teachers' practices, we propose a sample task in TOOLBOX 8.6 which can be done on a teacher education programme or, better still, in the supportive environment of an informal teacher development group.

> **Toolbox 8.6 Exploring values guiding your teaching practices**
>
> Ask your colleague/mentor/friend to ask you: *What's important to you about language teaching?* Get them to note down exactly (word by word) what the answer is in your own words (this is very important). If they don't quite catch what you said, or are unsure of the exact phrasing, tell them that they can ask you to repeat what you said. The answers should be written down as they are expressed without changing the wording. They should then ask: *What else is important to you about language teaching?* The questions should be repeated until at least ten values are listed.
>
> **Follow-up:**
>
> 1. Look at your list of values and reflect on the ways in which they are oriented towards teaching, learning, language, learners, self or

Motivating Learners, Motivating Teachers

something else. Is there anything important you feel is missing? Add it to the list.
2. Circle the values that are most significant and which you would describe as your core values. Where do you think they come from and how are they connected with who you are, your worldviews and to the world around you? Allow a few days to decide which values you want to work on, and give yourself time to explore what these values mean to you, perhaps talking about them with a colleague or reading around relevant philosophies of education.
3. Thinking about your top values, ask yourself:

- What are the behaviours that I use to fulfil these values? To what extent is the environment I create in my language classroom a reflection of what is important to me?
- What do I want to change?
- In what way can the L2 vision principles for the language classroom described in this book assist me in this process?

Note down your reflections in a journal and discuss anything important that has emerged from this exercise with your colleagues/classmates/mentor/friends.

8.3 Generating images of ideal language teacher selves

We have emphasised throughout this book that the idea of vision implies a sensory experience generated through our imagination of what can be, and it is this image that ultimately moves us to action. This is just as true about teachers as about students. As with the current situation characterising the study of student vision, we have yet to see substantial empirical work on the construction of language teachers' selves in their teaching practice. We know, however, that teachers routinely generate images of themselves and their practice – an interesting example of recent research has been Feryok and Pryde's (2012) study on the role of imaging as an 'orienting activity' – and there is also some evidence indicating that the more vivid, specific and coherent the images are that the teachers construct, the more likely they are to develop their practices in the desired directions as they embark on their teaching career (see McElhone *et al.*'s 2009 investigation in ILLUSTRATION 8.4).

Illustration 8.4 On the role of vision in teacher development

McElhone *et al.* (2009) have investigated a cohort of new literacy teachers in their pre-service and in-service years by specifically focusing on their visions of good teaching in relation to the development of their professional practice. The researchers evaluated the teachers' practice in a quantitative way by

(Re-)igniting the flame of teacher vision

assigning scores to them, and based on these ratings they divided the group into three subgroups: (1) those whose practice developed, (2) those whose practice remained stable over the period of investigation and (3) those whose practice weakened. Interestingly, the teachers with improved practice were those who held the most coherent and specific images of ideal teaching.

So, the question is: how do we help teachers to construct such images? The answer is no different from what we have already suggested in Part II of this book: like learners, teachers, too, can benefit from a variety of techniques for envisioning their desired future end states (i.e. imagery focused on the outcome) as well as visualising the actual strategies for achieving them (i.e. imagery focused on the process). They, too, can profit from activities such as guided imagery or creative narrative tasks concerning the imagined future (e.g. visualising inspiring teaching moments or writing a letter from the future to the present self) – indeed, virtually all the techniques we have covered in Part II offer potential for the construction and enhancement of ideal language teachers' selves. For instance, Maggie regularly uses a writing task at the beginning of her Communicative Language Teaching course in which she asks the course participants to write a journal entry entitled 'The Teacher I Would Ideally Like to Become'. This enables the (student) teachers to begin the process of constructing and articulating their desired teaching personas. For further illustration on what guided imagery may look like when adopted for language teachers, TOOLBOX 8.7 presents a sample guided imagery exercise adapted from Hammerness (2006), while ILLUSTRATION 8.5 describes an outcome of such an exercise, a classroom teacher's expressive vision of a learning environment that fosters a genuine culture of inquiry and growth.

Toolbox 8.7 Guided imagery (imagery streaming) prompts: My ideal classroom ... (adapted from Hammerness 2006: 93)

Imagine that you are taking me on a tour around your ideal classroom. You can look around the room and you can hear and see the activities going on ...

- What do you see, feel and hear when you walk around your ideal classroom?
- What are you doing in your ideal classroom? What is your role? Why?
- What are your students doing in this ideal classroom? What role(s) do the students play? Why?
- What kinds of things are the students learning in your ideal classroom? For instance, what activities, topics or texts are they working on? Why are those important for them to learn?
- What is the relationship between what goes on in your ideal classroom and the kind of society you would like to see in the twenty-first century?

Motivating Learners, Motivating Teachers

> **Illustration 8.5 Kelly's vision: fostering a learning culture (Hammerness 2006: 30–1)**

When describing her vision in a written statement while a fifth-year teacher at Blackwell High School, Kelly does not talk about the physical layout of the classroom, but rather portrays the atmosphere of the classroom. Her vision is one in which students and teacher explore scientific questions together in an atmosphere of 'excitement, earnestness, and life'. Investigations are shaped by student interest rather than by teacher's choice or textbook topics. The environment is charged with excitement; Kelly sees herself 'surrounded' by students who have questions 'burgeoning' from them, and she sees herself responding with 'guidance, coaching, and shared enthusiasm'. She also imagines students asking one another the same questions 'with the same demand and expectation they ask of me, as though they knew the question was their own, not mine, thus making the answer more important to discover'. Students are learning to question and challenge information they've encountered and are learning to think critically through real-world problems: They 'investigate and offer solutions to complex situations which often have no answer, while developing skills and reflecting on their learning'. Kelly imagines students working in a variety of different forms determined by what is appropriate to the task at hand: 'some in groups, some individually, in discussions and research working on problems that are real-world, practical'.

8.4 Sparking creative tension

Let us recall for a moment Maggie's theory of Language Teacher Conceptual Change (LTCC; Kubanyiova 2012) that we briefly described in Section 1.5. If the material in this book has resonated with you and you have begun to generate vivid images of yourself as a 'visionary' language teacher, we can say with confidence that the 'Nice-but-not-for-me' path in the LTCC model is not the one you have embarked on. Does this mean, however, that your vision will inevitably transform your teaching practice? The honest answer is: only if some further conditions are met.

The LTCC model suggests that with regard to the change of teacher beliefs, the crucial condition is becoming aware of a *dissonance* between the desired and the actual teaching selves. Before we discuss specific strategies for generating such dissonance (in Section 8.4.1), let us illustrate what such 'creative tension' looks like in action. ILLUSTRATION 8.6 describes the moment when an experienced English language instructor was confronted with an uncomfortable truth: her teaching, which she had always thought of as effective, actually contradicted her ideals

(Re-)igniting the flame of teacher vision

grounded in specific philosophies of teaching. She had always been confident about herself as a teacher, but, at some point, something did not feel right and – as she recounts later – it was this emotional tension that led her to look at her work with new eyes and new commitment. Without a conscious awareness of dissonance, the chances are that nothing much would have changed for her in the long run.

> **Illustration 8.6 Encountering dissonance: Lynne Herndon's (2002: 35) account**
>
> New job. New semester. New curriculum. A new opportunity to re-envision my teaching. A chance to put into practice the insights I had gleaned from my previous teaching experiences as well as the theory I had absorbed during my intensive MATESOL program the summer before. But how?
>
> I had been teaching English to mainstream and ESL students in private and public schools for several years. Although I was well practiced as a teacher of writing, my real love was reading, and my students and colleagues generally appreciated my skills as a literature teacher. I had learned how to choose literary works that the students enjoyed, how to craft study guides that delved into the key themes of a text, and how to lead students in provocative class discussions. I was an effective teacher, no doubt, but somehow my teaching didn't feel right to me.
>
> My training had emphasised the importance of allowing students ownership over the reading and writing process, a philosophical orientation that I embraced in theory but failed to follow fully in practice. Perhaps my love of literature was part of the problem. As I prepared a lesson plan, my excitement about a reading would sweep over me and thoughts would begin to race through my head. In the classroom, my ideas too often predominated, and my voice was too often the most assured in the room. Although students generally enjoyed and benefited from my classes, in the end the literature we studied belonged more to me than it did to them. My new teaching position provided me with a chance to shift the balance. But how?

Herndon's narrative in ILLUSTRATION 8.6 illustrates well the key role that discrepancy, tension or dissonance play in prompting self-regulatory action. We know from research on both possible selves and language teacher conceptual change that meaningful development occurs only when teachers become aware of a discrepancy between their vision and reality, and experience what has sometimes been termed *emotional dissonance* (Golombek and Johnson 2004; Kubanyiova 2012). To put it simply, teachers must feel at least a little uneasy about the current status quo in order to want to change it, which is a similar idea to the one forming the basis of Higgins's self-discrepancy theory described in

139

Motivating Learners, Motivating Teachers

Section 1.2. Senge (1990/2006: 139–40) referred to this uneasiness as 'creative tension':

> People often have great difficulty talking about their visions, even when the visions are clear. Why? Because we are acutely aware of the gaps between our vision and reality. 'I would like to start my own company,' but 'I don't have the capital.' Or, 'I would like to pursue the profession that I really love,' but 'I've got to make a living.' These gaps can make a vision seem unrealistic or fanciful. They can discourage us or make us feel hopeless. But the gap between vision and current reality is also a source of energy. If there was no gap, there would be no need for any action to move toward the vision. Indeed, the gap is the source of creative energy. We call this gap creative tension.

Fettes (2005: 5) summarised succinctly how this tension works in education: 'it is when teachers are confronted by a mismatch between their imagination and their experience that transformation is most likely to occur'. This principle explains one of Zoltán's most significant teaching-related episodes, one which left an indelible mark on his subsequent practice – see ILLUSTRATION 8.7.

> **Illustration 8.7 A perspective-changing evening talk (Zoltán)**
>
> In the summer of 1985, immediately after graduating as a teacher of English in Budapest, I had the chance to attend a two-week teacher training course at Pilgrims Language School in Canterbury. On one of the very first evenings, as we were expecting some initial orientation talk, a man in his thirties came in, glared at us and asked in what I thought was a strong Scottish accent, 'What's the point of doing all this?' (or something to this effect). And then, in some 20 minutes he did an excellent job in describing how soul-destroyingly pointless, depressing, sad, miserable, dismal and demotivating language teaching can be if our focus is only on making sure that our students get the proper tense right in a sentence. I cannot recollect his exact words, but I know that I came away with a shock of realisation that even with a seemingly technical subject such as the teaching of a foreign language, it might be possible to go beyond the technicalities of the language code and to offer something much more precious to the students than the rules of using the 'if conditional': the opportunity to get to know ourselves better, to form true relationships and to enrich our identities. The lecturer did not explain how this could be done (or indeed what exactly these lofty concepts meant), but for me that evening talk was enough to convince me that there is no point in the whole

education business unless we at least aim for such higher-order goals. Looking back, I can pinpoint that evening in Canterbury as one of the main lessons that taught me that if we want it to, the language classroom can become a far more exciting, inspiring and meaningful environment than a mere venue for preparing students for the next language proficiency test. In some ways, my vision was ignited then.

8.4.1 Strategies of generating creative tension

How can creative tension be generated? In other words, what kind of stimulus is needed to enlighten us, to make us gasp, to shake us out of our comfort zones and to uproot our visions so that they can be planted in a more fertile soil? It is difficult to offer very specific recipes, because different people need different sorts of 'dissonance impetus' to help them see what they think they have always known from a fresh perspective. Here are four common approaches that have been found generally useful in both initial teacher education and in-service teacher development programmes:

- *Peer observation.* Observing other teachers' classes is a surprisingly enlightening (and equally surprisingly underutilised) experience, because being faced with someone else's practice inevitably works as a mirror that highlights the differences between their and our own conduct, thereby leading to critical self-reflection. This also works from the receiving end: having colleagues observe our own classes and give us feedback is an admittedly face-threatening but immensely instructive process that can trigger off genuine changes.
- *'Self-observation': watching ourselves on video.* This, again, is a rarely employed method (which probably has something to do with the technical issues involved) even though it offers an ideal opportunity for self-reflection: we can become our own judges. Anyone who has done it will know that seeing ourselves in action immediately propels us out of our comfort zones because being faced with our own mannerisms is not exactly comfortable viewing. Yet, the tension created in this way has massive transformational capacity.
- *Collecting student feedback.* Regularly collecting student feedback through short questionnaires (see TOOLBOX 8.8 for guidelines on how to construct student evaluation questionnaires and feedback forms) can offer a great deal of constructive information and can also reveal some uncomfortable truths. Furthermore, relaying the feedback to the students subsequently can be a powerful group-building exercise.

Motivating Learners, Motivating Teachers

> **Toolbox 8.8 Guidelines for constructing student evaluation questionnaires and feedback forms**
>
> We have found that questions are often less effective in eliciting meaningful answers in feedback forms than a few unfinished sentence beginnings that the respondents need to complete. A good sentence completion item should be worded so that it directs the respondent's attention to a well-defined issue/area. For example:
>
> - *One thing I liked about this activity is* ....
> - *One thing I didn't like about this activity is* ....
> - *I found this activity* ....
>
> The strength of such a quick feedback instrument is that it takes up only a few minutes of classroom time and can still produce an accurate estimate of the class's overall attitudinal temperature.
>
> Another, more common way of collecting feedback is through asking a few open-ended questions such as the following typical sequence:
>
> - *What were the most effective aspects of this course?*
> - *What were the least effective aspects of this course?*
> - *How could this course be further improved?*
>
> Two practical suggestions: first, we have found that the number of questions should be limited to a maximum of three, or else the form will look too demanding and therefore may be demotivating for students to fill in. If you want more detailed feedback, a qualitative interview is the right procedure. Second, the form appears more doable – and therefore user-friendly – if you mark a few blank lines after each question.

- *Focus-group interview.* Focus-group interviews involve having a semi-structured discussion with a small group of teachers (usually 6–12), with the interviewer acting more like a facilitator than an 'interrogator'. The technique is based on the collective experience of group brainstorming, that is, participants thinking together, inspiring and challenging each other, and reacting to the emerging issues and points. For this reason, focus groups are ideal for programme evaluation – to assess the effectiveness of a particular course and to understand what was or was not working and why.
- *Action research.* Action research (or exploratory practice) is a generic term for a family of related research methods conducted by, or in cooperation with, teachers for the purpose of gaining a better understanding of their educational environment and improving the effectiveness

(Re-)igniting the flame of teacher vision

of their teaching. This is a more ambitious (and time-consuming!) form of gathering relevant classroom data, and two good recent overviews of the practicalities of conducting action research are Allwright and Hanks (2009) and Burns (2010).

Besides obtaining some sort of feedback to act as a trigger for critical self-reflection, teachers can also interrogate, and if necessary challenge, established ways of thinking about motivational teaching through narrating their own stories, especially when the prompts ask them to focus on the creative conflicts in their own practice (TOOLBOX 8.9 offers a series of story prompts that can be used for this purpose).

> **Toolbox 8.9 Story prompts for critical reflection (adapted from Blunt 2001)**
> - Can you talk about a time when you taught a specific course / group of students and suddenly realised how much you didn't know?
> - Was there ever a time that you felt you failed in a job badly?
> - Did you have a time in your teaching when you worked with students who accomplished well beyond what you or anyone may have expected?
> - Did you ever go through a personal/professional crisis that helped you realise and begin to live out important values that may have been previously obscured from you?
> - Did you ever take part in an event where you felt you put your career on the line?
> - Was there ever a time you felt you couldn't go on or were about to give up?
> - Did you ever do something that no one knew about but which gives you a great sense of accomplishment today?

Such a conscious and in-depth examination of one's teaching practice is a good way of putting one's vision to the test. Embarking on such an adventure may yield disconcerting or upsetting results, as shown in ILLUSTRATION 8.8, which presents an interview extract from Maggie's research with language teachers. As the text demonstrates, being willing to face the actual impact of her vision on her practice, Monika came to a deeply unsettling realisation: the practices modelled in her specific teaching environment that she had gradually adopted made her students scared. This awakening was a key moment for Monika to see that the vision she was actually pursuing was not her own and that the consequences of her actions were in stark contrast to the vision she had originally started her career with. In the end, Monika's creative tension helped her to return to her original vision and to remain true to it.

> **Illustration 8.8 Monika's confrontation with her vision of teacher as 'Captain' (Kubanyiova 2012: 198)**
>
> Extract from an interview with Monika, a practising L2 teacher:
>
>> ... I sort of started to search for my place, like what type of teacher I will be and so that is where it was all going ... I was never happy with my classes. It worried me too. But I didn't know what I was doing wrong. Who would tell me? This is how it should be, you must keep the order and maintain your authority no matter what and that's when it's good. But actually the kids were afraid of me. There were a great number of those who were afraid of me. Now I am able to look at it face to face, yes, it's true, they were frightened ...
>
> As a result of an in-service course that Monika participated in, she gradually came to adopt a different approach:
>
>> a kind of an open approach, a healthy partnership, not a hierarchy ... So [the course] certainly was a very significant turning point. Sure, not immediately from the start, but ... it came as a lightning from the sky, as a kind of salvation. I then found myself there. I found myself and I knew what to do with it.

9 Guarding the flame of teacher vision

> I am not afraid of storms, for I am learning how to sail my ship.
> *Louisa May Alcott (1832–1888)*

In an analysis of threats to teacher motivation, Dörnyei and Ushioda (2011) explain that although teachers are highly qualified, motivated professionals with a vision to pursue a largely fulfilling job, the profession is struggling with serious difficulties that overshadow the satisfaction with the inherent qualities of teaching. In their overview, they list six particular issues that keep eroding teacher motivation, especially for those working in the state sector: (1) the exceptionally high stress level inherent to the job; (2) the increasing restrictions infringing teaching autonomy (by externally imposed curricula, tests, methods and other directives); (3) the fragile self-efficacy of practitioners, most of whom are undertrained in areas concerning group leadership and classroom management; (4) the difficulty of maintaining an intellectual challenge in the face of repetitive content and routinised classroom practices; (5) an inadequate career structure to generate effective motivational contingent paths; and (6) the economic conditions, which are usually worse than those of other service professions (e.g. lawyers and doctors).

How can we guard the flame of vision to teach in the face of such adversities? In this last chapter we are going to attempt some answers to this question even if these answers are unlikely to offer a solution to every classroom practitioner. After all, teachers are exposed to a wide array of voices – both real and metaphorical – that quietly (and sometimes not so quietly) erode their visions, trying to convince them that these visions are impossible, unrealistic, uneconomical, ineffective, undesirable or downright ridiculous. And when the pressures from the environment get too intense, the voices of opposition too loud and the constraints too stifling, the cumulative effect of these can become a tangible threat that pushes us to lower our expectations, give up our dreams and put up with whatever the system is asking us to put up with. The pathway to teacher burnout is wide and well-trodden, but it is not the only route by any means!

9.1 Staying connected to the original vision in the face of detrimental ought-to self-images

The essence of this section can be summed up in one short recommendation: *make sure that the vision you entertain is your own*. Teaching would undoubtedly be a more attractive job if it were only their ideal selves that teachers needed to pursue in their work. This is, unfortunately, rarely (if ever) the case and the everyday reality of teachers' work brings with it numerous external pressures, demands and requirements. As a result many, if not most, teachers feel a growing pressure to live up to others' expectations rather than to live out their own dreams.

We saw earlier (e.g. in Chapter 1) that possible selves theory subsumes the various externally driven incentives and duties under the notion of the ought-to self, and we can view the specific representation of the various teaching-related responsibilities and obligations as forming the notion of the ought-to L2 teacher selves. There are many stakeholders in the language teaching enterprise – from parents, colleagues and heads of department to school managers, education boards and ministries of education – and therefore a teacher can have a whole array of ought-to teaching selves depending on whose expectations he/she strives to (or is forced to) comply with. Thus, in many teachers' minds there is a distinct imbalance between their deeply cherished visions of who they would like to become as language teaching professionals and the multitude of externally imposed images of what good teachers ought to do and who they ought to be. Indeed, if teachers are not careful, other people's images of teaching can gradually sneak into their consciousness and become internalised. As a result, these imported images can start squeezing out the ideal self-image from teachers' working self-concept, and they no longer see the purposes, philosophies and values that originally brought them into teaching.

Herein lies the problem, but this is also where we find a potential solution: to be vigilant and to consciously remember that even when we have to follow external guidelines, the imposed ought-to images do *not* have to become our own. In other words, even when we need to make compromises, these can be guided by principled decisions to respond to the external pressures (e.g. teaching to the test) while at the same time allowing our vision to shine through in locally appropriate ways. Past research has shown that if teachers manage to keep the flame of vision alight, the desired images of the future *do* have the potential to override extrinsic influences in the teachers' mindsets. However, when the vision falters, the mundane constraints of the teaching environment can rapidly assume full control. In her pioneering overview of the motivation and work satisfaction of language teachers, Martha Pennington (1995: 19–20) has expressed this same idea very clearly as follows:

> Where an employee's future-oriented, long-term outlook is positive, there is less attention to the more immediate, quotidian framework. However, where the broad outlook is unsatisfactory and there seems

little chance of career aspirations being met in a given work context, the employee's attention shifts to the immediate frame of reference, which assumes comparatively great importance.

9.2 Building resilience through vision boosters and safety zones

In this section, our specific focus is on visualisation techniques that have been devised to assist teachers to develop resilience and to arm themselves against adversity. As Morosini (2010: 49) explains, 'the capacity to dream means being able to courageously condition your imagination to shape hopeful images of the future even in the face of extraordinary adversity'. Mental imagery has been a key theme throughout this book, and it has also been found useful for facilitating various aspects of teachers' practice; for example, Jagla (1994: 14) recommends it for lesson planning (a point echoed by Thornbury 1999 with regard to language teachers as well), and this advice can also come in useful in the planning stages of a potentially risky idea, approach or task:

> The ability to imagine is an essential ingredient to good teaching. One needs to be able to picture how an idea might be played out with a particular group of students in order to decide how to best present the idea in a lesson. Good lesson planning in general is picturing your students doing whatever it is you have planned for them and 'seeing' how Johnny or Mary might respond in your mind's eye. You might decide to alter your approach as you picture yourself going through the lesson.

Building resilience through visualisation can be of two (related) types: first, teachers can use imagery as a mental rehearsal of specific activities or lessons to immunise themselves against difficult situations and to boost their willingness to experiment with new approaches. The second type of imagery involves visual boosters for strengthening the teaching vision and renewing the commitment to one's ideal language teacher self.

The first approach – building *general resilience* – can employ similar techniques to the ones proposed in Part II in connection with student vision. ILLUSTRATION 9.1 describes a scenario when a teacher trainer led her student teachers to utilise meta-imagery control skills to restructure a negative situation, not unlike the way athletes use this technique to improve on their skills (see Section 3.1). Simply changing the teacher's facial expression and body language during the imagined scene made a real difference. Fletcher (2000) further notes that this technique is effective not only because it offers a concrete tool that teachers can use to deal with a difficult scenario but also because it can be applied to regain

Motivating Learners, Motivating Teachers

positive energy and a sense of well-being *after* a difficult experience in class. If used as part of a post-lesson reflection process, this type of imagery can prepare teachers for handling threatening situations in the future and building more positive relationships with their students.

Illustration 9.1 Just smile! (Fletcher 2000: 240)

I encouraged the group to think themselves into a classroom situation where they were teaching but things did not go quite as they had hoped and planned. In their visualisation I encouraged them to pick up on how the class and they were reacting – perhaps the children were not paying attention, maybe someone walked in and disrupted the flow of the lesson. I asked them to focus on their own face and body language – to step outside themselves and audit the effect of the situation upon them. There were giggles of amusement and nervousness from the group! I invited them to change the situation just marginally by changing their facial expression to a smile – and I watched as some of the members of my group duly began to relax their facial muscles and gently settle into their chairs. I asked them to see what was happening in front of them and to subtly replay the situation so things went a little better than they first remembered – what might they change? My message was that they could put some of the negative feelings on one side and increase their feeling of well-being through using visualisation.

A further resource in the visualisation armoury includes short regular *boosters* of language teacher vision, which are examples of what is called the 'positive imagery approach' (Singer 2006: 111) in psychology. They typically involve highly pleasurable, relaxing or inspirational images (often of nature scenes) to counteract anxiety and to build up one's overall motivational stamina. TOOLBOX 9.1 presents a guided imagery script illustrating this method in which the imagined and highly uplifting feeling of a butterfly emerging from its cocoon is drawn on in order to make a motivational declaration.

Toolbox 9.1 Guided imagery: butterfly (adapted from Edwards 2009)

Relax deeply, and then imagine yourself curled up inside a dark cocoon, which envelops you so closely that you can barely breathe. How does it feel? (Safe? Constricting? Suffocating? Secure? Lonely? Dull? Scary?) When you feel a desire to break free, gently stretch out – feel the cocoon easily ripping open, letting in the sunlight. You emerge as a beautiful butterfly, with wings ready to unfurl.

Guarding the flame of teacher vision

When you are ready, stretch your wings and fly into the forest. Flutter here and there amongst the trees, sensing the life all around you – the plants, birds, animals and insects. Feel yourself as a part of this living forest. And now fly up above the forest, and take on a human form. Look down on the trees, lakes and mountains far below as you soar through the air ... When you are ready, fly towards a mountain peak, and land. Stand on top of this mountain, and shout out to the world below: 'I am ready to be the best teacher I can be!' 'I am ready to take courage to be the teacher I want to be!' (or whatever feels appropriate and right for you). Then gently come back to the room.

Another way of boosting resilience concerns visual reminders of positive past examples of our ideal selves in action. When asked to reflect on her vision of the teacher she would ideally like to become, Tojiniso Olimnazarova, an English language teacher from Tajikistan, recalled various uplifting images of past experiences, including the one described in ILLUSTRATION 9.2. A regular priming of such images can work as effective resilience builders in the face of adversity.

Illustration 9.2 Remembering the positive moments (Olimnazarova, personal communication, 2012)

Before my present job, for ten years I was working for an English programme in my country, and once one of my Afghani students, a teacher himself, wrote to me the following:

Dear Teacher Toji,
Personally, I have selected you as a MODEL TEACHER, and I myself model on you as a teacher, and I will apply in my future career what teaching skills I learnt from you. I was influenced by your good personality, attitude, forbearance, curiosity and decisiveness. Russell, an English philosopher, says: 'No man can be a good teacher unless he has feelings of warm affection [like parents' affection to their children] toward his pupils and a genuine desire to impart to them what he believes to be of value.' We found you as kind as Russell defines a good teacher.

I was really HAPPY to receive something like this from my student. I understand it would be very difficult to leave every student with such feelings; however, I really wish I could.

A final shielding strategy we would like to present here concerns creating *trustworthy spaces* or *safety zones* within the educational environment. Guarding the flame of an emerging and often fragile vision requires a setting that will be supportive of such deeply personal agendas. Although we are well aware that many language teachers work

Motivating Learners, Motivating Teachers

in contexts which do not readily offer such support, there is evidence in the literature that creating safety zones of like-minded colleagues can and has been done (e.g. Edge 1992). We take inspiration from the work of Casbon, Shagoury and Smith (2005), who have formulated a set of ground rules, or 'touchstones', for creating trustworthy spaces for teacher interaction in which teachers' identities and visions are nurtured (see TOOLBOX 9.2). A support group adopting principles of this nature can turn into a fertile culture in which the stem cell of vision can grow into a potent transforming agent.

> **Toolbox 9.2 Touchstones for creating trustworthy spaces for teacher interaction (adapted from Casbon *et al.* 2005: 362)**
> - Come with 100% of ourselves.
> - Presume welcome and extend welcome.
> - Believe that it is possible to go away more refreshed than when you came.
> - Interact with others through invitation, not invasion; opportunity, not demand.
> - Avoid trying to fix others.
> - Be open to learning from one another.
> - Turn to inquiry and wonder when the going gets tough.
> - Listen to the silence.
> - Observe confidentiality.

9.3 Processing our fears and turning adversity into allies

Every time we decide to try something new in our classroom, we take a risk: the class may go really well, but it may also fail miserably. It is this fear of failure that we wish to address in this section, because understanding its source holds important cues as to why some teachers may discard the dream of being 'visionary teachers' while others invest energy into attaining it even when difficulties start to kick in. The fear that Jane Tompkins (1996) describes in ILLUSTRATION 9.3 – and which can occur in varying degrees when teachers try something new in their classes – is likely to lead to the former scenario (i.e. watering down or abandoning our visions).

> **Illustration 9.3 Jane Tompkins's (1996: 1) ultimate nightmare**
> I'm in front of the class on the first day of school, and for some reason, I'm totally unprepared. (How did this happen?) Throat tight, I fake a smile, grab for words, tell an anecdote, anything to hold their attention. But the

> strangers in rows in front of me aren't having any. They start to shuffle and murmur; they turn their heads away. Then chairs scrape back, and I realize it's actually happened. The students are walking out on me. I have finally gotten what I deserve.

Fears of this type usually threaten the teachers' sense of self because they are ultimately rooted in their desire to preserve their self-image, which is more central to their self-concept than the desire to create environments in which learners' vision can be ignited. Until the sources of such fear are dealt with, any situation that carries a risk of self-exposure and embarrassment is likely to threaten the teachers' vision. Therefore, from a practical perspective, a crucial step in helping teachers to guard the flame of their vision is to help them to understand the sources of their feared selves and then to encourage them either to embrace their fears as an essential part of the teaching process (as we will see in the next section) or, if necessary, to replace them with alternative visions that are more conducive both to the students' learning and to the teachers' well-being. We offer the following task – TOOLBOX 9.3 – with this aim in mind.

Toolbox 9.3 Understanding your fears

This task should ideally take place in conjunction with a discussion on the nature of fear in language teaching. Step 3 would be a natural place for such input.

Step 1: Brainstorm

Brainstorm your fears about what might happen if you tried to implement the vision-based approach in your language teaching. (e.g. *Students won't like it. Colleagues will disrespect me. Parents will think I'm not serious enough. Students won't learn anything. They will just mess about and I won't get through my coursebook. I will appear foolish in front of the students ...*)

Step 2: Visualise

Imagine your worst-case scenario of 'what might happen' if you tried some new ideas from this book in your classroom, incorporating your greatest fears into this visualisation. Include all your senses: what do you see, hear, feel?

Step 3: Analyse

Share your visualisation in your group or write about it in a journal. Where do you think your fear comes from? How does it relate to your vision of a good language teacher? How might you address your fears? Or your visions?

9.3.1 Turning adversity into an ally

Adversity can deal a death blow to our visions, but with appropriate processing it can be turned into an ally. That something unpleasant can become beneficial is a known phenomenon in several areas of psychology. For example, when groups develop, they often go through a rugged transition phase that does not seem like an improvement in several respects: while the initial formation phase was usually orderly, with students doing their best to avoid any disruptions, during the subsequent transition phase members feel free to enter into arguments and debates. Peace is often replaced by conflicts and tensions, sometimes only brewing under the surface but at times erupting in a seemingly unexpected and illogical manner. The main lesson from group dynamics research is that this 'storming phase' is not necessarily bad from the long-term perspective. As long as the process is managed well so that it does lead to sorting out some underlying issues rather than to mere hostility, it is likely to strengthen the group (see Dörnyei and Murphey 2003 for a more detailed discussion).

A further example, even closer to home, is the fact that – as we have seen in Chapter 7 – a classic principle in possible selves theory has been that for maximum effectiveness, a desired future self should be offset by a corresponding feared self. Thus, in this case it is explicitly stated that having a vivid sense of a dispreferred outcome is not only *not* harmful, but is actually beneficial provided it is balanced with a corresponding positive self-image in the same domain: we can be motivated to do something both to reach a desired outcome *and* to avoid an adverse one. In sum, some fears are essential for strengthening teachers' determination to act on their ideal selves, a point made expressively by Parker Palmer (2007: 39):

> My fear that I am teaching poorly may be not a sign of failure but evidence that I care about my craft. My fear that a topic will explode in the classroom may be not a warning to flee from it but a signal that the topic must be addressed.

One important component of Maggie's model of Language Teacher Conceptual Change (LTCC, Kubanyiova 2012) concerns what she called Reality Check Appraisal, which refers to teachers' evaluation of their internal and external resources in relation to new ideas, educational developments or reforms. It can involve, for example, the teachers' assessment of their own self-efficacy (i.e. the belief as to whether they have the ability to make a positive impact on the learners through implementing the new ideas), contextual constraints such as time and resources (which may prevent teachers from experimenting with new approaches) or students' expectations (which may be at odds with

Guarding the flame of teacher vision

some of the key assumptions of the new material). An interesting finding was that although the contextual constraints and pressures were almost identical for all teacher participants in Maggie's research project, some of them interpreted the situation as a threat and therefore a clue to quickly put out the flame of an emerging new vision, while others approached the same constraints as a challenge to be tackled rather than avoided (which is not unlike the well-known anecdote about the two marketing scouts reporting on the shoeless situation in a specific region of Africa; see ILLUSTRATION 9.4). It all depended on the nature of their initial reality check appraisal.

Illustration 9.4 Is it a threat or an ally? (from Zander and Zander 2000: 9)

A shoe factory sends two marketing scouts to a region of Africa to study the prospects for expanding business. One sends back a telegram saying,

SITUATION HOPELESS STOP NO ONE WEARS SHOES

The other writes back triumphantly,

GLORIOUS BUSINESS OPPORTUNITY STOP THEY HAVE NO SHOES

One of the main tenets of responding to adversity in a constructive manner is to hold our nerves and engage with the negative issue instead of going on the defensive. ILLUSTRATION 9.5 describes a nightmare moment that many of us are dreading: a hostile challenge by a student. The teacher, Rachel Kessler (2002), honestly admits that a similar moment would have been deeply upsetting for her in the past and most of us can fully sympathise, as we too would have felt the humiliation and self-doubt that situations like these can generate. On the day of this episode, however, Kessler decided to put into practice her conviction that adversity can be seen as an opportunity to grow, and she remembers clearly the feeling of gratitude for the guidance she had received from the 'trouble-maker', Sue Ellen, with no hint of defensiveness or anxiety.

Illustration 9.5 Turn your critics into allies (Kessler 2002: 141–3)

'If you continue to lead this workshop the way you've just led this first hour, it will be completely useless for me.'
  Sue Ellen's voice comes from the back of the room, high up on the last tier of this choral room.

> 'I will go back in September,' she continues, 'and be completely unprepared to bring any of this work into my classroom or present any of this information to my colleagues, which they are expecting me to do.'
>
> Her words are like a swift blow to my midsection. After the shock, I take a breath and continuing to look straight at this woman, I respond. 'Thank you, that's exactly the guidance I was looking for. Francisco,' I say now turning to my colleague, 'please move the overhead projector so we can start the lecture.'

This mature attitude requires the learning of how to shift the focus away from our self-image and set our gaze on the opportunities that a seeming attack or scepticism from a range of stakeholders opens up for our personal growth as visionary teachers. TOOLBOX 9.4 lists five concrete recommendations on how to develop this disposition and how to spot an ally where others may see an enemy.

> **Toolbox 9.4 Five strategies to process adversity (based on Kessler 2002)**
> - Learn to be open to perceiving what is happening right now.
> - Develop responsiveness to the needs of this moment.
> - Become flexible enough to shift gears.
> - Be prepared with the repertoire, creativity and imagination to invent a new approach in the moment.
> - Remember to be humble and honest enough to simply pause and acknowledge if a new approach has not yet arrived.

9.4 Sustaining hope

The notion of possible selves and hope have been inextricably bound together ever since Markus and Nurius's (1986) initial paper introducing the concept; as they stated, 'positive possible selves can be exceedingly liberating because they foster hope that the present self is not immutable' (p. 963), and then added: 'when we perceive ourselves, we see not only our present capacities and states but also our potential: what we hope to become, what we plan to do, what we are worried will happen, and so on' (p. 964). We have cited ample evidence in the previous chapters that vision can take someone to unexpected places or achievements, and in this final section we would like to underscore the fact that all these positive outcomes were grounded in the fact that the visionary individual in question had never given up hope. Vision – as conceptualised in relation to desired *possible* selves – rests in hope, and to paraphrase the proverbial message that we started our Introduction with ('Where there is no vision, the people perish'), we can affirm, 'Where there is no hope, the vision perishes.' This view is confirmed by Rick Snyder's *hope theory* (see ILLUSTRATION 9.6), which highlights the ability of high-hope people to find routes to achieving difficult or even seemingly unattainable goals, in contrast to low-hope people who do not display flexibility to find alternative routes when the primary pathway is blocked.

Illustration 9.6 On high-hope people in Snyder's (2002) hope theory

Rick Snyder (1944–2006) was one of the founders of 'positive psychology', best known for his work on hope. The following extracts are taken from his 2002 paper that summarises his views, entitled 'Hope Theory: Rainbows in the Mind'.

> 'Hope is defined as the perceived capability to derive pathways to desired goals, and motivate oneself via agency thinking to use those pathways.' (p. 249)

> 'Contrary to my early views that extremely difficult goals were not applicable to hope because they truly were unattainable (viz., the "abandon all hope ye who enter here" sign on the doorway to hell [in Dante's *The Divine Comedy*] – where nothing is possible), I have learned that high-hope people occasionally alter those seeming absolute failure situations so as to attain the impossible.' (p. 251)

> 'For a high-hope person pursuing a specific goal … entails the production of one plausible route, with a concomitant sense of confidence in this route … Beyond the primary route, the high-hope person also should be very good at producing plausible alternate routes … High-hope people describe themselves as being flexible thinkers who are facile at finding alternate routes, whereas low-hope persons report that they are less flexible and do not produce these additional routes.' (p. 251)

> 'This reminds me of the rainbow that frequently is used as a symbol of hope. A rainbow is a prism that sends shards of multicoloured light in various directions. It lifts our spirits and makes us think of what is possible. Hope is the same – a personal rainbow of the mind.' (p. 269)

Thus, the main message of this short concluding section is that we should stick to our hopes, or rather – what is more practical – we should always try and find an angle or aspect of the future that offers hope.

Sustaining hope is not merely a function of an optimistic temperament; as we argued in Section 1.5, it is our belief that spreading safety nets (e.g. building support groups) and providing plenty of models and practice runs can turn a threat into a challenge and give the participants hope that walking on water is not something people are born with, but rather a skill that anyone can develop if they learn to trust their vision and persevere in their practice.

Conclusion

We have come to the end of a long journey. Quite frankly, we did not know the exact details and destinations of our travels when we set out; all we had was a strong conviction that vision matters, and we were keen to unfold the practicalities of this conviction. Looking back, we have covered a lot of ground, from narratives to guided imagery and from avatars to creative tension. It might be therefore useful to take stock now and see how all the various details hang together and (we hope) make sense with respect to an emerging bigger picture. TOOLBOX 2.1 and TOOLBOX 8.1 offered a framework for motivating learners and teachers through vision, with each component elaborated on in a subsequent chapter of this book. In order to sum up what we have tried to say, here is a list of the main vision-building blocks we have described in these chapters:

	FOCUS ON THE STUDENTS
CREATING THE LANGUAGE LEARNER'S VISION (Chapter 2)	The logical first step in a visionary motivational programme is to help learners to create desired future selves, that is, construct visions of whom they could become as L2 users and what knowing an L2 could add to their lives.
Understanding students' current identity concerns and lived experiences	Future self-images are rooted in people's present reality; therefore, we need to understand the students' identity concerns, that is, who they are and what unique life experiences, dreams and worries they bring into the classroom.
Providing regular tasters of desired future states	The teacher's role is not to construct a specific future image for the students but to create opportunities that will allow them to 'taste', explore and try out various versions of their possible selves; we need to taste the future in order to desire it!
Applying guided imagery	Mental imagery is an effective performance enhancement technique with considerable motivating power, and it can be used as a tool for establishing new desired future selves.
Applying guided narratives	Personal/autobiographical narratives are the tools people use to deal with the complexity of the world around them and therefore narratives are a powerful means for crafting current and future self-images.
Ensuring ample exposure to role models	Role models are known to be highly effective in changing people's attitudes and outlook; a positive role model can raise the observers' hopes for the future and thus motivate them to pursue similar excellence.

STRENGTHENING THE VISION THROUGH IMAGERY ENHANCEMENT (Chapter 3)	The more intensive the imagery accompanying the vision, the more powerful the vision; therefore, we need to help students to see their desired language selves with more clarity and, consequently, with more urgency for action.
Training imagery skills	Methods of imagery enhancement have been successfully explored in several domains in the past, indicating that imagery skills can be consciously developed and utilised to strengthen the students' vision.
Building creative visual and narrative tasks into the teaching routine	Student vision can be bolstered by building creative visual and narrative activities into our teaching practice, utilising the rich collection of visual aids and story techniques available in language teaching methodology.
Encouraging students to keep learning journals	A learning journal is, in effect, an ongoing personal narrative in which students interact with the teaching materials, thereby shaping not only the instructional intake but also their own emerging academic and personal identities.
Harnessing the power of virtual worlds	The rapid development of virtual online environments opens up exciting new opportunities, because they allow mental images of future selves to be 'embodied' by digital realities, thereby making the images more vivid, elaborate and in some sense more 'real'.
Strengthening the whole group's vision	An effective way of strengthening the learners' individual vision is to generate and strengthen the collective vision of the whole learner group they belong to.
SUBSTANTIATING THE VISION BY MAKING IT PLAUSIBLE (Chapter 4)	Possible selves are only effective insomuch as learners perceive them as plausible; therefore, students need to anchor their ideal L2 self-images in a sense of realistic expectations.
Cultivating realistic beliefs about language learning	A real danger in vision-formation is constructing a 'story of self-deception' made up of projections of unrealistic desires; therefore, optimal future selves need to take into account realistic beliefs about the individual's own capabilities and the skills and strategies required for attaining the goal.
Creating channels for constructive reality self-checks	Constructive reality self-checks are crucial because they enable the wishful thinkers to face reality and the pessimists to understand that, with appropriate strategies, achieving success in an L2 is a realistic possibility.
Eliminating obstacles and barriers	In order to pre-empt the subversive role of real or imagined barriers, a visionary training programme must address the question of any possible obstacles head-on.
TRANSFORMING THE VISION INTO ACTION (Chapter 5)	'Vision without action is daydream': future self-guides are productive only if they are accompanied by a set of concrete action plans, that is, by a blueprint of concrete pathways that will lead to them.

Conclusion

Providing students with models of self-relevant roadmaps	Many learners can see their destination but not the path to it; therefore, exposing language learners to realistic models of roadmaps to their L2 selves is a critical step in enabling them to construct and execute their L2 visions.
Mapping out pathways to success through visualisation	While envisioning a positive outcome in one's future can instil a sense of general motivation in the individual, in order to translate this 'hype' into actual hard work, we need also to visualise the 'how' element.
Providing students with individual guidance	Offering students one-to-one time to discuss their action plans constitutes very effective support, and making these tutorials salient also gives purpose and closure to the students' previous preparation.
KEEPING THE VISION ALIVE (Chapter 6)	Everybody has several distinct possible selves that are stored in their memory and compete for attention in the person's limited 'working self-concept'; therefore, in order to keep our vision alive, we need to activate it regularly so that it does not get squeezed out by other life concerns.
Including regular reminders and 'priming stimuli' in the teaching content	One way of keeping the vision alive is to include regular prompts in the teaching content that are related to the desired goals.
Engaging learners' transportable identities	Students can experience (metaphorical) transportation to their future vision only when they are connected to their 'transportable identities' (i.e. their genuine, context-independent, real selves) rather than to artificial student roles/identities.
Helping to re-envisage 'broken' visions	Even the most treasured ideal self-images can become outdated, impossible or simply 'out of sync' as time goes on, resulting in wrong or broken visions that need to be revisited and re-imagined.
COUNTERBALANCING THE VISION BY CONSIDERING FAILURE (Chapter 7)	A classic principle in possible selves theory is that for maximum effectiveness as a motivational resource, a desired future self should be offset by a corresponding feared self.
Offering regular reminders of the negative consequences of not succeeding	For the negative counterbalancing function of the feared self to be effective in evoking the 'getting away' urge, it needs to be made and kept salient through reminders of the consequences of failure.
Foregrounding the ought-to self	The ought-to self is driven by an avoidance tendency, the wish to avoid undesirable outcomes such as disappointing people or receiving actual punishment; accordingly, one way of counterbalancing the vision is to highlight the ought-to L2 self.
Integrating images of feared selves into visualisations?	The jury is still out as to whether the powerful process of visualising failure can have such a negative effect on some learners' self-esteem that it should be seen as taking the 'counterbalancing' of the ideal self too far.

FOCUS ON THE TEACHERS	
(RE-)IGNITING THE FLAME OF TEACHER VISION (Chapter 8)	The primary condition for the motivational capacity of possible selves is that they have to exist; therefore igniting, or if necessary re-igniting, the flame of teacher vision is the single most important step in any motivational agenda for classroom practitioners.
Understanding who we are for insights into who we want to become	The seeds of any future teaching vision are contained in the teachers' past experiences; therefore, a vision-generating process needs to start with self-reflection on our gifts, past learning experiences and the influential encounters that originally brought us into teaching.
Engaging with the 'whys': values, moral purposes and teaching philosophies	An essential part of how we imagine ourselves as teachers rests on the answers to the following questions: Why do we want to become a teacher? What do we believe teaching and teachers are for? and Why and how do languages matter?
Generating images of ideal language teacher selves	It is the sensory experience of what can be that ultimately moves us to action; therefore, the more vivid, specific and coherent the images the teachers construct, the more likely they are to develop their practices in the desired direction.
Sparking creative tension	Real transformation occurs only when teachers become aware of a discrepancy between their vision and reality, thereby experiencing some 'creative tension'.
GUARDING THE FLAME OF TEACHER VISION (Chapter 9)	When the pressures from the teaching environment get too intense and the constraints too stifling, teacher vision can come under real threat and needs active protection.
Staying connected to the original vision in the face of detrimental ought-to self-images	Many teachers feel a growing pressure to live up to others' expectations rather than to live out their own dreams; resisting the ongoing challenge of the multitude of extrinsic self-images that try to squeeze out the ideal self-image from our working self-concept requires principled effort.
Building resilience through vision boosters and safety zones	Visualisation techniques and support groups can be used to assist teachers to develop resilience and to arm themselves against adversity.
Processing our fears and turning adversity into allies	A crucial step in helping teachers to guard the flame of their vision is to help them to process their fears and other adversities constructively by viewing them as useful signals and turning them into opportunities for development.
Sustaining hope	Where there is no hope, the vision perishes!

It is important to reiterate here the point we made at the beginning of Part II, namely that the set of motivational principles and facets that are included in the above tables should not be seen as components of a

Conclusion

linear, step-by-step programme that requires each building block to be fully implemented before moving on to the next. Rather, the best way to look at the principles for motivating through vision is to use these components as a flexible framework or as a user-friendly guide that can help teachers to make informed decisions about the tools that are at their disposal in specific situations.

You are the message!

While we were collecting materials for this book and preparing the manuscript, we could not help noticing that the tenor of the emerging text often deviated from what we would normally expect from a book on applied linguistics. Having thought about it, we believe that our proclivity for a lofty sentiment has been due to the fact that we were focusing on the highest-order motivational construct, vision, that freely transfers from one domain to another as it concerns some of the ultimate Wh- questions of human behaviour. In fact, this unique character of vision explains why we felt it necessary to complement the part on student vision with a part that focuses on teacher vision: while there are several practical techniques and procedures that can facilitate the generation of a constructive vision, ultimately the essence of vision cannot really be taught as such but only modelled. Hence our final thought for the day: *You are the message!*

Of course, this is not a new idea by any means, as variations of the 'you must be the change that you wish to see in the world' tenet (usually attributed to Mahatma Gandhi) have been around as a source of inspiration for several decades, and a similar notion is expressed by the 'practice what you preach' phrase. Indeed, it has been stated by many in various forms that whether we are aware of it or not, we are continuously enacting our various ideal and ought-to selves in the classroom, and our students are sensitive to this and respond to the implicit messages. As Hermanson (2009: 10–11) puts it, 'Whether you are presenting to a large audience or mentoring a youngster, what you are offering is deeper than your words or techniques. What you are offering is your Self.' This is why Tompkins (1990: 656) concludes that our classrooms function as some sort of an acid test for what we really stand for:

> I've come to realise that the classroom is a microcosm of the world; it is the chance we have to practice whatever ideals we may cherish. The kind of classroom situation one creates is the acid test of what it is one really stands for.

It follows from the above that there might be cases when the visions we enact with our behaviour may not be those that we explicitly articulate and espouse. In other words, the messages we send in the classroom may not necessarily be the ones we wish to convey, and the lack of harmony between what we practise and what we preach may reduce the impact that we make on the students. This is why Carl Rogers (1983) considered *congruence* – that is, the ability to behave according to our true self and to be real and authentic without hiding behind facades or roles – one of the three key prerequisites of the modern educator. Some of the activities in Part III offer guidelines on how to align ourselves more tightly with the images of classrooms we wish to emulate for our students – it is worth a try, because if we are successful, there is a good chance that our students will follow suit.

References

Allwright, D. and Hanks, J. (2009). *The developing language learner: An introduction to exploratory practice.* Basingstoke: Palgrave Macmillan.
Arnold, J. (1999). Visualization: Language learning with the mind's eye. In J. Arnold (ed.), *Affect in language learning* (pp. 260–78). Cambridge: Cambridge University Press.
Arnold, J., Puchta, H. and Rinvolucri, M. (2007). *Imagine that! Mental imagery in the EFL classroom.* Cambridge: Cambridge University Press & Helbling.
Bailey, K. M. (1996). The best laid plans: Teachers' in-class decisions to depart from their lesson plans. In K. M. Bailey and D. Nunan (eds.), *Voices from the language classroom* (pp. 15–40). Cambridge: Cambridge University Press.
Bailey, K. M., Bergthold, B., Braunstein, B., Jagodzinski Fleishman, N., Holbrook, M. P., Tuman, J., Waissbluth, X. and Zambo, L. (1996). The language learner's autobiography: Examining 'apprenticeship of observation'. In D. Freeman and J. Richards (eds.), *Teacher learning in language teaching* (pp. 11–29). Cambridge: Cambridge University Press.
Bandura, A. (1997). *Self-efficacy: The exercise of control.* New York: Freeman.
Barth, R. S. (1990). *Improving schools from within: Teachers, parents, and principals can make the difference.* San Francisco: Jossey-Bass Publishers.
Bass, B. M. and Riggio, R. E. (2006). *Transformational leadership* (2nd edn). Mahwah, NJ: Lawrence Erlbaum.
Berkovits, S. (2005). *Guided imagery: Successful techniques to improve school performance and self-esteem.* Duluth, MN: Whole Person Associates.
Blunt, R. (2001). Leaders and stories: Growing the next generation, conveying values, and shaping character. *The Public Manager*, 30(1): 458.
Bolman, L. G. and Deal, T. E. (2008). *Reframing organizations: Artistry, choice, and leadership.* San Francisco, CA: Jossey-Bass.
Borg, S. (2003). Teacher cognition in language teaching: A review of research on what language teachers think, know, believe, and do. *Language Teaching*, 36: 81–109.
Borrero, N. (2011). Entering teaching for and with love: Visions of pre-service urban teachers. *Journal of Urban Learning, Teaching, and Research*, 7: 18–26.
Boyatzis, R. E. and Akrivou, K. (2006). The ideal self as the driver of intentional change. *Journal of Management Development*, 25(7): 624–42.
Bruner, J. (1987). Life as narrative. *Social Research*, 54(1): 11–32.
Buckingham, J. E. (2009). Imaginary friends: Using guided imagery, line drawings and webquests to incorporate culture into the foreign language curriculum. *AYMAT Individual Thesis / SMAT IPP Collection, Paper 480.* Retrieved from http://digitalcollections.sit.edu/ipp_collection/480
Burns, A. (2010). *Doing action research in English language teaching.* New York: Routledge.

Cantor, N. (1990). From thought to behavior: 'Having' and 'doing' in the study of personality and cognition. *American Psychologist*, 45(6): 735–50.

Carver, C. C., Lawrence, J. W. and Scheier, M. F. (1999). Self-discrepancies and affect: Incorporating the role of feared selves. *Personality and Social Psychology Bulletin*, 25: 783–92.

Carver, C. S., Reynolds, S. L. and Scheier, M. F. (1994). The possible selves of optimists and pessimists. *Journal of Research in Personality*, 28: 133–41.

Casbon, C. H., Shagoury, R. and Smith, G. A. (2005). Rediscovering the call to teach: A new vision for professional and personal development. *Language Arts*, 82(5): 359–66.

Celce-Murcia, M., Brinton, D. M. and Snow, M. A. (eds.) (2013). *Teaching English as a second or foreign language* (4th edn). Boston, MA: National Geographic Learning / Cengage Learning.

Chan, L. H. (2012). The use of mental imagery in L2 motivation. Paper presented at the Annual Conference of the American Association for Applied Linguistics (AAAL), Boston, MA.

Churches, R. and Terry, R. (2007). *NLP for teachers: How to be a highly effective teacher*. Carmarthen: Crown House.

Clark, J. M. and Paivio, A. (1991). Dual coding theory and education. *Educational Psychology Review*, 3(3): 149–210.

Clark, M. C. and Rossiter, M. (2008). Narrative learning in adulthood. *New Directions for Adult and Continuing Education*, 2008(119): 61–70.

Cohen, A. D. and Macaro, E. (eds.) (2007). *Language learner strategies: Thirty years of research and practice*. Oxford: Oxford University Press.

Collier-Meek, M. A., Fallon, L. M., Johnson, A. H., Sanetti, L. M. H. and Delcampo, M. A. (2012). Constructing self-modeling videos: Procedures and technology. *Psychology in Schools*, 49(1): 3–14.

Conway, M. A. and Pleydell-Pearce, C. W. (2000). The construction of autobiographical memories in the self-memory system. *Psychological Review*, 107(2): 261–88.

Cox, R. H. (2012). *Sport psychology: Concepts and applications* (7th edn). New York: McGraw-Hill.

Crookes, G. (2009). *Values, philosophies, and beliefs in TESOL: Making a statement*. Cambridge: Cambridge University Press.

Csikszentmihalyi, M. (1988). The flow experience and its significance for human psychology. In M. Csikszentmihalyi and I. S. Csikszentmihalyi (eds.), *Optimal experience: Psychological studies of flow in consciousness* (pp. 15–35). Cambridge: Cambridge University Press.

Day, R. and Bamford, J. (2002). Top ten principles for teaching extensive reading. *Reading in a Foreign Language*, 14(2): 136–41. Retrieved from http://nflrc.hawaii.edu/rfl/october2002/day/day.html

Dewey, J. (1897). My pedagogic creed. *School Journal*, 54(3): 77–80.

Do, T. M. (2012). Re-imagining ideal L2 selves in the study abroad context: A study of Vietnamese postgraduate students in the UK. Unpublished MA module assignment, University of Birmingham.

References

Dörnyei, Z. (1994). Motivation and motivating in the foreign language classroom. *Modern Language Journal*, 78: 273–84.

Dörnyei, Z. (2000). Motivation in action: Towards a process-oriented conceptualisation of student motivation. *British Journal of Educational Psychology*, 70: 519–38.

Dörnyei, Z. (2001). *Motivational strategies in the language classroom*. Cambridge: Cambridge University Press.

Dörnyei, Z. (2005). *The psychology of the language learner: Individual differences in second language acquisition*. Mahwah, NJ: Lawrence Erlbaum.

Dörnyei, Z. (2009). The L2 Motivational Self System. In Z. Dörnyei and E. Ushioda (eds.), *Motivation, language identity and the L2 self* (pp. 9–42). Bristol: Multilingual Matters.

Dörnyei, Z. (2014). Motivation in second language learning. In M. Celce-Murcia, D. M. Brinton and M. A. Snow (eds.), *Teaching English as a second or foreign language* (4th edn, pp. 518–31). Boston, MA: National Geographic Learning / Cengage Learning.

Dörnyei, Z. and Chan, L. (2013). Motivation and vision: An analysis of future L2 self-images, sensory styles, and imagery capacity across two target languages. *Language Learning*, 63(3): 437–62.

Dörnyei, Z. and Kormos, J. (2000). The role of individual and social variables in oral task performance. *Language Teaching Research*, 4: 275–300.

Dörnyei, Z. and Murphey, T. (2003). *Group dynamics in the language classroom*. Cambridge: Cambridge University Press.

Dörnyei, Z. and Ushioda, E. (2011). *Teaching and researching motivation* (2nd edn). Harlow: Longman.

Dowrick, P. W. (2012). Self modeling: Expanding the theories of learning. *Psychology in Schools*, 49(1): 30–41.

Dunkel, C., Kelts, D. and Coon, B. (2006). Possible selves as mechanisms of change in therapy. In C. Dunkel and J. Kerpelman (eds.), *Possible selves: Theory, research and applications* (pp. 187–204). New York: Nova Science.

Edge, J. (1992). *Cooperative development: Professional self-development through cooperation with colleagues*. Harlow: Longman.

Edwards, G. (2009). *Living magically: A new vision of reality*. London: Piatkus.

Erikson, M. G. (2007). The meaning of the future: Toward a more specific definition of possible selves. *Review of General Psychology*, 11(4): 348–58.

Feryok, A. and Pryde, M. (2012). Images as orienting activity: Using theory to inform classroom practices. *Teachers and Teaching: theory and practice*, 18(4): 441–54.

Fettes, M. (2005). Imaginative transformation in teacher education. *Teaching Education*, 16(1): 3–11.

Fezler, W. (1989). *Creative imagery: How to visualize in all five senses*. New York: Simon & Schuster.

Finke, R. (1990). *Creative imagery: Discoveries and inventions in visualization*. Hillsdale, NJ: Lawrence Erlbaum.

Fletcher, S. (2000). A role for imagery in mentoring. *Career Development International*, 5(4): 235–43.

Fox, J. and Bailenson, J. N. (2009). Virtual self-modeling: The effects of vicarious reinforcement and identification on exercise behaviors. *Media Psychology*, 12: 1–25.

The Freedom Writers and Gruwell, E. (1999). *The Freedom Writers diary: How a teacher and 150 teens used writing to change themselves and the world around them*. New York: Broadway Books.

Fugitt, E. D. (1983). *'He hit me back first!' Creative visualization activities for parenting and teaching*. Rolling Hills Estates, CA: Jalmar Press.

Fukada, Y., Fukuda, T., Falout, J. and Murphey, T. (2011). Increasing motivation with possible selves. In A. Stewart (ed.), *JALT 2010 Conference Proceedings* (pp. 337–49). Tokyo: JALT.

Gallucci, S. (2011). Language learning, identities and emotions during the year abroad: Case studies of British Erasmus students in Italy. Unpublished PhD thesis, University of Birmingham.

Gardner, R. C. (1985). *Social psychology and second language learning: The role of attitudes and motivation*. London: Edward Arnold.

Gardner, R. C. (2001). Integrative motivation and second language acquisition. In Z. Dörnyei and R. Schmidt (eds.), *Motivation and second language acquisition* (pp. 1–20). Honolulu, HI: University of Hawaii Press.

Gardner, R. C. and MacIntyre, P. D. (1993). On the measurement of affective variables in second language learning. *Language Learning*, 43: 157–94.

Gawain, S. (2002). *Creative visualization: Using the power of your imagination to create what you want in your life*. Novato, CA: Nataraj Publishing.

Gerngross, G., Puchta, H. and Thornbury, S. (2006). *Teaching grammar creatively*. Crawley: Helbling Languages.

Gladwell, M. (2008). *Outliers: The story of success*. London: Penguin Books.

Goldstein, B. (2008). *Working with images: A resource book for the language classroom*. Cambridge: Cambridge University Press.

Gollwitzer, P. M. (1999). Implementation intentions: Strong effects of simple plans. *American Psychologist*, 54(7): 493–503.

Golombek, P. R. (2009). Personal practical knowledge in L2 teacher education. In A. Burns and J. C. Richards (eds.), *The Cambridge guide to second language teacher education* (pp. 155–62). Cambridge: Cambridge University Press.

Golombek, P. R. and Johnson, K. E. (2004). Narrative inquiry as a mediational space: Examining emotional and cognitive dissonance in second-language teachers' development. *Teachers and Teaching: Theory and Practice*, 10(3): 307–27.

Goodman, J. (1988). Constructing a practical philosophy of teaching: A study of pre-service teachers' professional perspectives. *Teaching and Teacher Education*, 4(2): 121–37.

Gould, D., Damarjian, N. and Greenleaf, C. (2002). Imagery training for peak performance. In J. L. Van Raalte and B. W. Brewer (eds.), *Exploring sport and exercise psychology* (2nd edn, pp. 49–74). Washington, DC: American Psychological Association.

Green, M. C. and Brock, T. C. (2000). The role of transportation in the persuasiveness of public narratives. *Journal of Personality and Social Psychology*, **79**(5): 701–21.

Green, M. C. and Donahue, J. K. (2009). Simulated worlds: Transportation into narratives. In K. D. Markman, W. M. P. Klein and J. A. Suhr (eds.), *Handbook of imagination and mental simulation* (pp. 241–54). New York: Psychology Press.

Griffiths, C. (ed.) (2008). *Lessons from good language learners*. Cambridge: Cambridge University Press.

Gruwell, E. (2007). *Teach with your heart: Lessons I learned from the Freedom Writers*. New York: Broadway Books.

Gruwell, E. and The Freedom Writers Foundation. (2007). *The Freedom Writers diary: Teacher's guide*. New York: Broadway Books.

Hadfield, J. (2012, September). A second self. *English Teaching professional*, **82**: 46–7.

Hadfield, J. and Dörnyei, Z. (2013). *Motivation and the ideal self*. London: Longman.

Hadfield, J. and Hadfield, C. (2008). *Introduction to teaching English*. Oxford: Oxford University Press.

Hale, B. (2005). *Imagery training*. Leeds: National Coaching Foundation.

Hall, C. R., Mack, D. E., Paivio, A. and Hausenblas, H. A. (1998). Imagery use by athletes: Development of the sport imagery questionnaire. *International Journal of Sport Psychology*, **29**: 73–89.

Hall, E., Hall, C., Stradling, P. and Young, D. (2006). *Guided imagery: Creative interventions in counselling and psychotherapy*. London: Sage.

Hammerness, K. (2006). *Seeing through teachers' eyes: Professional ideals and classroom practices*. New York: Teachers College Press.

Henry, A. (2011). Examining the impact of L2 English on L3 selves: A case study. *International Journal of Multilingualism*, **8**(3): 235–55.

Hermanson, K. (2009). *Getting messy: A guide to taking risks and opening the imagination for teachers, trainers, coaches and mentors*. San Rafael, CA: Rawberry Books.

Herndon, L. D. (2002). Putting theory into practice: Letting my students learn to read. In K. E. Johnson and P. R. Golombek (eds.), *Teachers' narrative inquiry as professional development* (pp. 35–51). New York: Cambridge University Press.

Hershfield, H. E., Goldstein, D. G., Sharpe, W. F., Fox, J., Yeykelis, L., Carstensen, L. L. et al. (2011). Increasing saving behavior through age-progressed renderings of the future self. *Journal of Marketing Research*, **48**: 823–37.

Higgins, E. T. (1987). Self-discrepancy: A theory relating self and affect. *Psychological Review*, **94**: 319–40.

Higgins, E. T. (1998). Promotion and prevention: Regulatory focus as a motivational principle. *Advances in Experimental Social Psychology*, **30**: 1–46.

Higgins, E. T., Roney, C. J. R., Crowe, E. and Hymes, C. (1994). Ideal versus ought predilections for approach and avoidance: Distinct self-regulatory systems. *Journal of Personality and Social Psychology*, 66(2): 276–86.

Hiver, P. V. (2013). The interplay of possible language teacher selves in professional development choices. *Language Teaching Research*, 17(2): 210–27.

Hock, M. F., Deshler, D. D. and Schumaker, J. B. (2006). Enhancing student motivation through the pursuit of possible selves. In C. Dunkel and J. Kerpelman (eds.), *Possible selves: Theory, research and application* (pp. 205–21). New York: Nova Science.

Hoffman, E. (1989). *Lost in translation: A life in a new language*. London: Vintage.

Horn, I. S., Nolen, S. B., Ward, C. and Campbell, S. S. (2008). Developing practices in multiple worlds: The role of identity in learning to teach. *Teacher Education Quarterly*, 35(3): 61–72.

Horowitz, M. J. (1983). *Image formation and psychotherapy*. Northvale, NJ: Jason Aronson.

Horwitz, E. K. (1988). The beliefs about language learning of beginning university foreign language students. *Modern Language Journal*, 72: 283–94.

Jagla, V. M. (1994). *Teachers' everyday use of imagination and intuition: In pursuit of the elusive image*. Albany, NY: State University of New York Press.

Johnson, K. E. (1994). The emerging beliefs and instructional practices of preservice English as a second language teachers. *Teaching and Teacher Education*, 10(4): 439–52.

Johnson, K. E. (1999). *Understanding language teaching: Reasoning in action*. Boston: Heinle & Heinle.

Johnson, K. E. and Golombek, P. R. (eds.) (2002). *Teachers' narrative inquiry as professional development*. New York: Cambridge University Press.

Johnston, B. (2003). *Values in English language teaching*. Mahwah, NJ: Lawrence Erlbaum.

Jones, K. (2012). Visualising success: An imagery intervention programme to increase two students' confidence and motivation in a foreign language. Unpublished MA dissertation, School of English, University of Nottingham.

Kaplan, A. (1993). *French lessons: A memoir*. Chicago: University of Chicago Press.

Kaushik, R. M., Kaushik, R., Mahajan, S. K. and Rajesh, V. (2006). Effects of mental relaxation and slow breathing in essential hypertension. *Complementary Therapies in Medicine*, 14(2): 120–6.

Keddie, J. (2009). *Images*. Oxford: Oxford University Press.

Kennedy, M. M. (2006). Knowledge and vision in teaching. *Journal of Teacher Education*, 57(3): 205–11.

Kenyon, G. M. and Randall, W. L. (1997). *Restorying our lives: Personal growth through autobiographical reflection*. Westport, CT: Praeger.

Kessler, R. (2002). Adversity as ally. In S. M. Intrator (ed.), *Stories of the courage to teach: Honoring the teacher's heart* (pp. 141–51). San Francisco, CA: Jossey-Bass.

References

Klinger, E. (2009). Daydreaming and fantasizing: Thought flow and motivation. In K. D. Markman, W. M. P. Klein and J. A. Suhr (eds.), *Handbook of imagination and mental simulation* (pp. 225–39). New York: Psychology Press.
Knäuper, B., Roseman, M., Johnson, P. J. and Krantz, L. H. (2009). Using mental imagery to enhance the effectiveness of implementation intentions. *Current Psychology*, 28: 181–6.
Kormos, J., Kiddle, T. and Csizér, K. (2011). Systems of goals, attitudes, and self-related beliefs in second-language-learning motivation. *Applied Linguistics*, 32(5): 495–516.
Kouzes, J. M. and Posner, B. Z. (2009). To lead, create a shared vision. *Harvard Business Review*, January: 20–1.
Krystowiak, D. (2012). Massively Multiplayer Online Games as a support tool for learning a second language. Unpublished MA module assignment. University of Birmingham.
Kubanyiova, M. (2006). Developing a motivational teaching practice in EFL teachers in Slovakia: Challenges of promoting teacher change in EFL contexts. *TESL-EJ*. Special Issue: *Language Education Research in International Contexts*, 10(2): 1–17. Retrieved from http://www.tesl-ej.org/ej38/a5.pdf
Kubanyiova, M. (2009). Possible selves in language teacher development. In Z. Dörnyei and E. Ushioda (eds.), *Motivation, language identity and the L2 self* (pp. 314–32). Bristol: Multilingual Matters.
Kubanyiova, M. (2012). *Teacher development in action: Understanding language teachers' conceptual change*. Basingstoke: Palgrave Macmillan.
Larsen-Freeman, D. (2000a). An attitude of inquiry: TESOL as a science. *Journal of the Imagination in Language Learning*, 5. Retrieved 6 April 2004, from http://www.njcu.edu/cill/vol5/larsen-freeman.html
Larsen-Freeman, D. (2000b). *Techniques and principles in language teaching* (2nd edn). Oxford: Oxford University Press.
Leary, M. R. (2007). Motivational and emotional aspects of the self. *Annual Review of Psychology*, 58: 317–44.
Lee, J. J. and Hoadley, C. M. (2007). Leveraging identity to make learning fun: Possible selves and experiential learning in Massively Multiplayer Online Games (MMOGs). *Innovate*, 3(6). Retrieved 30 April 2013, from http://www.innovateonline.info/pdf/vol3_issue6/Leveraging_Identity_to_Make_Learning_Fun-__Possible_Selves_and_Experiential_Learning_in_Massively_Multiplayer_Online_Games_(MMOGs).pdf
Leuner, H., Horn, G. and Klessmann, E. (1983). *Guided affective imagery with children and adolescents*. New York: Plenum.
Levin, I. M. (2000). Vision revisited: Telling the story of the future. *Journal of Applied Behavioral Science*, 36(1): 91–107.
Lewin, K. (1952). *Field theory in social science: Selected theoretical papers by Kurt Lewin*. London: Tavistock.
Libby, L. K. and Eibach, R. P. (2009). Seeing the links among the personal past, present, and future: How imagery perspective in mental simulation functions in defining the temporally extended self. In K. D. Markman,

169

W. M. P. Klein and J. A. Suhr (eds.), *Handbook of imagination and mental simulation* (pp. 359–72). New York: Psychology Press.

Libby, L. K. and Eibach, R. P. (2011). Self-enhancement or self-coherence? Why people shift visual perspective in mental images of the personal past and future. *Personality and Social Psychology Bulletin*, 37(5): 714–26.

Libby, L. K., Shaeffer, E. M., Eibach, R. P. and Slemmer, J. A. (2007). Picture yourself at the polls: Visual perspective in mental imagery affects self-perception and behavior. *Psychological Science*, 18: 199–203.

Lightbown, P. M. and Spada, N. (2013). *How languages are learned* (4th edn). Oxford: Oxford University Press.

Lockwood, P. and Kunda, Z. (1997). Superstars and me: Predicting the impact of role models on the self. *Journal of Personality and Social Psychology*, 73(1): 91–103.

Lortie, D. (1975). *Schoolteacher: A sociological study*. Chicago: University of Chicago Press.

MacIntyre, P. D. and Gregersen, T. (2012). Emotions that facilitate language learning: The positive-broadening power of the imagination. *Studies in Second Language Learning and Teaching*, 2(2): 193–213.

MacIntyre, T. and Moran, A. P. (2007). A qualitative investigation of meta-imagery processes and imagery direction among elite athletes. *Journal of Imagery Research in Sport and Physical Activity*, 2(1): 1–20.

Magid, M. (2011). A validation and application of the L2 Motivational Self System among Chinese learners of English. Unpublished PhD thesis. University of Nottingham.

Magid, M. (2012). The L2 Motivational Self System from a Chinese perspective: A mixed methods study. *Journal of Applied Linguistics*, 6(1): 69–90.

Magid, M. and Chan, L. H. (2012). Motivating English learners by helping them visualise their Ideal L2 Self: Lessons from two motivational programmes. *Innovation in Language Learning and Teaching*, 6(2): 113–25.

Maley, A., Duff, A. and Grellet, F. (1981). *The mind's eye: Using pictures creatively in language learning*. Cambridge: Cambridge University Press.

Markus, H. and Nurius, P. (1986). Possible selves. *American Psychologist*, 41: 954–69.

Markus, H. and Nurius, P. (1987). Possible selves: The interface between motivation and the self-concept. In K. Yardley and T. Honess (eds.), *Self and identity: Psychosocial perspectives* (pp. 157–72). Chichester: John Wiley & Sons.

Markus, H. and Ruvolo, A. (1989). Possible selves: Personalized representations of goals. In L. A. Pervin (ed.), *Goal concepts in personality and social psychology* (pp. 211–41). Hillsdale, NJ: Lawrence Erlbaum.

Markus, H. R. (2006). Foreword. In C. Dunkel and J. Kerpelman (eds.), *Possible selves: Theory, research and applications* (pp. xi–xiv). New York: Nova Science.

McAdams, D. P. (1993). *The stories we live by: Personal myths and the making of the self*. New York: Guilford Press.

References

McAdams, D. P. (2001). The psychology of life stories. *Journal of General Psychology*, 5(2): 100–22.

McAdams, D. P. and Pals, J. L. (2006). A new Big Five: Fundamental principles for an integrative science of personality. *American Psychologist*, 61(3): 204–17.

McElhone, D., Hebhard, H., Scot, R. and Connie, J. (2009). The role of vision in trajectories of literacy practice among new teachers. *Studying Teacher Education*, 5(2): 147–58.

McGonigal, J. (2011). *Reality is broken*. London: Jonathan Cape.

Meek, R. (2007). The parenting possible selves of young fathers in prison. *Psychology Crime and Law*, 13: 371–82.

Mendelsohn, D. J. (ed.) (1999). *Expanding our vision*. Toronto: Oxford University Press.

Mercer, S. (2011). *Towards an understanding of language learner self-concept*. Dordrecht: Springer.

Morgan, J. and Rinvolucri, M. (1983). *Once upon a time: Stories in the language classroom*. Cambridge: Cambridge University Press.

Morosini, P. (2010). *Seven keys to imagination: Creating the future by imagining the unthinkable – and delivering it*. London: Marshall Cavendish.

Morris, T., Spittle, M. and Watt, A. P. (2005). *Imagery in sport*. Champaign, IL: Human Kinetics.

Moulton, S. T. and Kosslyn, S. M. (2009). Imagining predictions: Mental imagery as mental emulation. *Philosophical Transactions of the Royal Society B*, 364: 1273–80.

Murdock, M. (1987). *Spinning inward: Using guided imagery with children for learning, creativity and relaxation*. Boston, MA: Shambhala.

Murphey, T. and Arao, H. (2001). Changing reported beliefs through near peer role modeling. *TESL-EJ*, 5(3): 1–15.

Murray, G., Gao, X. and Lamb, T. (eds.) (2011). *Identity, motivation and autonomy in language learning*. Bristol: Multilingual Matters.

Noels, K. A. (2003). Learning Spanish as a second language: Learners' orientations and perceptions of their teachers' communication style. In Z. Dörnyei (ed.), *Attitudes, orientations, and motivations in language learning* (pp. 97–136). Oxford: Blackwell.

Noels, K. A. (2009). The internalisation of language learning into the self and social identity. In Z. Dörnyei and E. Ushioda (eds.), *Motivation, language identity and the L2 self* (pp. 295–313). Bristol: Multilingual Matters.

Norman, C. C. and Aron, A. (2003). Aspects of possible self that predict motivation to achieve or avoid it. *Journal of Experimental Social Psychology*, 39: 500–7.

Norton, B. (2000). *Identity and language learning: Social processes and educational practice*. Harlow: Pearson.

Norton, B. (2001). Non-participation, imagined communities and the language classroom. In M. P. Breen (ed.), *Learner contributions to language learning: New directions in research* (pp. 159–71). Harlow: Longman.

Norton, B. and Toohey, K. (2001). Changing perspectives on good language learners. *TESOL Quarterly*, 35(2): 307–22.

Norton, J. D. (2013). Chasing the light: Einstein's most famous thought experiment. In M. Frappier, L. Meynell and J. R. Brown (eds.), *Thought experiments in science, philosophy, and the arts* (pp. 123–40). London: Routledge.

Ortberg, J. (2001). *If you want to walk on water, you've got to get out of the boat*. Grand Rapids, MI: Zondervan.

Oyserman, D. (2009). Identity-based motivation: Implications for action-readiness, procedural-readiness, and consumer behavior. *Journal of Consumer Psychology*, 19: 250–60.

Oyserman, D. and James, L. (2009). Possible selves: From content to process. In K. Markman, W. M. P. Klein and J. A. Suhr (eds.), *The handbook of imagination and mental simulation* (pp. 373–94). New York: Psychology Press.

Oyserman, D. and Markus, H. R. (1990). Possible selves and delinquency. *Journal of Personality and Social Psychology*, 59: 112–25.

Oyserman, D., Bybee, D. and Terry, K. (2006). Possible selves and academic outcomes: How and when possible selves impel action. *Journal of Personality and Social Psychology*, 91(1): 188–204.

Oyserman, D., Johnson, E. and James, L. (2011). Seeing the destination but not the path: Effects of socioeconomic disadvantage on school-focused possible self content and linked behavioral strategies. *Self and Identity*, 10(4): 474–92.

Oyserman, D., Terry, K. and Bybee, D. (2002). A possible selves intervention to enhance school involvement. *Journal of Adolescence*, 25: 313–26.

Paivio, A. (1985). Cognitive and motivational functions on imagery in human performance. *Canadian Journal of Applied Sport Sciences*, 10: 22S–28S.

Paivio, A. (1986). *Mental representations: A dual coding approach*. New York: Oxford University Press.

Palmer, A. (1999). Joseph Campbell: An inspiration and role model for language teachers. In D. J. Mendelsohn (ed.), *Expanding our vision: Insights for language teachers* (pp. 5–16). Toronto: Oxford University Press.

Palmer, P. J. (2007). *The courage to teach: Exploring the inner landscape of a teacher's life* (10th edn). San Francisco, CA: Jossey-Bass.

Papi, M. and Abdollahzadeh, E. (2012). Teacher motivational practice, student motivation, and possible L2 selves: An examination in the Iranian EFL context. *Language Learning*, 62(2): 571–94.

Pennington, M. C. (1995). Work satisfaction, motivation and commitment in teaching English as a second language. Unpublished ms., University of Luton, UK (ERIC Document Reproduction Service No. Ed 404850).

Peterson, K. D. and Deal, T. E. (1998). How leaders influence the culture of schools. *Educational Leadership*, 56(1): 28–30.

Petit, P. (2002). *To reach the clouds: My high-wire walk between the Twin Towers*. London: Faber and Faber.

References

Pizzolato, J. E. (2006). Achieving college student possible selves: Navigating the space between commitment and achievement of long-term identity goals. *Cultural Diversity and Ethnic Minority Psychology*, 12(1): 57–69.

Polkinghorne, D. E. (1988). *Narrative knowing and the human sciences.* Albany, NY: State University of New York Press.

Reisberg, D. and Heuer, F. (2005). Visuospatial images. In P. Shah and A. Miyake (eds.), *The Cambridge handbook of visuospatial thinking* (pp. 35–80). Cambridge: Cambridge University Press.

Richards, K. (2006). 'Being the teacher': Identity and classroom conversation. *Applied Linguistics*, 27(1): 51–77.

Rogers, C. R. (1983). *Freedom to learn for the 80s.* Columbus, OH: Merrill.

Ruvolo, A. P. and Markus, H. R. (1992). Possible selves and performance: The power of self-relevant imagery. *Social Cognition*, 10(1): 95–124.

Rymal, A. M. and Ste-Marie, D. M. (2009). Does self-modeling affect imagery ability or vividness? *Journal of Imagery Research in Sport and Physical Activity*, 4(1): 1–14.

Sampson, R. (2012). The language-learning self, self-enhancement activities, and self perceptual change. *Language Teaching Research*, 16(3): 317–35.

Schön, D. A. (1983). *The reflective practitioner: How professionals think in action.* New York: Basic Books.

Senge, P. M. (1990/2006). *The fifth discipline.* London: Random House.

Senior, R. M. (2006). *The experience of language teaching.* Cambridge: Cambridge University Press.

Sharkey, J. and Johnson, K. E. (eds.) (2003). *The TESOL Quarterly dialogues: Rethinking issues of language, culture, and power.* Alexandria, VA: TESOL.

Sheldon, K. M. and Lyubomirsky, S. (2006). How to increase and sustain positive emotion: The effects of expressing gratitude and visualizing best possible selves. *Journal of Positive Psychology*, 1(2): 73–82.

Simons, J. (October, 1996). Competition plans and routines. Paper presented at the National Coaching Congress of the Australian Track and Field Coaches Association.

Sinek, S. (2009). *Start with why: How great leaders inspire everyone to take action.* New York: Penguin.

Singer, J. L. (2006). *Imagery in psychotherapy.* Washington, DC: American Psychological Association.

Snyder, C. R. (2002). Hope theory: Rainbows in the mind. *Psychological Inquiry*, 13(4): 249–75.

Souter, T. (2006). *Anything I can do, you can do better: How to unlock your creative dreams and change your lives.* London: Vermilion.

Spiro, J. (2007). *Storybuilding.* Oxford: Oxford University Press.

Stevick, E. W. (1986). *Images and options in the language classroom.* Cambridge: Cambridge University Press.

Stevick, E. W. (1990). *Humanism in language teaching: A critical perspective.* Oxford: Oxford University Press.

Stopa, L. (2009). How to use imagery in cognitive-behavioural therapy. In L. Stopa (ed.), *Imagery and the threatened self: Perspectives*

on mental imagery and the self in cognitive therapy (pp. 65–93). London: Routledge.
Stuart, C. and Thurlow, D. (2000). Making it their own: Preservice teachers' experiences, beliefs, and classroom practices. *Journal of Teacher Education*, 51(2): 113–21.
Suits, B. (1978). *The grasshopper: Games, life, and Utopia*. Toronto: University of Toronto Press.
Szpunar, K. K. and McDermott, K. B. (2009). Episodic future thought: Remembering the past to imagine the future. In K. D. Markman, W. M. P. Klein and J. A. Suhr (eds.), *Handbook of imagination and mental simulation* (pp. 119–29). New York: Psychology Press.
Taylor, S. E. and Pham, L. B. (1996). Mental simulation, motivation, and action. In P. Gollwitzer (ed.), *The psychology of action* (pp. 219–35). New York: Guildford Press.
Taylor, S. E., Pham, L. B., Rivkin, I. D. and Armor, D. A. (1998). Harnessing the imagination: Mental simulation, self-regulation, and coping. *American Psychologist*, 53(4): 429–39.
Thornbury, S. (1999). Lesson art and design. *ELT Journal*, 53(1): 4–11.
Thorne, S. L. (2008). Transcultural communication in open internet environments and massively multiplayer online games. In S. Magnan (ed.), *Mediating discourse online* (pp. 305–27). Amsterdam: Benjamins.
Thorne, S. L. and Black, R. W. (2007). Language and literacy development in computer-mediated contexts and communities. *Annual Review of Applied Linguistics*, 27: 133–60.
Thorne, S. L., Black, R. W. and Sykes, J. M. (2009). Second language use, socialization, and learning in internet interest communities and online gaming. *The Modern Language Journal*, 93(Focus issue), 802–21.
Tompkins, J. (1990). Pedagogy of the distressed. *College English*, 52(6): 653–60.
Tompkins, J. (1996). *A life in school: What the teacher learned*. New York: Basic Books.
Tudor, I. (1996). *Learner-centredness as language education*. Cambridge: Cambridge University Press.
Ushioda, E. (2001). Language learning at university: Exploring the role of motivational thinking. In Z. Dörnyei and R. Schmidt (eds.), *Motivation and second language acquisition* (pp. 91–124). Honolulu, HI: University of Hawaii Press.
Ushioda, E. (2008). Motivation and good language learners. In C. Griffiths (ed.), *Lessons from good language learners* (pp. 19–34). Cambridge: Cambridge University Press.
Ushioda, E. (2011). Motivating learners to speak as themselves. In G. Murray, X. Gao and M. Lamb (eds.), *Identity, motivation and autonomy in language learning* (pp. 14–33). Bristol: Multilingual Matters.
van der Helm, R. (2009). The vision phenomenon: Towards a theoretical underpinning of visions of the future and the process of envisioning. *Futures*, 41: 96–104.

References

van Lier, L. (2007). Action-based teaching, autonomy and identity. *Innovation in Language Learning and Teaching*, 1(1): 46–65.
Vasquez, N. A. and Buehler, R. (2007). Seeing future success: Does imagery perspective influence achievement motivation? *Personality and Social Psychology Bulletin*, 33, 1392–405.
Wajnryb, R. (2003). *Stories: Narrative activities for the language classroom.* Cambridge: Cambridge University Press.
Wang, C. and Burris, M. A. (1997). Photovoice: Concept, methodology, and use for participatory needs assessment. *Health Education & Behavior*, 24(3): 369–87.
Watt, H. M. G. and Richardson, P. W. (2008). Motivations, perceptions, and aspirations concerning teaching as a career for different types of beginning teachers. *Learning and Instruction*, 18: 408–28.
Weinberg, R. (2008). Does imagery work? Effects on performance and mental skills. *Journal of Imagery Research in Sport and Physical Activity*, 3(1): 1–21.
Wenger, W. and Poe, R. (1996). *The Einstein factor.* New York: Three Rivers Press.
Whitty, M. (2002). Possible selves: Exploring the utility of a narrative approach. *Identity: An International Journal of Theory and Research*, 2(3): 213–30.
Wong, M. S. and Canagarajah, S. (eds.) (2009). *Christian and critical English language educators in dialogue: Pedagogical and ethical dilemmas.* New York: Routledge.
Wright, A. (1989). *Pictures for language learning.* Cambridge: Cambridge University Press.
Wright, A. (2009). *Storytelling with children* (2nd edn). Oxford: Oxford University Press.
Wright, A. and Hill, D. A. (2008). *Writing stories: Developing language skills through story making.* Crawley: Helbling Languages.
Xin, B. (2012). Generating and enhancing vision for language learning: A successful motivated L2 learner's experience. Unpublished MA module assignment, School of English, University of Nottingham.
Zander, R. S. and Zander, B. (2000). *The art of possibility: Transforming professional and personal life.* Boston, MA: Harvard Business Review Press.
Zentner, M. and Renaud, O. (2007). Origins of adolescents' ideal self: An intergenerational perspective. *Journal of Personality and Social Psychology*, 92(3): 557–74.
Zhen, Y. (in preparation). Chinese university students' willingness to communicate in L2: A complexity theory perspective. Unpublished PhD thesis, University of Birmingham.
Zheng, D., Young, M. F., Wagner, M. M. and Brewer, R. A. (2009). Negotiation for action: English language learning in game-based virtual worlds. *Modern Language Journal*, 93(4): 489–511.
Zimmerman, D. (1998). Identity, context, interaction. In C. Antaki and S. Widdicombe (eds.), *Identities in talk* (pp. 87–106). London: Sage.

Index

10,000-hour rule 91

action
  relationship to self characteristics 11
  transforming the vision into 99–106
action-based teaching 35–6
action plans 99–101
  individual guidance for students 105–6
  mapping out pathways through visualisation 103–5
  relevant roadmaps for learners 101–3
action research 142–3
agency, and self-image construction 35–6
Alcott, Louisa May 145
ambitions subsumed by the vision 100
American Dream 15–16
anxiety, 'immunising' against 70–1
Apple 131
Arnold, Jane 17
athletes
  as role models 63
  imagery training 66, 67
  see also sport psychology
attributions 21
authentic L2 experience 109
autobiographical narratives 57–9
  about the future 59–60
  of students 43
Avatar English 80
avatars and virtual environments (VEs) 79–80
awareness raising 34

back-to-the-future language learning history 73
Bandura, Albert 63
barriers to realising a possible self 97–8
Barth, Ronald 123
Beethoven, Ludwig van 15
Best Possible Selves writing project 37–8
'bliss', finding your 126–7
body language of teachers 147–8
brainstorming 100
breathing exercises 54–5, 67
'broken' visions, helping to re-envisage 112–13
Bruner, Jerome 57, 73

Campbell, Joseph 126, 129
career meetings 106
career structure for teachers 145
celebrity culture, influence on possible selves 35
celebrity role models 63
Chan, Letty 38, 48–9, 50, 53–4
children, use of imagery techniques 66–7
China, importance of face 117
classroom activities
  creative visual and narrative tasks 72–7
  cultivating realistic learner beliefs 92
  engaging learners' transportable identities 109–12
  personalising the learning tasks 110–12
  preparing a motivational speech 88–9
  priming stimuli 107–9
  vision-reminders 107
  warm-up activities 107–8
classroom-based social research 42–5
classroom management issues 145
classroom newsletter 64
classroom practices
  building in creative visual and narrative tasks 72–7
  collecting student feedback 141–2
  differences between teachers 22–4, 26–8
  lack of intellectual challenge for teachers 145
  motivating power of role models 64
  repetitive content and routinised practices 145
  transformation by teachers 3
cognitive-situated period (1990s) 21
cognitive theory, dual coding theory 16–17
collaborative research by language learners 42–5
collective vision *see* group vision
Comic Life 73
communicating the collective vision effectively 87–9
communicative activities, engaging learners' transportable identities 110–12
communicative roles, discourse identity 110
conceptual change
  and educational philosophy of teachers 130–4

176

Index

conditions for 124
see also Language Teacher Conceptual Change (LTCC) model
confidence, and positive visualisation 119–20
congruence of messages sent by teachers 162
constructing a vision, meaning of 34–5
core identity 110
counterbalancing the vision by considering failure 114–21
creating the language learner's vision 32, 34–64
creative tension
  as driver of transformation 138–44
  strategies for generating 141–4
creative visual survey 73
critical reflection, story prompts 143
cross-modal priming 108

daydreaming 15–16
desensitisation procedures 66, 70–1, 120
desired future states, providing tasters of 45–7
desired self, balanced with feared self 114–15
Dewey, John 1
diaries, use by students 42–5
difficult situations
  preparation to handle 147–8
  strategies for 153–4
discourse identity 110
dissonance
  and creative tension 138–44
  driver for conceptual change 28
Do, Tra Mi 112
dual coding theory (Paivio) 16–17
duties and obligations of learners 116–18
dynamic systems perspective on motivation 21
economic conditions for teachers 145
education as vision building 1
educational potential of imagery 66
Einstein, Albert 15, 62
elaborating the vision 65–6
emotional dissonance 138–44
ethnography in the classroom 44
examinations, motivational effect 116
experience-based images 45–7
exploratory practice 142–3
external barriers to realising a possible self 97

external pressures on teachers 145, 146
extracurricular activities 109
extrinsic motivation 21

face, importance in China 117
failure
  avoidance as motivation 114–21
  effects of consideration by learners 118–21
feared self
  balanced with desired self 114–15
  integrating into visualisations 118–21
  motivational aspect 114–16
  teachers 26, 150–1
  used by teachers as an ally 152–4
feedback from students 141–2
Filipovic, Zlata 75, 77, 78
finding your 'bliss' 126–7
first-person perspective on imagery 18–20
flexible thinking 155
flow experience 74, 127
focus-group interviews 142
Frank, Anne 75, 77–8
Freedom Writers Foundation 75, 77–8, 84
Freedom Writers movie 39
French Lessons (Kaplan) 76
Frost, Robert 44–5
future-centred narratives, writing 59–60
future history technique 48
future L2 selves 20
future self-guides 12
  conditions for ability to motivate 13–14
  utilising approach and avoid tendencies 114–15
future self-image 31
  ability to generate 13
  activating and re-activating 107
  and personal narratives 58–9
  compatibility with other aspects of self-concept 13
  counteracting feared possible self 14
  distinct difference from current self 13
  elaboration and vividness 13
  existence of a roadmap towards 13–14
  need for effort to achieve 13
  need for regular activation to maintain 14
  negative consequences of failing to achieve 14
  plausibility of 13
  procedural strategies to achieve 13–14

177

Index

games, vision and motivational potential of 80–2
Gardner, Robert 20–1
Gies, Miep 75, 77–8
Gladwell, Malcolm 91
goal intentions 103
goals, and vision 9–10
Golden Circle concept 131
'group chronicle' creation 86
group dynamics 83
  storming phase 152
group goal-setting strategies 83
group leadership, issues for teachers 145
group vision
  communicating it effectively 87–9
  creating a 'group chronicle' 86
  mission of the group 83–4
  modelling through transformational leadership 86–7
  pooling individual narratives 84–6
  story sharing session 85–6
  strengthening a shared vision 82–9
growing the vision 99–100
Gruwell, Erin (Ms G) 39–41, 75, 77–8, 84
guided imagery
  applying 48–57
  conditions for effective application 52–4
  constructing ideal teacher selves 137–8
  creating your own imagery scripts 56–7
  dealing with resistance to 52–3
  definition 49
  for teachers 24–5
  introductory exercises 54–6
  positive imagery approach 148–9
  types of 49–52
  use in sport psychology 14
  use of past memories 18
guided narratives, application 57–62
guided selection 34

Harley-Davidson 131
Herndon, Lynne 139
Hesburgh, Theodore 65
high-hope people 155
Hoffman, Eva 76
hope
  and teacher vision 154–6
  turning a threat into a challenge 28
hope theory 155
humanism (Stevick) 39

ideal L2 self 21, 22
  motivational intervention 38
  providing tasters of 45–7
ideal L2 teacher self 25, 26, 125–7
  generating images 136–8
Ideal Self Tree 38
ideal self, as a future self-guide 12
ideal self-image, sources of influence on 34–5
identity
  and motivation 21
  and narrative 58–9
  levels in social interaction 109–10
  possible selves theory 11–14
identity concerns of students, understanding by teachers 38–45
image formation 1
image portfolio 72
image-seeds 45
image streaming 50–2
  of a future history 59–60
imagery
  focus on process 103–4
  functions in performance 16–17
  mental rehearsal aspect 17
  motivational aspect 17
  role in language education 17–18
  use of past memories 18
  see also guided imagery; mental imagery; visualisation
imagery direction 119–20
imagery enhancement, training methods 66–71
imagery in psychology 16–17
imagery perspective 18–20
imagery training
  in sport 67
  principles 67–9
  workout routines 69–71
'immunisation' against stressful situations 119–20
implementation intentions 103–4
inspirational leadership, Golden Circle concept 131–4
institutional identity 110
instrumental orientation/motivation 21
integrative life narratives 58
integrative orientation/motivation 21
intellectual challenge, teachers' lack of 145
interactional identity 110

Index

internet research 108
intrinsic motivation 21
investment, motivation as 21

job interview, scripted imagery 50
Jones, Katherine 118

Kaplan, Alice 76
Kennedy, John F. 131
Kessler, Rachel 153–4
King, Martin Luther, Jr 2, 131
Klinger, Eric 15–16
Krystowiak, Dawid 81–2

L2 (second language) learning
  future L2 selves 20
  possible L2 selves 20
  vision as a motivational force 4
L2 learning experience 22
L2 motivation research, history of 20–1
L2 Motivational Self System 20, 21–2, 38
  ideal L2 self 22
  L2 learning experience 22
  ought-to L2 self 22
Lang Lang 63
language attitudes 34–5
language education, role of imagery 17–18
language learner's vision, creating 32, 34–64
language learning, and identity 11
language learning autobiographies, teachers 127–9
language tasks 100
Language Teacher Conceptual Change (LTCC) model 5, 26–8, 138, 152
Lawrence, T. E. 90
leadership 86
learner agency 35–6
learner autonomy 35
learner-centredness (Tudor) 39
learner identity 35
learner motivation, and educational philosophy of teachers 130–4
learners
  empowering the 'pessimists' 93–5
  engaging their transportable identities 109–12
  feedback from 141–2
  help with seeing the path 101–3
  hostile challenge to teacher 153–4

individual guidance on action plans 105–6
influence of lived experiences 38–45
misconceptions about language learning 90–2
motivational aspect of the ought-to self 116–18
narrative research techniques 42–5
'over-optimistic' beliefs 95–6
personalised learning 91
realistic beliefs about language learning 90–2
reasonable criteria for success 91
reminders of negative consequences of not succeeding 115–16
self-relevant roadmaps to their L2 selves 101–3
summary of vision-building principles 157–9
techniques for understanding their stories 42–5
types of unrealistic beliefs 92–6
understanding current identity concerns 38–45
learning contract 100
learning histories 43
learning journals, encouraging students to keep 77–8
learning modes 111
lesson planning, use of visualisation 147
Levin, Ira 10, 86
Lewin, Kurt 5
long-term goals 100
  visualisation 104
Lost in Translation (Hoffman) 76
low-hope people 155

Magid, Michael 38, 50, 53–4
Mahatma Gandhi 161
mapping pathways to success, use of visualisation 103–5
Markus (2006) 15–16
massively multiplayer online games (MMOGs) 80–2
master identity 110
McAdams, Dan 58
Meister Eckhart 31
memories of past events, link to future mental images 18
mental imagery 14–20

Index

applying guided imagery 48–57
 as mental rehearsal 147–8
 as vision boosters 147
 frequency of 15–16
 in psychology 16–17
 potency of 15–16
 range of applications 14, 15
 see also imagery; visualisation
mental rehearsal aspect of imagery 17
mental time travel 18
Mercer, Sarah 42
meta-imagery control skills 147–8
motivating learners, meaning of 2
motivation
 and vision 2, 3–4
 as investment 21
 role in language teacher development 22–8
 self-discrepancy theory 12
 theories of 3
 see also L2 motivation
motivational aspect of imagery 17
motivational capacity of vision 10–14
motivational change/evolution studies 21
motivational intervention programmes 36–8
motivational potential of virtual worlds 79–80
motivational self-regulation 36
motivational speech, classroom activity 88–9
Ms G see Gruwell, Erin
Muhammad Ali 48
Murdoch, Maureen 52–3
Murphey, Tim 63–4, 85

narrative learning 77–8
narratives
 applying guided narratives 57–62
 autobiographical story about the future 59–60
 creating of a group vision 84–6
 importance in human experience 57–9
 pooling individual narratives 84–6
 retelling the past in a different light 60–1
 story sharing session 85-6
 teachers' language learning experience 127–9
 telling your future story creatively 73
 transportation power of 73–7
near peer role models 63–4, 85
negative attitudes as a barrier to possible self 97

negative counterbalance to positive visions 114–16
negative feelings, using visualisation to help cope with 147–8
new socio-dynamic approaches to motivation (2000s) 21
newslettering 64, 85
Nicklaus, Jack 68–9
non-verbal imagery system 17
Norton, Bonny 39, 42–3

observational learning 62
Olimnazarova, Tojiniso 149
Olympic Games 63
online gaming spaces 80–2
operationalizing the vision 99–100
Ortberg, John 27
ought-to L2 self 21, 22
ought-to L2 teacher self 26
 detrimental effects on teacher vision 145–7
ought-to self 12
 as a barrier to possible selves 98
 as motivational force 116–18
 situations where there is no obvious one 117–18
out-of-class projects 109
outcome simulation 103
over-optimistic learner beliefs 95–6

Paivio, Allan, dual coding theory 16–17
Palmer, Adrian 125, 126
Palmer, Parker 152
parent meetings 106
parents, influence on possible selves 34
past–future link 18
past learning experiences, influence on teachers 127–9
peer group influences 35
peer observation 141
Pennington, Martha 146–7
perceived control over attainment of possible self 97
personal life stories 57–9
personal vision 9
personalised goals 10
personalising communicative tasks 108, 109
personalising language activities 110–12
personality development, and life narratives 58–9
perspective on imagined scenes 18–20

Index

pessimistic learner beliefs 93–5
Petit, Philippe 8–9
phobias 66, 70–1, 120
Photo Story 73
photovoice technique 43, 44, 73
plausible nature of the vision 90–8
Podborski, Steve 120
positive imagery approach 66, 148–9
positive psychology 155
positive role models 62–4
positive visualisation, and confidence 119–20
possible L2 selves 20
possible selves
   and hope 154–6
   and language teacher development 25–7
   as visions of what might be 11–12
   eliminating obstacles and barriers 97–8
   ideal teacher selves 125–7
   motivational intervention programmes 36–8
   opportunities to experience 45–7
   ought-to self as a barrier 98
   potential of online gaming 80–2
   power of virtual environments 79–80
   providing tasters of 45–7
   realistic expectations 91–2
   sources of ideas about 34–5
   strength-based approach 94–5
Possible Selves programme 37, 97–8, 99–100, 105–6
possible selves theory 11–14, 31–2
   and the L2 Motivational Self System 22
   feared self 114–15
Possible Selves Tree 37, 38, 98
post-lesson reflection process 147–8
pressure, effects on students 115–16
priming technique 107–9
priming the negative consequences of not succeeding 115–16
process-oriented conceptualisation of motivation 21
process-oriented imagery 103–4
progress monitoring and recording 100
psychology, dual coding theory 16–17

Quick Set Routine 69

realism in imagery training 68
realistic beliefs about language learning 90–2
Reality Check Appraisal 152

reality checks 90
reality self-checks, creating channels for 92–6
reflection
   on language learning autobiographies 127–9
   on the purpose of language teaching 130–6
   post-lesson reflection process 147–8
reflection-on-action 134–6
reflective journals 44
regularity of imagery training 68
reinforcement in imagery training 68
relaxation and imagery training 67
remembering the past to imagine the future 18
resonance, inspiration for conceptual change 28
responsibilities, and the ought-to self 12
Richards, K. 39
roadmaps to success 101–3
Rogers, Carl 162
role models 35, 62–4, 130
Roux, Michel, Jr 45, 46

safety net, turning a threat into a challenge 28
safety zones 149–50
School-to-Jobs programme 37, 97, 98, 105, 106
scripted fantasy 49
scripted imagery 49–50
second language see L2
Second Life virtual environment 78, 79, 80
self-actualisation 126
self-confidence 21
self-created avatars 79
self-deception and vision formation 91
self-defining moments in language learning histories 61–2
self-determination theory 36
self-discrepancy theory 12, 139–40
self-efficacy 21
   assessment by teachers 152
   fragility in teachers 145
self-generated imagery 50–2
self-image and personal narratives 58–9
self-observation (on video) 141
self-regulatory learning 36
self system
   dynamic nature of 11
   possible selves theory 11–14

Index

sensory experience of vision 10
sensory modes, cross-modal priming 108
Shakespeare, William 14
Shaw, George Bernard 98
short-term goals 100
   visualisation 104
Sinek, Simon 131
situated analysis of motivation 21
situated identity 110
situation-specific motives 21
situational constraints 97
Snyder, Rick 155
social barriers to possible selves 98
social duties, and the ought-to self 12
social interaction, levels of identity 109–10
social position/role, situational identity 110
social pressures on learners 116–18
social psychological period (1959–1990) 20–1
socio-dynamic approaches to motivation (2000s) 21
Socratic imagery 49
Souter, Tessa 101, 102–3
Southwest Airlines 131
sport psychology 70
   imagery direction 119–20
   imagery training 14, 66, 67
   Paivio's dual coding model 17
   use of vision 10
Star Wars 114
Stevens, Cat 44–5
Stevick, Earl 17, 39
stock-taking, vision review 112–13
story prompts for critical reflection 143
storytelling *see* narratives
strategy boards 105
strength-based approach
   developing ideal teacher selves 126–7
   possible selves 94–5
strengthening the vision, imagery enhancement 65–89
stress levels in teaching 145
students *see* learners
substantiating the vision by making it plausible 90–8
Suits, Bernard 80
Swift, Jonathan 34
systematic desensitisation technique 66, 70–1, 120

task-execution strategies 100
teacher autonomy, restrictions on 145
teacher burnout 145
teacher cognitions 23–4
teacher conceptual change, creating conditions for 27–8
teacher development
   how to inspire trainees 28
   role of motivation and vision 22–8
teacher education, 'apprenticeship of observation' 127–9
teacher motivation
   aspects of 123–4
   conditions for conceptual change 124
   guarding the flame of teacher vision 145–56
   influence on learners' motivation 24–5
   (re-)igniting the flame of teacher vision 125–44
   threats to 145
   through vision 124
teacher practice, use of mental imagery 147–50
teacher–student talk (Richards) 39
teacher support groups 149–50
teacher vision
   building resilience 147–50
   detrimental ought-to self-images 145–7
   erosion of 145
   ideal teacher selves 125–7
   recognising our talents and passions 126–7
   strategies to process adversity 153–4
   summary of vision-building principles 159–60
   sustaining hope 154–6
   turning adversity into an ally 152–4
   understanding sources of fear 150–1
   understanding who we are 125–30
   vision boosters 147–50
teachers
   as classroom ethnographers 44
   creative tension as driver of transformation 138–44
   differences in classroom behaviours 22–4, 26–8
   empowering pessimistic learners 93–5
   framework for motivational practice 4–5
   guiding images 24–5
   ideal language teacher selves 25
   images of teaching 24–5
   Reality Check Appraisal 152

Index

reflection on the purpose of language teaching 130–6
responses to new ideas and material 22–4, 26–8
revisiting past learning experiences 127–9
transformation of classroom practice 3
transformational leadership 3
treading softly with 'over-optimistic' learners 95–6
understanding identity concerns of students 38–45
understanding why we chose the profession 129–30
using imagery to construct ideal teacher selves 136–8
vision for change and improvement 3
teaching philosophies 130–4
third-person perspective on imagery 18–20
Toffler, Alvin 107
Tompkins, Jane 150–1
Total Physical Response method 70
training imagery skills 66–71
transactional leadership 86
transformation, driven by creative tension 138–44
transformational leadership 3, 86–7
transforming the 'unteachable' (illustration) 39–41
transportable identity
  definition 110
  engaging in learners 109–12
transportation experience 73–7
Transportation-Imagery Model 74
transportation questionnaire 76–7
transportation theory 73–4
trustworthy spaces 149–50
Tudor, I. 39
turning points in language learning histories 61–2
Twain, Mark 8

unrealistic positivity 96

values that guide teaching practices 132–3, 134–6
van der Helm, R. 9
video self-modelling (VSM) 71
virtual environments (VEs) 78–82
  and possible selves 79–80
  avatars 79–80
  motivational power 79–80
  online gaming spaces 80–2
  types of 78–9
vision
  and desire for deliberate change 9
  and language teacher conceptual change 27–8
  and the future 9
  and the ideal 9
  and the L2 Motivational Self System 22
  as a force for learning 1–2
  as a high-order construct 28–9
  danger of self-deception 91
  defining aspects 9
  distinction from goals 9–10
  example of Philippe Petit 8–9
  future research directions 28–9
  keeping it alive for learners 107–13
  motivational capacity 2, 3–4, 10–14
  of teachers 3
  personal vision 9
  possible selves theory 11–14
  role in language learning 1–2
  role in language teacher development 22–8
  sensory experience of 10
  strengthening the whole group's vision 82–9
  transforming into action 99–106
  types of 9
  what it is 9–10
  why it matters 9–10
vision-based approach 3–4
vision board of ideal L2 self 47
vision boosters for teachers 147–50
vision building
  application of the principles 160–2
  summary of principles for students 157–9
  summary of principles for teachers 159–60
  the teacher is the message 161–2
vision-centred teaching practice
  counterbalancing by considering failure 32, 114–21
  creating the language learner's vision 32, 34–64
  framework 32–3
  keeping the vision alive 32, 107–13
  motivational conditions 32
  motivational practice 32
  strengthening the vision 32, 65–89

183

Index

substantiating the vision 32, 90–8
transforming the vision into action 32, 99–106
vision-immersion opportunities 45–7
vision journal 72
vision-relevant rituals 108
vision-reminders 107–13
vision review 112–13
visionary programme design 36–8
visionary training programmes 97
visions of what might be, possible selves 11–12
visual reminders of positive past examples 149
visual representations of pathways to success 105
visualisation
  integrating images of feared selves 118–21
  student awareness of 48–9
  use by teachers 147–50
  see also imagery; mental imagery

writing an autobiographical story about the future 59–60